E
872
M64

Mollenhoff, Clark R

The President who failed : Carter out of control / Clark R. Mollenhoff. — New York : Macmillan ; London : Collier Macmillan, c1980.

xix, 264 p. ; 24 cm.

Includes index.
ISBN 0-02-921750-4

1. United States—Politics and government—1977- . 2. Carter, Jimmy, 1924- . I. Title.

E872.M64 973.926'092'4 79-6767
MARC

Library of Congress 79

THE PRESIDENT WHO FAILED

Books by Clark R. Mollenhoff

Washington Cover-up
Tentacles of Power
Despoilers of Democracy
The Pentagon
George Romney: Mormon in Politics
Strike Force
Game Plan for Disaster
The Man Who Pardoned Nixon
The Investigative Reporter: Courthouse to White House

THE PRESIDENT WHO FAILED

Carter Out of Control

Clark R. Mollenhoff

MACMILLAN PUBLISHING CO., INC.
NEW YORK
COLLIER MACMILLAN PUBLISHERS
LONDON

Macmillan Publishing Co., Inc.
866 Third Avenue, New York, N.Y. 10022

Collier Macmillan Canada, Ltd.

Library of Congress Catalog Card Number: 79-6767

Printed in the United States of America

printing number

1 2 3 4 5 6 7 8 9 10

Library of Congress Cataloging in Publication Data

Mollenhoff, Clark R.
The President who failed.

1. United States--Politics and government--1977-
2. Carter, Jimmy, date I. Title.
E872.M64 973.926'092'4 79-6767
ISBN 0-02-921750-4

CONTENTS

FOREWORD

Sometimes an exposure involves an abuse so blatant or titillating that it blazes its own path to recognition. But more often, the uncovering of a scandal requires a great cooperative act of perception that ripples across society.

The most crucial level of perception is that of the press itself. If the press at large ignores a fledgling exposé, if editors scorn its incompleteness or fail to grasp its importance, if reporters do not jump in to widen the beachhead, if press conferences do not confront officials over it, if columnists do not elaborate its ramifications, then it will not survive to reach those levels where public advocates take it up, where investigative agencies begin to grind, where mass opinion demands redress.

Rightly do newsmen rail against bureaucratic secrecy, political cover-up, and judicial hostility, but the great graveyard of investigative stories is to be found in apathetic newsrooms. In *The President Who Failed* Clark Mollenhoff has swept together out from the dark corners of the Carter administration facts that myopic editors have failed to perceive, facts that should have been laid out on the front pages for readers to ponder. Yet, these facts have been largely discarded or ignored in editorial offices across the fifty states.

The picture that emerges is not one that America really wants to see so soon after Watergate. Americans have been rocked by one new shock after another until they now tend to hide from disagreeable news. Nor are the exposers any more eager than the exposed to engage in another angry, protracted, bitter-end investigation that might traumatize the nation all over again.

The first time I called upon Jimmy Carter in the White House, I tried to explain how I felt. "Because I played a leading part," I said, "in exposing some of the corruption that went on under Richard Nixon, I feel a duty to restore balance and respect. . . . I am looking for stories that would restore faith in the system, faith in the Oval Office." This brought a diffident smile to the face of the new President who came to power preaching morality to post-Watergate America. He deplored "the sordid occurrances of the past." He agreed that the American people looked to him to bring a new sense of integrity and idealism to Washington. "So I think I do have, in spite of partisan divisions, the good wishes of the American people," he told me.

The tragedy of the Carter presidency is that he has foolishly squandered those good wishes. Jimmy Carter has let down a people who wanted to believe in him, who wished for his success. He promised that he would never lie to them, yet his administration has been caught in one awkward lie after another. He promised strong leadership, yet he has withdrawn into long periods of indecision, passivity and paralysis. He has never tired of uttering his Billy Graham sermonettes. He has preached against drug abuse and indiscriminate sex. "I have asked my own White House staff," he said early in 1977, "to protect the integrity of their families. We need a better family life . . . so those of you who are living in sin, I hope you'll get married. Those of you who have left your spouses, go back home." But he has been unable to impress his standards upon his immediate subordinates. Both the President's son, Chip Carter, and top aide, Hamilton Jordan, have left their wives. Several witnesses have also reported seeing Carter aides at sex and drug parties, with Jordan leading the revelry.

Like Richard Nixon before him, Carter has tended to insulate himself from the Washington whirl and to use his staff as a buffer. He has a desire for solitude and a craving for an orderly environment, undisturbed by trivial interruptions of internecine discord. "I value solitude," he once told me, "I kind of hunger after loneliness." So Carter tried to isolate himself from unnecessary turmoil, dealing regularly only with those trusted, select few whose faces and accents were familiar to him. The trouble with all this is that a seething enterprise like America cannot be led from a glass bubble. Subordinates suddenly catapulted from the backwaters of Georgia to the peaks of power in Washington will succumb to the heady atmosphere there. They will find true security only in their good-ole-boy ties with their own limited group.

As outsiders, they will distrust the insiders who know their way around the marble maze. Even the President's own appointees, the top two thousand in government, will be given minimal initiative and will not be trusted with sensitive information. The clique at the center will feel threatened by the professionals who will press closely around. Suspicion and hostility at the center will eventually permeate the organization. Professionals who are blocked from access to the President will grow uneasy and will begin to connive. Subordinates denied trust will become untrustworthy.

This scenario is all too familiar to those of us who witnessed the Nixon presidency first commit the blunders and then the crimes that produced the greatest political scandal in American history. We hardly expected to see the same scenarios repeated within the decade by the Carter presidency. Yet, already, we have witnessed the creeping corruption, the quiet cover-ups, the pious denials.

This time there is no pack of reporters hot on the trail of the White House conspirators: most reporters and editors do not want to believe the evidence before them. This time there is no Special Prosecutor pulling together all of the pieces of the scandal. The investigations that have been forced on Jimmy Carter's Justice Department have been fragmented. Half a dozen grand juries have viewed isolated parts of the donkey, but the prosecutors are making no effort to put the animal together, and no one is really trying to pin the tail to the donkey.

Not without reluctance, I have made an effort to dig up facts that the Carter crowd has sought to cover up. I have published many of the sordid details in my column for an audience that has largely lost its savor for political scandal. But it takes a book such as Clark Mollenhoff has written to put the whole story into focus. Mollenhoff has done a painstaking job of assembling the facts. His book offers an investigative reporter's view of Jimmy Carter: a stark, black-and-white portrait of a President who had great promise but, sadly, failed in his first term. After the Carter presidency fades into history, a more comprehensive book than this can perhaps be written about the malfeasance, misfeasance, and nonfeasance of the Carter administration. But until then, this doggedly detailed record is the most thorough and objective record available.

Clark Mollenhoff is uniquely qualified to write this book. I have known him for thirty years, first as a formidable rival and, more recently, as a member of my investigative team. He is an indomitable, sometimes intimidating, reporter, a giant both in physical size and in journalistic zeal who has won more prizes for investigative reporting than anyone in Washington. Every American who takes his citizenship seriously should read Clark Mollenhoff's book.

JACK ANDERSON

PREFACE

I Voted for Jimmy Carter

This book is not an effort to assess Jimmy Carter as a human being, but it is an effort to analyze his performance as President of the United States. I do not intend to recount again the stories of his roots, his boyhood, his youth or his early manhood to identify these experiences with the decisions he has made as President. Much of that has been written, rewritten, overwritten and psychoanalyzed by his admirers and by his critics. I will leave the interesting chores of analyzing his spiritual and intellectual development to the psychiatrists, the psychologists and those authors and journalists who make claims to having expertise in identifying (after the fact) those flaws of character in our leaders that we all should have noted before casting our ballots.

Hordes of political writers have already written countless stories of how this ambitious, determined and intelligent farmer-businessman from Plains, Georgia, outwitted the professional politicians in a game plan written by Hamilton Jordon, who was his administrative aide in the Georgia governor's office. They have written long and detailed accounts of every step of the primary route from the Iowa caucuses through the crucial Pennsylvania primary, and on through the Democratic Convention and the general election.

It is not my intention to hash over the real and imagined inconsistencies and misrepresentations of Mr. Carter's campaign, or to compare his duplicity with the duplicity of other major candidates who have won, or tried to win, this nation's most coveted office. It is my intention to analyze Jimmy Carter's performance as a President, and to do it in as objective a manner as is humanly possible.

I voted for Jimmy Carter in November 1976. I was not partisan or ideological in casting that vote, but felt that I had done as careful and objective a study of the alternatives before me and before the country. Let me explain the reasons why I cast my vote for Jimmy Carter.

In the post-Watergate era Jimmy Carter said what I wanted to hear about the importance of open government and the corrupting influence of a secret government that did not want to be accountable to the Congress and the press. He criticized the evils of political appointments in the Justice Department and the resulting bad impact of political influences on investigations and prosecutions. Candidate Carter viewed "executive privilege" as the pernicious vehicle for cover-up of the crimes and the lies told by President Nixon.

Candidate Carter said he would not lie to us and, in clear and certain terms, he emphasized this with his often repeated comment, "You can count on that." He also spoke much about the importance of having "competent" people in government and stressed that point in his campaign book, *Why Not the Best?*

While I accepted the fact that as President Mr. Carter might not be able to live up to the letter on those unqualified promises, I hoped and believed that he meant what he said about the importance of competence and integrity in government, and that he would not permit political expediency to abandon those vital goals. I was willing to rationalize that those promises were made in the heat of a campaign he wanted to win, and that he did not wish to become ensnarled in the complicated business of explaining over and over the proper qualifications he intended to give to his promises.

It is quite possible that I was too much inclined to want to believe Candidate Carter because of my sharp disappointment with President Gerald Ford on a number of specific issues. Although I had been a long-time friend and admirer of Ford in his days as a congressman, I was angered at his pattern of outright deceptions in statements and actions leading up to the unconditional pardon of Richard M. Nixon. I was also disappointed by his misrepresentations on a number of other issues in the area of labor and agricultural policy which I had followed closely as Washington Bureau Chief for the *Des Moines Register*.

President Ford permitted widespread use of "executive privilege" by Secretary of State Henry Kissinger and others in the aftermath of Watergate. Approving and condoning the use of "executive privilege" constituted an obstruction of justice in my view and in the view of a number of senators and congressmen. I also felt that Ford was arrogant and deceptive in his repetition of the self-serving claim that he was running "an open administration." I had often heard him discuss the evils of "executive privilege" and the importance of total accountability to Congress and the press when Democrats were in the White House.

Thus I leaned toward Carter in the early campaign despite the fact that I had been unimpressed when he was in Washington for meetings with newsmen in 1975 and 1976. When Candidate Carter was one of the featured speakers at the Little Dinner of The Gridiron Club in December 1975, I received a negative impression. The Gridiron Club holds its so-called Little Dinner every December. It is a social and business get together and provides the opportunity for reporters and political leaders to get to know each other in a relaxed and pleasant forum. Several speakers are selected to entertain around some basic theme of contemporary political interest. Each speaker gives a brief, and hopefully witty, speech to show off his ability to be entertaining, and briefly serious. Most of the speakers regard it as a rare opportunity to show their talents to a group which includes more than sixty of the nation's top newsmen. This is particularly true when it involves speakers who are announced or unannounced candidates for either the Democratic or Republican nominations for President.

The December 1975 Little Dinner featured a half-dozen of the men who had indicated an interest in the Democratic nomination for President in 1976. That impressive list of speakers included Jimmy Carter, whose major claim to fame at that time was that he was a one-term governor of Georgia who had the audacity to seriously think he might win the Democratic nomination. To most of us he was the "Jimmy Who?" of cartoon fame.

One reason that I and others remember that Jimmy Carter spoke at the December 1975 dinner was because of a tasteless bathroom joke that he told in a feeble effort at humor. This type of story might be told and appreciated in a men's locker room or at a convention of traveling salesmen, but it was out of place at a Gridiron Dinner where there were unwritten traditions that ruled out dirty jokes or off-color remarks.

Carter's speech was an embarrassment to the audience, and the light laughter was pointed more at Carter than with him. Senior members of the Gridiron Club—men who would have laughed at the joke in another setting—commented critically and sagaciously, "Jimmy Carter bombed out. He showed his caliber. He will never win the Democratic nomination."

The Gridiron members' reaction was not based upon the substance of the Carter joke but on his lack of understanding of the forum and of the impact that his little speech might have on a number of prominent reporters and columnists. I do not recall whether I made personal comment at the time, but my reaction was in line with the majority thinking. It was unfortunate that he didn't have someone among his political advisers who could have taken the time to make a simple inquiry on the type of speech expected in the Gridiron forum. I contrasted it to the great care that John F. Kennedy and Robert F. Kennedy took with their Gridiron speeches in earlier years to hit the formula of quick one-liners filled with self-deprecating Washington humor and a few subtle barbs aimed at political opponents.

While the tasteless Gridiron speech soured many Washington political writers on Jimmy Carter, it was a speech that went unreported under Gridiron tradition and thus unnoticed in the Democratic caucuses in Iowa a month later. Jimmy Carter's big win in the Iowa caucuses more than overcame the political injury he had inflicted upon himself with his off-the-record speech before the Gridiron Club members.

When the Carter political phenomenon started I could hardly believe it, and by the time he became a credible candidate I had read his book *Why Not the Best?* and noted that he proudly wrote of his years in the Navy with Admiral Hyman Rickover's elite crew. As a long-time admirer and friend of Admiral Rickover, I called the Admiral to get his personal assessment of former Navy Lieutenant James Earl Carter, who had served under him in the naval nuclear propulsion program.

Admiral Rickover confirmed the general details that Jimmy Carter had related about the meetings the two men had had. He said he had selected Carter for the nuclear program because he felt Carter was intelligent, well qualified for the job and a conscientious worker. But Admiral Rickover balked at giving an overall assessment of Carter as a candidate for President, even on an off-the-record basis with a reporter with whom he had excellent relations over a number of years.

"I am not going to make any statement about Jimmy Carter or

any of the other candidates that might drag me and my programs into the political campaigns,'' Admiral Rickover said.

''My programs are too important to get them involved in any political campaign, and I expect them to go on far beyond the next election [November 1976],'' the proud and effective father of the nuclear submarine program declared. ''If I would say something that might be helpful to Carter his opponents might hold it against me and my programs. If I would say something that might be harmful to Carter, he or his people might hold it against my programs.''

It was impossible to get any indication from Admiral Rickover as to whether he believed the man who was campaigning as his protégé would make a good President. However, it was a plus, in my thinking, that Jimmy Carter had been selected by Rickover, and that he wrote and spoke with admiration of the crusty old Admiral who paid attention to the details on his job and was often highly critical of the incompetence of military officers and high-ranking civilian Pentagon officials who simply did not know their jobs.

After Carter won the Democratic nomination he continued to speak in terms of an open and accountable government, and the few inconsistencies that developed seemed to me to be inconsequential quibbling over terminology. Even the unfortunate *Playboy* interview in which Candidate Carter made the admission that he had many times ''lusted'' for women other than his wife was only the result of a poor choice of words in making the point to the interviewer that he had never had sexual relations with anyone but his wife. It may have been poor judgment to have agreed to the *Playboy* interview, but I blamed Press Secretary Jody Powell, who unwisely got himself and Jimmy Carter committed to the interview before fully realizing the subjects that would be discussed or the negative impact that would result from a ''born again'' candidate agreeing to any interview for *Playboy*—an example of a candidate's not doing his homework.

Looking back on 1976, it was probably my irritation with President Ford on the Nixon pardon that kept me in Carter's corner as much as a specific affirmative position that Carter took on any domestic or international issue. In the course of the campaign, Carter convinced me and millions of others that he would institute some higher ethical standards in government, would choose highly competent people as his appointees without regard for party label and would take politics out of the appointments in the Justice Department. If he remained true to these simple principles, it would be as far as I was concerned a long step forward.

My first disillusionment after Carter was in command came with his failure to do anything to restore Air Force Cost Analyst A. Ernest Fitzgerald to cost-cutting duties on major Pentagon weapon systems, and with the appointment of Dr. Harold Brown —one of Robert S. McNamara's whiz kids—as Secretary of Defense.

The large number of Georgians brought to Washington for the White House staff had to be a disappointment to those of us who believed he would carry out his pledge to cut the White House staff by one-third. (The White House staff was actually increased by more than one hundred people in the first months Carter was President. This was justified by the large increase in mail flowing from President Carter's promotion of the populist theme that he wanted to hear directly from the voters.)

The naming of Atlanta attorney Griffin Bell as Attorney General struck Republicans and many Democrats as inconsistent with Carter's pledge to take politics out of the Justice Department. What was the difference between this appointment of a political supporter and friend and Richard Nixon's naming of his political supporter and friend, John N. Mitchell, as his first Attorney General?

It was a shock to Democrats and Republicans alike when Ray Marshall, nominated by Carter as Secretary of Labor, made statements indicating endorsement of the unionization of the military services. To save his nomination, Marshall, with pressure from the White House, said his position had been misunderstood.

It was disturbing to such an old Georgia friend of President Carter as Jack Nelson, Washington Bureau Chief for the *Los Angeles Times,* that the President and his White House staff did not perceive the seriousness of the banking problems of T. Bertram Lance earlier than they did. It would have been to the advantage of Lance and President Carter to have requested that Lance step aside immediately as Director of the Office of Management and Budget, and to have avoided any appearance of a continued personal relationship.

Those following the Lance controversy closely had to conclude that the Carter White House had no top level people who could assess evidence of serious law violations in an objective manner. Georgians were investigating other Georgians, and still more sympathetic Georgians were reviewing the reports and concluding erroneously in most cases that no law violations or unethical conduct was involved.

Even after the Lance affair and the controversy over the political firing of United States Attorney David Marston, the White House Counsel's office under Atlanta lawyer Robert Lipshutz was not competent in analyzing a serious conflict of interest in an appointment to the Commodity Futures Trading Commission —an agency responsible for the regulation integrity in the trillion-dollar-a-year commodity trading industry.

It was difficult to comprehend why the Carter White House would force the resignation of Joel (Jay) Solomon as administrator of the corruption-ridden General Service Administration (GSA) in the midst of Solomon's aggressive clean-up of corruption and mismanagement. Solomon, a Tennessee businessman, was a Carter appointee, and the job he was doing in exposing scandals at the GSA had nearly unanimous approval from the press and the public.

Likewise, it was difficult to understand why President Carter for months tolerated the embarrassing, independent comments of Ambassador to the United Nations Andrew Young, while sharply rebuking and firing such dissenters as former Congresswoman Bella Abzug and White House Assistant Midge Costanza.

It was incomprehensible how President Carter, who had said his Energy program would be the moral equivalent of war, permitted his White House to force Energy Secretary James Schlesinger to accept political appointments that undermined the integrity and competency of that important new agency.

These are only a few of the actions of the Carter administration that I will analyze in trying to show how political personnel selection and a lack of a competent fact-finding arm in the White House compounded the very enormous problems that the White House faced in its first three years in office.

Not the least of these problems was the public perception of Hamilton Jordan, who refused to bend his own undisciplined life style to the political needs of the Carter White House. In the process Jordan gained a reputation as a ruthless political barbarian, a Washington swinger, a social slob and an incompetent administrator. The result was that his denials of charges that he sniffed cocaine were discounted sharply, because he admitted that he frequented the places where the charges originated.

Equally distressing to those who had voted for Carter was the reluctance of Attorney General Bell to name a special prosecutor when charges of possible crimes were made against high officials of the Carter Administration or against political friends or relatives of President Carter. The Justice Department under Griffin Bell, and later under Attorney General Benjamin Civiletti, seemed intent upon establishing a reputation for foot-dragging and political cover-up that was reminiscent of the Watergate era in the Nixon administration.

To properly analyze those cases that have resulted in the sharp fall of the political popularity of Jimmy Carter, it is necessary to scrutinize in detail the controversial events and ask this vital question, "What did the President know and when did he know it?"

In addition to asking and trying to answer that vital question, which dominated the investigation of the Watergate cover-up, I shall seek the answer to another question—when the first cannot be answered with precision—on the specific responsibility of Jimmy Carter for actions by his administration. The additional question that must be asked if there is to be the full accountability that President Carter promised us in the post-Watergate era is, "What should a reasonably effective President have known, and when should he have known it?"

In precise terms, we should determine if President Carter and the Carter White House can be permitted to avoid responsibility for the widespread use of the equivalent of "executive privilege" in his administration with the technical explanation that "executive privilege" is not invoked until President Carter has given his personal approval to its use. Acceptance of such a self-serving explanation means, and has meant, that department and agency heads use the "executive privilege" theory to block Congress, the courts and the press from access to documents and testimony, while the White House proudly boasts that President Carter has never invoked the despicable doctrine.

While I am sure that there are many things President Carter has done for the nation that are admirable, it is not my intention to explore those achievements, for they have been overshadowed by a series of unfortunate events that have destroyed Mr. Carter's image as a leader of the free world.

I do not wish to picture him as a willfully dishonest man who has corrupted all or any part of the federal government. On the contrary, I believe that he was basically a well-motivated man with a burning desire to be President. I am sure that he wanted to be a good President at the time he took office, and did not believe that any of the appointments he made (of Georgians or of others) represented any political sell-out of principles.

However, during his presidency, Mr. Carter has thoughtlessly made compromises and accommodations without understanding the full implication of those actions. He has tried to hide the embarrassing details of faulty decisions and has drifted into the dangerous rhetoric of self-deception and cover-up. Those were the major crimes of Watergate when Mr. Nixon and his top aides tried to hide behind the unjustified claims of "executive privilege."

Regardless of his motivations, I believe the Carter record demonstrates that the abuses of executive branch power did not end with Watergate.

CHAPTER ONE

Why Not the Best?

Ernie Fitzgerald was the most celebrated whistleblower of recent years on government cost overruns. By the time of the 1976 political campaign, Fitzgerald had been battling the Pentagon bureaucracy for nearly eight years. He had originally committed the sin of telling the unvarnished truth to a congressional subcommittee investigating massive overruns on the Lockheed C-5A program. The matter started when Fitzgerald, Deputy for Management Systems in Air Force Headquarters, failed to abide by the instructions of his Air Force superior to give misleading and false testimony to the Joint Economic Subcommittee.

From the date of that testimony in November 1968, he had been subjected to persistent criticism and harassment. In the last days of the Johnson administration, less than a week after he had told the offending truths about the C-5A costs, he was asked to falsify his testimony. Then an effort was made illegally to remove his career tenure by contending that "a computer error" had been responsible for his job security.

For a time, Ernie Fitzgerald had tried to believe that someone in the upper echelon of the Air Force would have the integrity to step in and stop the harassment. It was, after all, as Senator William Proxmire (D.—Wis.) informed the Pentagon, a violation of the law for Air Force officials to retaliate in any manner against a witness who had given truthful testimony to Congress, even if that truthful testimony was embarrassing to the Pentagon brass. As Senator Proxmire explained, unless the truthful officials—the so-called whistleblowers—were protected from the wrath of their superiors there would be no way to get the facts on the corruption, waste and mismanagement at the Pentagon, which was costing billions of dollars every year.

However, in the course of Ernie Fitzgerald's successful fight against efforts to fire him by both the Johnson and Nixon administrations, he did come to learn the sad reality that the Justice Department would not prosecute—or even effectively investigate—the obvious violations of the law by high officials of the Pentagon, and it was to take more than five years in a civil lawsuit, carried forward with the help of the American Civil Liberties Union (ACLU), to obtain a federal court order directing that he be reinstated in his Air Force job and be given back pay.

Even then the Defense Secretaries and the Air Force Secretaries in the Nixon and Ford administrations complied only in the technical sense of putting him back on the payroll, meanwhile refusing to restore him to cost-cutting duties on the C-5A program or comparable major weapons systems. While doling out millions and billions in cost overruns on the C-5A, the F-111 warplane, and other mismanaged programs, the Air Force quibbled, cut and trimmed on the amount of back pay it finally awarded the truth-telling cost cutter.

In the nearly eight years since he had responded truthfully to Senator Proxmire's questions on the cost of the C-5A jet transport, Fitzgerald had learned the mournful reality of Admiral Hyman Rickover's wise advice to Defense Department employees. "If you must sin, sin against God, not against the bureaucracy. God may forgive you, but the bureaucracy never will," Admiral Rickover commented on many occasions relative to his experience with the Navy in getting the nuclear submarine program moving.

Ernie Fitzgerald was a long-time admirer of the crusty old admiral who had fought so many battles against incompetence, waste and corruption, which were a hazard to every major Defense Department program.

And one of the foremost reasons that Fitzgerald was favorably disposed in 1976 toward Democratic Candidate Jimmy Carter was that Carter had at one time served in Admiral Rickover's elite group. Although Carter had been a junior officer in Rickover's group for only a few years, Fitzgerald reasoned that he must have had some qualities of competence and integrity to pass muster before the tough-minded and discerning Rickover.

Moreover, Candidate Carter had made specific reference to the attempts of the Nixon and Ford administrations to fire Fitzgerald after he had given his truthful testimony about the nearly $2 billion in cost overruns on the Lockheed C-5A jet transport program. In pledging to "squeeze the fat" out of the Pentagon budget, the Democratic candidate declared that there would be "no Fitzgerald cases" in a Carter Administration.

Jimmy Carter used a Rickover comment as the title for his political campaign biography, *Why Not the Best?* As Carter related the story in his book, Admiral Rickover was questioning him about some of his grades that had fallen below perfection. Rickover asked Carter if he had done his best on those subjects. When Carter replied that he had not done his best, he quoted Rickover as replying: "Why not the best?"

That was a question Ernie Fitzgerald had asked himself many times as his cost analysis job took him through the maze of corruption, incompetence, politics and waste that was the Air Force way on all major weapons systems. The best price and the best performance were rarely given any priority in a system in which a handful of Senators and Congressmen and a few big defense contractors dominated the scene.

The efforts to falsify the cost and performance record on the C-5A Galaxy jet transport were not isolated incidents of corruption and cover-up. Fitzgerald was also knowledgeable about the political boondoggle on the decision to buy the F-111 warplane from General Dynamics for a price that was initially higher than Boeing's price by at least $400 million, and which eventually ran into the billions. As is made clear in the December 1970 Report of the Permanent Subcommittee on Investigations, when McNamara and his top aides were caught with a decision that they could not justify, they tried to pressure witnesses to give false testimony and rigged false performance and cost reports to Congress.

What Ernie Fitzgerald thought amazing was that even as the F-111 scandal was being exposed, the top Air Force officials were engaging in the same type of false and deceptive tactics to hide from Congress the truth about cost and performance on the C-5A.

Fitzgerald thought optimistically that if Jimmy Carter could just eliminate one-third the waste at the Pentagon, it would mean that billions could be saved or made available for other programs. As far as Ernie Fitzgerald was concerned, Candidate Carter was saying altogether the right things about squeezing the fat out of the Pentagon budget, and his speeches indicated that he recognized the importance of protecting honest government employees from retaliation by the bureaucracy.

Candidate Carter repeatedly stressed the importance of eliminating corruption and mismanagement from the federal government and pointed to the vital role of government employees in exposing and eliminating this waste of tax dollars. The former Georgia Governor declared that it was essential that honest employees of the federal government feel free to tell the truth about specific examples of corruption and mismanagement if the Congress, the public and the President were to find evidence of bad government. In the prepared text of a speech given in Alexandria, Virginia, home of many middle and lower level employees of the Pentagon, Carter had mentioned the Fitzgerald case specifically as the kind of Pentagon retaliation against a truthful government employee "that would not be tolerated" in a Carter administration. Reporters had told Fitzgerald that Carter had also included comments about his case in off-the-cuff remarks to a number of audiences, which included large numbers of government employees.

Friends and supporters of Ernie Fitzgerald active in the Carter campaign assured him that Carter was deeply concerned about the treatment Fitzgerald had received at the hands of Pentagon superiors and was interested in Ernie's views on specific steps to stop the mismanagement and waste of Defense dollars. These assurances came from men and women who were later to be placed in high positions in the White House and at the Pentagon. Fitzgerald did in fact submit a report with ideas on how to cut waste and mismanagement in the Defense Department, and he was sounded out as to his availability for a subcabinet-level post in the Defense Department.

Fitzgerald was not a naive citizen. He was an expert cost analyst and student of government and politics and acted like a decent and intelligent student of government. He did not expect Jimmy Carter to perform all of the miracles of reorganization and efficiency that he pledged. Carter's stress on honesty and integrity had its appeal to Fitzgerald, and he was particularly moved by Carter's emphasis on the importance of basic honesty and truth in the operation of government.

Certainly President Lyndon B. Johnson, symbol of Washington wheeling and dealing, said little about honesty and truth. While Presidents Richard M. Nixon and Gerald R. Ford spoke about it from time to time, the record of their performance on Watergate scandals and the Nixon pardon demonstrated deceptions, duplicity and outright falsifications. Presidents such as Johnson, Nixon and Ford had demonstrated an unwillingness to interfere with the corruption and mismanagement that was wasting billions of dollars annually at the Pentagon. Each had turned a deaf ear to the pleas of the truthful government officials who were persecuted for their truths about Defense Department waste.

Certainly Jimmy Carter—the self-proclaimed Rickover protégé—would be a step up out of the morass of the Johnson, Nixon and Ford years when the impetus for Defense Department corruption had seemed to be stimulated by the political pressures from the White House itself.

As Fitzgerald followed the 1976 political campaign, he was mildly distressed that Candidate Carter was caught taking apparently inconsistent positions on what his government policy would be on abortion and the deregulation of natural gas. Also, there were some questions about whether he had courted pro-segregationist Alabama Governor George Wallace's support in running for Governor in Georgia.

However, Fitzgerald recognized that nearly all candidates for president engage in a certain amount of contrived fuzziness on such highly volatile issues during political campaigns. Certainly, any inconsistencies in Carter's statements could be more than matched by the established record of duplicity in President Ford's administration.

While Fitzgerald thought it was "stupid" for the Democratic candidate to have agreed to sit for an interview for *Playboy* magazine with Robert Scheer, a free-lance journalist, the Air Force cost expert did not believe the mistake was important. It was embarrassing for Carter to be quoted as saying he had "looked on a lot of women with lust," but in the light of the accompanying assertion that he had never made love to any woman but his wife, it was not a moral issue as Fitzgerald saw it. Fitzgerald's view was that Carter and Jody Powell, his press man, had used poor judgment in agreeing to the interview for *Playboy,* and that Carter had been inept in his choice of words in discussing the life style of some of his campaign aides.

To Fitzgerald, it seemed that Carter's campaign "bloopers" were kept to a reasonable minimum for an "outsider" to the Washington political scene who was relying to a large extent upon a young and relatively inexperienced group of political advisers. Certainly all of the flap about the "ethnic purity" comment did not merit the controversy it caused.

President Ford frequently misspoke himself, after all, on national and international issues, and Fitzgerald felt that fumbled rhetoric was not a real issue. He felt rather that the real issues dealt with:

the waste and corruption in the buying of military weapons systems as well as the purchasing policies of other departments

a genuine reform of the Civil Service system so it would provide a real protection for government workers who wanted to do something about the corruption and mismanagement in government

an open, honest and accountable executive branch that would dedicate itself to eradication of the waste of billions of dollars

It was from firsthand experience that Fitzgerald knew there had been no real effort to meet these basic issues in the Johnson, Nixon or Ford administration. With Jimmy Carter in the White House there might be a chance to get away from the old cliques and the old ways that had permitted, and even encouraged, the wasting of tax money as was done on the F-111 warplane and the C-5A jet transport. The Johnson, Nixon and Ford administrations had taken part in the questionable awards of these multibillion-dollar contracts and the multimillion-dollar government bailouts when the contracts went sour.

While Fitzgerald was not convinced that Jimmy Carter was necessarily the best man in the nation for the presidency, the former Georgia Governor certainly looked like "the best" of the selections available. He seemed to be an intense, serious and intelligent man with a strong contempt for Washington insiders. He was forthright in his criticism of the falsifications and wheeling-dealing that permeated so much of the nation's federal government operations.

And, as a native of Alabama, Fitzgerald could understand how Carter might have considered some association with segregationist George Wallace as essential to a victory in his campaign for state office in Georgia. It appeared that Carter's record as Governor of Georgia was sufficiently supportive of civil rights to win large support in the black community in Georgia. By 1976 there seemed little doubt as to the sincerity of Carter's commitment to integration and even to affirmative action programs.

Although Carter appeared to be too much of a loner, and too dependent upon a small Georgia clique, Fitzgerald believed it was better to err in leaning a little too far in that direction than to be a captive of the establishment sharks.

For these reasons, and because he had been shocked by President Ford's pardoning of Richard Nixon, Fitzgerald and his wife, Nell, decided to vote for Carter on November 2, 1976. Although Nell Fitzgerald was working for a local Democratic candidate, a personal friend and neighbor, neither she nor her husband was a political partisan of either the Democratic or the Republican parties. Thus they cast their votes for Carter when they voted at the Franklin Sherman School in McLean, Virginia shortly after 7 A.M. As Fitzgerald drove to his office at the Pentagon, he mused about the tougher spending policies he hoped would be enforced if Jimmy Carter was elected.

Because former Senator Eugene McCarthy, a liberal Democrat from Minnesota, was in the race as an independent candidate, it was a cliffhanger election, and President Ford did not concede defeat until shortly after 11 A.M. on November 3. It was the closest presidential election in this century. Carter won his 297 electoral votes in 23 states and the District of Columbia. Ford won 241 electoral votes in 27 states. Carter was hurt by the candidacy of Senator McCarthy, who polled more than 650,000 votes. In four states—Iowa, Maine, Oklahoma and Oregon—McCarthy polled more votes than the margin of Carter's loss to Ford.

Fitzgerald was pleased with Carter's victory and was hopeful that he would soon see evidence that Admiral Rickover's protégé —President-elect Jimmy Carter—would demonstrate his intention to break with the past and make war on corruption and mismanagement in the Defense Department.

CHAPTER TWO

First Disillusionment

Within a few days after the November 2, 1976, election, Air Force cost analyst Ernie Fitzgerald heard disturbing reports that former Air Force Secretary Harold Brown was among those being considered by President-elect Carter for Defense Secretary. Fitzgerald tried to convince himself that the reports could not be true. Dr. Brown had had a very significant role in the two major Defense Department debacles of the McNamara years. He had been Director of Defense Research and Engineering at the time Defense Secretary Robert S. McNamara gave the scandalous award of the F-111 warplane contract to General Dynamics in 1962, and he was Air Force Secretary when the equally scandalous C-5A jet transport contract was awarded to the Lockheed Aircraft Corporation a few years later.

It was Air Force Secretary Brown, in fact, who in November 1968 had severely criticized Fitzgerald for telling Senator William Proxmire (D.—Wis.) about the nearly $2 billion dollars in cost overruns on the C-5A contract. Fitzgerald recalled not only this, but also how, immediately after criticizing Fitzgerald, Brown had asked the Defense Department personnel office how Fitzgerald could be fired.

Fitzgerald believed it would be "a personal tragedy" if Brown was named as Defense Secretary, and that is precisely what he told a member of the Carter transition team who came to him seeking his views on a list of men being considered by President-elect Carter for the top Pentagon post.

He capsuled for the transition team his dispute with Brown, relating the story of Brown's criticism of his accurate testimony on the massive cost overruns on the C-5A program, and how Brown had been unmoved by his explanation that he had simply given truthful testimony in response to Senator Proxmire's questions. He told them of his surprise and disappointment at Brown's willingness to go along with the Air Force brass who were urging falsification and misrepresentations to the Joint Economic Committee on Defense Production.

The Carter transition team members said they would relay the information on Brown to their superiors, but they were interested mainly in Fitzgerald's view of the five men on the list being considered for Defense Secretary.

Briefly scanning the list, Fitzgerald commented that his assessment would have to be based upon "what Jimmy Carter is looking for in a Defense Secretary."

It was explained briefly that Carter was putting a priority on "ending the nuclear arms race" with the Soviet Union, and whether the men on the list were generally viewed as "hawks" or "doves."

"From a standpoint of technical knowledge on nuclear arms, Harold Brown is the best qualified man on the list," Fitzgerald said. "But he isn't much of a manager. If he is named, an effort should be made to get a top manager for the number two spot."

Fitzgerald emphasized again that the appointment of Brown would be "a personal tragedy to me," unless he and Brown could sit down ahead of time and work out their past differences.

Brown had served from 1969 to 1977 as President of California Institute of Technology in Pasadena. He had not been involved in the bitter struggle during the Nixon and Ford administrations that ended only when United States District Judge William Bryant found that Fitzgerald had been illegally fired and ordered his reinstatement. Certainly Fitzgerald, weary with the legal fight for reinstatement, had no desire to wage war with Harold Brown over an incident that was eight years old, and it was possible that Brown had mellowed and was willing to let bygones be bygones.

Fitzgerald told the transition team members that if Brown was to be Defense Secretary, he simply wanted an opportunity to make peace "so we can both get on with the job of cutting the waste in defense spending." While Dr. Brown was a politically pliable Air Force Secretary under Defense Secretary Robert S. McNamara, it was possible that an older and more mature Dr. Brown could emerge as a Defense Secretary.

After it was formally announced that Dr. Brown was Jimmy

Carter's selection to be Secretary of Defense, members of the Carter transition team encouraged Fitzgerald and his lawyers to believe that they would be given an early opportunity to sit down with Dr. Brown for a discussion of how Fitzgerald's cost-cutting talents could be best used in the new Carter administration. That meeting was never arranged, and Fitzgerald and his lawyers were told that Dr. Brown had rejected this suggestion by Carter's top aides.

At the confirmation hearing before the Senate Armed Services Committee, Dr. Brown told Senator Howard Metzenbaum, an Ohio Democrat, that he would give consideration to such a meeting with Fitzgerald, but he avoided a flat commitment. This was the last bit of evidence that Fitzgerald needed to convince him that Jimmy Carter and his top aides did not have the desire or the courage to fulfill the 1976 political campaign commitment to help honest government employees in exposing corruption and waste in government.

In following the Fitzgerald case, this reporter was surprised to discover in late December 1976 that one of Carter's top advisers was unaware of Dr. Brown's significant role in the two biggest procurement scandals in the McNamara Pentagon. The Carter organization could not conceivably have made a thoughtful and informed decision on whether Dr. Brown was "the best man for the job" without an examination of his role in the TFX scandal and the C-5A contract disaster. Dr. Brown, as the Report of the Permanent Subcommittee on Investigations made clear in December 1970, participated fully in the cover-ups of the award of the TFX fighter-bomber (F-111) contract to General Dynamics.

When Dr. Brown was head of research and engineering, he was initially opposed to the awarding of the multibillion-dollar contract to General Dynamics on technical engineering grounds. But later he took part in the production of a series of questionable McNamara studies to justify the award after the fact.

According to Senate investigators, when Dr. Brown was named by McNamara as Air Secretary in 1965, he took a full role in the production of deceptive reports on the progress of cost and performance that were an integral part of the cover-up.

Dr. Brown's role in the awarding of the multibillion-dollar C-5A contract to Lockheed was spelled out in detail by Fitzgerald in his well-documented book, *The High Priests of Waste*. Dr. Brown had been Air Force Secretary for only a few weeks at the time of the awarding of this controversial contract in 1965 and had a limited responsibility in connection with the award, but he had a major responsibility in the attempted cover-up of the overruns from Congress in 1968.

Fitzgerald related in his book that Dr. Brown was "on the right side" in approving pursuit of the C-5A contract cost overruns but later folded to the pressure and as Air Force Secretary became a central figure in attempting to keep the Proxmire committee in the dark on the $2 billion in cost overruns and related problems.

"You're a damned poor congressional witness," Dr. Brown was quoted by Fitzgerald as criticizing him for answering Senator Proxmire's questions truthfully. Fitzgerald said he was cut off by Dr. Brown in his effort to explain why he chose to expose the cost overruns rather than give false testimony. Fitzgerald related that Dr. Brown then retorted that Senator Richard Russell, the Georgia Democrat, had called to complain of implications that he (Russell) had brought pressure to continue the contract.

In his book (published in 1972) Fitzgerald wrote that Dr. Brown dismissed him curtly and with considerable irritation, and a few days later he was notified by the personnel office that he had lost his tenure in his Air Force cost analyst job. The Air Force personnel office falsely explained that Fitzgerald had no job security because "a computer error" had been responsible for his having received notice of job tenure a few months earlier.

When Fitzgerald successfully exposed that tactic as fraudulent, Dr. Brown made inquiry as to how Fitzgerald could legally be fired and received a memorandum a few days later on three ways that could be used to get rid of Fitzgerald despite his job tenure. One of those ways—a reduction in force—was actually used a few months later in the illegal effort to fire him.

The role of Dr. Brown on those two large Air Force contracts scarcely indicated the kind of respect for truth and integrity in defense contracting that President-elect Carter had promised.

It was a shock and a surprise to learn that Carter's decision to name Brown to the Defense Secretary post was made without awareness of the blots on Dr. Brown's past record. Although President-elect Carter might have had a good and sufficient reason for appointing a Defense Secretary despite such blemishes, he should have been apprised of the problem in sufficient detail to have asked some pointed questions about the circumstances regarding Brown's role in these two major military procurement fiascos.

Greg Schneiders, Deputy Assistant to Special Assistant to the

President Hamilton Jordan, subsequently explained that there had been such a rush to get appointments made that President Carter and other top aides just did not have the time to follow through on some campaign promises. Schneiders also told this reporter that President Carter had not forgotten his pledge to do something to assure that honest government whistleblowers would not be subject to retaliation and persecution. Certainly the Fitzgerald case—the most celebrated of the whistleblower cases—would not be forgotten.

Schneiders said he was aware that President Carter could gain a great amount of political credit by taking some direct action to straighten out Fitzgerald's case. It would be "a signal," he said, to all of the honest government employees that they could tell the truth about corruption and waste without fear of retaliation by superiors. Schneiders said that he and others in the White House were giving a high priority "to a real civil service reform" that would guarantee "no more Fitzgerald cases where government employees are fired for telling the truth."

There was no doubt about Greg Schneiders's sincerity, but it was soon apparent to him, and also to Fitzgerald, that he and his White House associates did not have the clout to oppose an adamant Defense Secretary Brown, who was unwilling to take any step to make peace with Fitzgerald or to use Fitzgerald's talents as a defense cost analyst. Secretary Brown was equally able in warding off suggestions and pressures from the Senate, particularly from Senators Proxmire and Metzenbaum.

Barred from cost analysis on major weapons, Fitzgerald did write some memorandums in 1976 that pointed out possible "illegality" of Air Force spending on an $800-million computer program.

That new dispute emerged in March and April 1977, in the first months of the Carter Administration, and demonstrated to Fitzgerald that it continued to be precarious to speak frankly about illegalities and mismanagement of one's Air Force superiors. The campaign promises of Jimmy Carter "to protect our federal employees from harassment and dismissal if they find out and report waste or dishonesty by their superiors" had no impact on the repressive and hostile climate in the Pentagon where Fitzgerald was working. As far as Fitzgerald was concerned, Richard M. Nixon or Gerald R. Ford might as well have been in the White House.

Ernie Fitzgerald did not learn until November 1979 that it was the Harold Brown as Air Secretary who on January 9, 1969, had advised incoming Air Secretary, Robert Seamans, that Fitzgerald "is of no use to the Air Force" because of his cooperation with Congress and should "be discouraged from remaining" with the Air Force. The ten-year-old Brown memorandum was unearthed by Fitzgerald's attorneys in litigation to get all of the facts leading up to Fitzgerald's illegal discharge by the Nixon administration. On that same January 9, 1969, when Brown was advising Seamans to get rid of Fitzgerald, the duplicitous Dr. Brown was expressing a contrary view in a letter to Senator William Proxmire. In a letter to Senator Proxmire, Brown said he was "shocked" that Proxmire would make a public statement that Fitzgerald was being treated unfairly by the Air Force. The Brown memorandum on his private advice to the incoming Secretary was hidden for more than ten years in the private files of the Pentagon while Brown and others contended Fitzgerald was dismissed in a "reduction in force" for economy reasons.

Fitzgerald's new controversy with his Air Force bosses in the Carter administration stemmed from a joint congressional report of December 10, 1975, that directed the Air Force to "terminate" a controversial computer program known as Advanced Logistics Systems (ALS). Because the Air Force contended that some parts of the $800-million program were "mission essential," Congress permitted programs specifically designated as "mission essential" to be exceptions to the termination directive.

Top Air Force brass then divided the $800-million computer project into dozens of smaller projects, classified each as "mission essential" and continued spending on virtually all parts of a program that Congress had directed to be "terminated."

Fitzgerald's first memorandums spelling out the waste and possible illegality (because the overall program had been terminated by Congress) were written in the summer of 1976. These memorandums were ignored by Fitzgerald's superiors and did not surface until the spring of 1977 in connection with congressional inquiries initiated by Representative John E. Moss, an able and aggressive California Democrat.

Surfacing at the same time as the Fitzgerald memorandums were the handwritten notes of Major General Robert L. Edge, Assistant Chief of Staff of the Air Force. These notes by General Edge stated that he was "not overly concerned" about the work on the "terminated" $800-million project. In his notes, General

Edge commented that Congress "doesn't know about" the continuation of the computer service project and added: "Why rock the boat unnecessarily?"

Representative Moss dashed off a letter to Secretary Brown characterizing General Edge's views and the continued spending on a "terminated" project as "a classic exhibition of contempt on the part of the Air Force for Congress." House and Senate appropriation committee members also expressed serious concern over Air Force disregard of orders to "terminate" the project.

General David C. Jones, Air Force Chief of Staff, contended he was unaware of the manner in which General Edge and others had handled the continuation of the program. While he denied that Air Force reports to Congress were false or fraudulent, he admitted they were anything but "timely and exhaustive" and promised a full investigation within the Air Force.

General Jones named Lieutenant General Charles E. Buckingham to conduct this internal Air Force probe. General Buckingham, comptroller of the Air Force, had been identified as one of the Air Force top brass who was trying to blame the computer foul-up on "Fitzgerald's vendetta against the Air Force." General Buckingham had bad-mouthed Fitzgerald as "biased" and, even before being named to the probe, had belittled the written evidence of the Air Force's disregard for the law and regulations in contract awards.

Four months into the Carter administration, Fitzgerald was thoroughly disgusted. Although his view on the illegality of the ALS program was supported by the Senate and House appropriations committee, he knew that those committee members would not carry on an effective fight to protect him from his superiors. The General Accounting Office (GAO) depth investigation on the Air Force handling of the computer program, which the committee had requested, could only recommend actions on the contract. He knew the GAO would not deal with the question of whether the actions of Air Force superiors constituted a violation of the laws making it illegal for any officials, civilian or military, to fire or otherwise retaliate against a government employee who gives accurate testimony before Congress.

The Carter administration did not fire Fitzgerald for his frank memorandums regarding possible illegalities on the $800-million computer program, but hostility to his honest independence was apparent at the highest levels in the Air Force and the Pentagon. A

Senate investigator received a call from an Air Force official who said that the Chief of Staff (Jones) "will not appear in the same room with Fitzgerald." Such resentment against Fitzgerald, whose offense was frank and honest testimony, was altogether inconsistent with Mr. Carter's pledge of a dedicated and effective effort to determine how money was being wasted by the Pentagon.

While Greg Schneiders insisted that he was as deeply concerned about the injustices Fitzgerald and others suffered, he was kept so busy as White House director of special projects that he had little time to do anything more than compile a file on a few cases of wronged whistleblowers and conduct a few interviews. A step in the right direction, yes, but not pushed as it should have been.

Those who took risks in their government careers to fight for honest and efficient government were not as politically important as the spokesmen for the draft dodgers and deserters of the Vietnam War. From a standpoint of political impact, those young men who had failed to carry out their responsibility in an unpopular war were more important than the men who told the Congress the truth about waste and mismanagement by the Pentagon—a truth Pentagon brass did not want Congress to learn.

Fitzgerald did not believe that Jimmy Carter's Pentagon was worse than Nixon's Defense Department, but from his personal standpoint he had outspoken champions among the House and Senate Democrats when a Republican was in the White House. Understandably, there was every reason for Democratic Congressmen and Senators to be more restrained in the first months of a new Democratic administration.

While President Carter engaged in televised "fireside chats" and "town meetings" to seek advice from the "average citizen" about running the government, he proved inaccessible to men of experience in cost cutting like Ernie Fitzgerald. Although the first months of the Carter administration were disillusioning for Fitzgerald, he tried to retain a faith in President Carter and to blame the problem on the inexperience and incompetence of some senior White House aides who were more interested in public relations gimmicks than in substantive improvement on programs.

By the end of Carter's first six months in office a good many of his supporters were having doubts about the ability, the intelligence and even the honesty of some of Carter's appointees.

CHAPTER THREE

Energy Policy and Political Expediency

Over a period of more than twenty years in Congress, Representative John E. Moss had made a national name for himself as a champion of open government and as an outspoken foe of government corruption and mismanagement. The aggressive California Democrat was recognized as "the Father of the Freedom of Information Act," and he had pushed this legislation through over the objections of President Lyndon B. Johnson.

He was a vociferous foe of "executive privilege" long before it became fashionable to oppose that secrecy doctrine in the Watergate cover-up of the Nixon administration. Moss contended that government secrecy fostered waste and corruption in the federal agencies, and he had consistently opposed it in Republican and Democratic administrations from President Eisenhower, through Presidents Kennedy and Johnson, and throughout the administration of President Nixon and Ford.

Also, Representative Moss was chairman of the Oversight Subcommittee of the House Commerce Committee, and had been a persistent investigator and critic of maladministration and secrecy in connection with various energy programs.

The California Democrat had looked with favor upon Carter early in 1976 because of the stress the former Georgia Governor was placing upon honesty and efficiency in government and on open information policies. Moss came out publicly in support of Carter in the days immediately following Carter's loss of the Maryland primary to California Governor Edmund G. (Jerry) Brown. Brown had aligned himself with the Maryland Democratic machine, then headed by corruption-tainted Governor Marvin Mandel, in a whirlwind campaign that netted him nearly 50 percent of the primary votes. Carter polled only 37 percent of the votes in the Maryland primary in one of the few setbacks he received in the 1976 primaries.

Carter was despondent about that defeat by Brown, and he needed the bolstering when Representative Moss—a symbol of open honest government—endorsed him in the face of the surprising political punch of his own California Governor.

"The nomination is still open," an exuberant Governor Brown had proclaimed in seeking to establish a bandwagon psychology. The Maryland primary had a reverse impact when John Moss rejected his bandwagon and endorsed Carter.

John Moss had been pleased when Carter won the Democratic nomination at New York City on July 15 after lashing out at "the disgrace of Watergate" and pledging an open, truthful government.

"It's time for us to take a look at our own government, to strip away the secrecy, to expose the unwarranted pressure of lobbyists, to eliminate waste, to release civil servants from bureaucratic chaos, to provide tough management," Carter had declared. It was a sentiment that had special appeal to Representative Moss.

"It's time for our government leaders to respect the law no less than the humblest citizen, so that we can end once and for all a double standard of justice. I see no reason why big shot crooks should go free and poor ones go to jail," Carter had told the Democratic convention.

Although Moss was disappointed that Democratic Candidate Carter did not challenge President Ford on the pardoning of Nixon, he was pleased that Walter Mondale made up for that oversight with a direct critical comment that the United States was "now led by a President who pardoned the person" who was responsible for "the worst political scandal in American history."

Moss was particularly pleased with Mondale's pledge of an "open government" with the comment: "We will let the healing sunshine of full public knowledge restore faith in the people's business."

In early August 1976, Moss found he was momentarily disapproving of Candidate Carter's praise for the "openness" of the Ford administration. Ironically, Carter's praise for Ford's "openness" came the same week that Representative Moss was criticizing President Ford for being an "imperial executive" whose information policies were "worse than those of Richard Nixon."

Moss, who had believed that Carter understood the misuses of "executive privilege" by Nixon and Ford, was distressed. The California Congressman directed his staff to prepare a memorandum for Carter explaining the problems that congressional investigating committees had with "cover-ups" by the Ford White House. It appeared that Jimmy Carter had accepted naively President Ford's self-serving claim that he ran an "open government" and had missed the significance of congressional and press complaints of Ford administration "cover-ups" at the FBI, CIA, Defense Department, State Department, Commerce Department, Justice Department and other agencies.

Carter aides told Moss that Carter's "lack of understanding" of the cover-ups by Ford was a result of his preoccupation with the long campaign for the Democratic nomination. Thus he had failed to associate the use of "executive privilege" against congressional committees with the open government issue. Those apologists for Carter assured Moss that Carter really believed in and understood the open government issue but had not related Ford's refusal to produce records for Congress with that issue.

Moss accepted Carter's explanations over the comments of some Carter critics who chose to believe that Carter's attitudes were tied to a strong streak of authoritarianism. Carter's critics contended Carter's praise of Ford's "openness" was a clever campaign device by a man who considered himself a shoo-in for the presidency and who did not wish his own comments to foreclose future use of "executive privilege."

Representative Moss rejected that thesis completely when the Carter campaign team members said they were sorry for mistakes about Ford's "openness" and solicited advice from the California Democrat in his area of expertise—government information policy. Moss had his staff members write memorandums of guidance for the Carter presidential campaign, and he was pleased to see Democratic Candidate Carter making use of some of this material in the last months of the campaign.

Throughout the fall campaign, the Carter headquarters in Atlanta was in touch with Frank Silbey, of Representative Moss's staff, for memorandums and advice on a wide range of maladministration and corruption in the Ford administration that had been under investigation by Representative Moss. Those included the misuse of "executive privilege" to bar Congress from the records of wiretapping kept by American Telephone and Telegraph Company, the questionable decisions to let a private oil company drain oil out of the Navy's Elk Hills oil reserves, a wide variety of conflicts of interest, and a number of abuses of the civil service merit system.

The civil service system abuses included a summary of the case of the illegal firing of Air Force cost analyst A. Ernest Fitzgerald. The memorandum on maladministration of the FEA included a summary of the heated controversy that Moss and Representative John Dingell, a Michigan Democrat, had with Douglas Robinson, an FEA lawyer, over the lack of prosecution of a Florida oil company for illegal overpricing of oil.

Frank Silbey reported to Moss that Carter's Atlanta headquarters showed an avid interest in facts dealing with the Ford administration's scandals, and that much of the material was being used by Jimmy Carter in his campaign.

While generally satisfied with Carter's campaign on the open government issue, Representative Moss had to wonder about the confusion on the energy policy issues and the seeming duplicity on the question of whether a Carter administration would support deregulation of natural gas. As chairman of the House Commerce Committee's oversight subcommittee, Moss had been deeply involved in investigations of the Ford administration's handling of the enforcement of laws by the Federal Energy Administration (FEA), and had been extremely critical of Ford for being a defender of the oil companies and the big energy interests. Midway in the campaign, Moss noted that Candidate Carter softened his criticism of Ford's energy policies, while a fuzziness developed on the question of whether there would be a deregulation of the natural gas prices.

Not until several weeks after Carter was elected did Representative Moss learn that Douglas Robinson, a controversial Ford administration lawyer, was a member of Jimmy Carter's transition team. Robinson had been a key member of Carter's energy policy staff during the last two months of the campaign after quitting his post as deputy counsel at the FEA in the Ford Administration.

Representative Moss had good reason to remember Robinson, for he and the staff of his commerce oversight subcommittee had clashed with the then deputy counsel for the FEA on the effectiveness of investigations and prosecutions on overcharges by oil companies.

"The things Robinson stands for are completely at odds with Jimmy Carter's campaign statements, and I am sure that he does not know of the nature of Robinson's opposition to prosecution of the Ven-Fuel Company in connection with overcharges of the Jacksonville [Florida] Electric Authority," Moss told this reporter in December 1976.

Moss said that after his "unfortunate experience" with Robinson as a witness before his commerce oversight subcommittee in the spring of 1975, he was "shocked to learn that this same Mr. Robinson was a Carter adviser on energy and a member of the transition team.

"I hope that his [Robinson's] role has not been important, and that when Governor Carter sees the transcript [of Robinson's testimony on the Ven-Fuel decision] he will make certain that Robinson's attitudes have no influence on his energy policy," Moss told me.

Moss confirmed to this reporter that he had "filed a strong note of protest" with the transition team in which he declared that "Robinson would be a bad influence on any administration.

"As a lawyer for the Ford administration's energy agency Robinson was a defender of the oil companies and the big energy interest," Moss said. "Testimony before the House oversight committee establishes clearly that he interfered with prosecution efforts of local enforcement officials and the United States Attorney's office in Jacksonville."

The outspoken California Democrat declared that "these are more than slight policy differences, for Robinson's actions were just plain bad government in my book."

Representative Moss felt so strongly on the Robinson issue that he tried to get in touch with President-elect Carter but failed. Then Moss tried to contact one of Carter's top advisers and again was advised that they were busy and unavailable.

This was a worse situation than he had ever faced in the Nixon or Ford administrations when he, as chairman of a House investigation subcommittee, could always get through to the President or to one of the staff people who could give him the satisfaction of an authoritative explanation or reply.

Although frustrated by his inability to get his message through directly to President-elect Carter, Representative Moss believed that a memorandum explaining his concern over Robinson and a copy of the transcript would be sufficient to end Robinson's influence on appointments in the energy field.

About the same time that Moss was expressing his concern over Robinson's possible influence on policy and personnel in the Carter administration, he and his staff learned that a long-time Carter supporter had been fired because of disagreements with Robinson on energy policy.

Joseph Browder, president of the Environmental Policy Center in Washington, had been one of a small group of Carter's energy advisers from the time he had prepared Carter's background paper on energy in 1974. During 1975 and 1976, Browder continued as an adviser to Carter on energy policy even as he was vice-president of the Environmental Policy Center. He had been "impressed with Carter's sincerity and his interest in the details of energy-environmental problems" in the many meetings they had had during the campaign for the Democratic presidential nomination.

Browder's role as a key adviser on energy issues continued until October 1976—a few weeks after Robinson resigned from the Ford administration and became an adviser to Stuart Eizenstat, Carter's chief adviser on domestic policy issues.

"In the middle of the political campaign, Robinson was arguing against criticism of the Ford administration's energy policies," Browder explained to the staff of the Moss subcommittee. "It was difficult to believe that Robinson, who had been a part of the much-criticized enforcement arm of FEA, was actually sitting in the Carter advisory group arguing against a criticism of Ford's energy policies."

Browder related that he had only one earlier dispute with what Carter was saying on the energy issue. That dispute involved a statement Carter made in the March primary campaign in Pennsylvania where he took a position on strip mining that was contrary to earlier positions on the same issue. That position on strip mining had "startled" Browder, and he called Carter for a direct discussion of the issue.

"We had a good talk, and he [Carter] corrected his position to where it had been," Browder said. "He [Carter] said my memorandums had not gotten through, that he was misinformed, and he was happy to be able to restate his position."

This and a number of other minor disputes over campaign

rhetoric on energy-related issues placed Browder in conflict with Eizenstat, one of the Georgians, who Browder characterized as "more interested in pleasing various political interests than in solid consistent policy."

"It appeared to me that Eizenstat was listening to some interests that were not in tune with what Carter had been saying," Browder said, but explained that he discussed these differences with Eizenstat in a civilized manner.

Browder said he first learned that Robinson had joined the Carter advisers in Atlanta from someone in Ralph Nader's group. Browder then initiated a call to Stu Eizenstat "to brief him on Robinson's appearance before the Moss oversight subcommittee."

"The next thing I knew he was working for Eizenstat, and I was hearing reports from congressional committees that John Hill [deputy administrator for FEA in the Ford administration] was complaining that I was picking on one of his boys [Robinson] who was in the Carter campaign.

"It was a ludicrous situation with Ford administration energy officials complaining about a long-time Carter energy adviser attacking his boy who was sitting in on all of our discussions," Browder said. He made no public complaint at that time because he did not want to rock the boat in the late stages of the Carter campaign and believed that Eizenstat simply might be using Robinson for political expediency. He felt certain that Robinson's influence would wane in the period immediately after Carter's election.

Instead of waning after the election, Robinson's influence increased, and as a result of Browder's disputes with Robinson, Browder was dropped from the Carter–Mondale transition team in mid-November.

Browder, disillusioned with many Carter aides, still clung to a belief in the sincerity of Jimmy Carter even as he told Congressional investigators and a few members of the press of conversations on energy policy that would have been politically embarrassing to the Carter campaign had they been known in the last weeks of the campaign.

Browder revealed that he had accused Frank Moore, a former Carter campaign fund-raiser, of making a deal with the oil industry to keep Carter energy advisers out of a meeting with oil industry representatives in exchange for a $200,000 campaign contribution.

Moore, later a special assistant to President Carter for congressional liaison, confirmed that Browder had accused him of making a deal with the oil industry at an October 4, 1976, meeting in Carter headquarters in Atlanta. He said he could not remember the details of the conversation, but he definitely did not tell Browder he had received $200,000 from the oil industry for the Carter campaign.

"I was trying to cool him [Browder] off, and I might have said something about him not knowing what it's like on the front line of the campaign, raising money," Moore said. "I do not remember the conversation in detail even now, but I know I did not say I had received $200,000 from the oil industry. I know I did not say there were commitments to the oil industry to keep energy adviser S. David Freeman away from Jimmy Carter."

Moore also said that a letter Carter wrote on October 19, 1976, to the governors of Texas, Oklahoma, Louisiana and New Mexico, pledging to deregulate prices of new natural gas, was not related to any campaign contributions from the oil industry. Moore said that representatives of the oil industry did contribute to Carter and that he could not remember the details except that it was not tied to any arrangement.

"It would have been illegal to make such a deal," Moore told this reporter. "Those who know Jimmy Carter know he had no commitments to special interests and would have no part of any deal. Those of us in the campaign knew how he felt about these things, and we knew he wouldn't stand for it."

Frank Moore clarified an earlier statement that he "did not recall a meeting with Browder" on October 4 by saying he did not regard his conversations with Browder to have constituted "a meeting."

"It was just a conversation as I was going through the [Atlanta] headquarters, being introduced to people," Moore explained. He said he did not recall how long he talked with Browder and two other campaign aides—Kathy Fletcher and James Rathlesberger—who were in the office.

Barbara Newman, a reporter for National Public Radio, taped Browder's explanation of his conversation with Frank Moore but was refused an interview with Moore for more than two weeks. Newman interviewed Fletcher and Rathlesberger and corroborated Browder's report that Moore had mentioned a sum of $200,000 from the oil industry.

Rathlesberger told Newman that he had heard Moore admit to

having promised gas and oil producers that Dave Freeman and another energy adviser, Lee White, would not be present in an August meeting Carter has scheduled with oil industry representatives.

Moore explained to this reporter in late January 1977 that he had avoided an interview with Newman because he was busy trying to reconstruct the events of the October encounter with Browder. He said he had discovered that two of his aides were present at the time and "both have told me that they have no recollection of any conversation about a $200,000 campaign contribution."

Moore declared that in October 1976 he was coordinating the campaign in the South "and wasn't even in the campaign fund business after December 1975." However, he acknowledged that he did talk with D. K. Davis of Dallas, an official of the Independent Petroleum Association, about getting support for Carter from the oil industry.

Although Moore said he did not request financial support for Carter, Davis volunteered to make a contribution because he liked Jimmy Carter. Davis also said that others in the industry would give no financial support if Dave Freeman was on the Carter energy team. Moore said he did not make a commitment to see that Freeman would not be present at Carter's meeting with the oil industry.

Davis told this reporter that he contributed some money to the Carter campaign but did not collect oil industry money for him and had no idea how much oil money might have been collected for Carter. Davis recalled that he did discuss Dave Freeman with Moore and that he told him "the oil industry perceived Freeman as a super-regulator" and "not a friend of the industry."

Moore acknowledged that he had a hand in removing Freeman's name from the roster of the energy meeting, but he said it was not related to his talk with Davis or any commitment to the oil and natural gas industry. "We looked over the list and it seemed to be overbalanced on the side of the environmentalists and I suggested that Freeman's name be dropped," Moore said. "It was not any part of an agreement. It was to bring better balance to the energy advisers list."

The proof that there was no deal to blackball Freeman, said Moore, is the fact that he later became a part of the Carter energy team and joined the White House staff as a senior energy adviser.

Barbara Newman's broadcasts and news stories prompted inquiries from Representative Moss and others about Moore's contacts with the oil industry and about the Carter letter to the Governors of Texas, Louisiana, New Mexico and Oklahoma pledging to deregulate the price of new gas. However, the White House, the FEA and the Justice Department were totally unresponsive to congressional inquiries.

White House Press Secretary Jody Powell was infuriated at being questioned as to how President Carter happened to use verbatim the text of an Oklahoma oil lobbyist's letter in his pledge to deregulate the price of new natural gas. Instead of trying to establish responsibility for this unusual bowing to special interests, Powell launched into an attack on the oil lobbyist who had told Barbara Newman that he was "surprised" a presidential candidate would adopt the oil industry language without change in the pledge to the governors of Texas, Oklahoma, New Mexico and Louisiana.

Press Secretary Powell viewed the oil lobbyist as the initiator of an attack on the Carter White House when, in fact, the lobbyist had only responded truthfully to Newman's questions about the authorship of the Carter campaign letter and his "surprise" and pleasure that it was accepted without change by Stuart Eizenstat's campaign issues office.

Representative Moss was distressed by the reports that Jimmy Carter had been induced to sign an oil lobbyist's letter as a campaign pledge. He was also concerned about the Carter administration's information policies and the resentment of legitimate press questions.

After President Carter was sworn into office on January 20, 1977, Representative Moss renewed his efforts to contact President Carter with regard to energy policy, government information policy and water policy in the Western states. Presidential Assistant Hamilton Jordan did not return his calls, nor did Secretary of the Interior Cecil Andrus in regard to water policy. The California Democrat's request for a meeting with President Carter went unanswered in a period when the President was proclaiming how accessible he was to members of Congress.

For weeks, Representative Moss remained hopeful that the lack of responsiveness of the Carter White House was the result of a young and inexperienced staff that would soon get its act together so it could be responsive to serious questions about energy, information policy and water policy in the Western states. He hoped it was not an example of clever stonewalling tactics, but Moss was afraid he was seeing evidence of a refusal to be accountable that was similar to that in the Nixon White House.

The months ahead were to be even more distressing to Moss and other House Democrats from a standpoint of information policy, energy policy and conflicts of interest.

CHAPTER FOUR

Labor's Man Marshall

President Carter pledged that his administration would not be subject to the pressures of special interest groups, but his choice for Labor Secretary was a man whose thinking was absolutely in tune with the AFL–CIO on controversial issues such as the repeal of Section 14 (B) of the Taft–Hartley Labor Law, which permitted the various states to enact the so-called right-to-work laws.

AFL–CIO President George Meany had indicated a preference for Harvard Economist John T. Dunlop, President Ford's former Secretary of Labor, but he was pleased in any event to give his approval to F. Ray Marshall, a pro-labor economist from the University of Texas. Not only was Marshall a strong advocate of the repeal of the Taft–Hartley Law to outlaw the various state right-to-work laws, but he was also an outspoken champion of legislation that would permit common situs picketing—long a goal of AFL–CIO building trade unions.

That was enough to win him the support of the AFL–CIO and the pro-labor bloc in the Senate Labor Committee including Chairman Harrison Williams, Democrat of New Jersey, and Senator Jacob Javits, the ranking Republican member from New York. On these two issues alone he was too much "the rubber stamp" of organized labor for the conservative Democrats and Republicans in the Senate, who argued that the Labor Secretary should represent all of the labor force of America regardless of whether they chose to belong to labor unions or not.

Most conservatives, of course, accepted the fact that any Democratic president would probably clear his nominee for the Labor Secretary post with George Meany despite any campaign pledges to reject the pressures of special interests. They were prepared to state their opposition to a basic pro-union philosophy but planned to vote for his confirmation unless they found some serious problem with his qualifications or his integrity.

However, Secretary-designate Marshall created a serious problem for himself at the confirmation hearing when he stated that he would support unionization of the military services. This was above and beyond anything that the AFL–CIO had requested, even though some of the AFL–CIO unions (specifically the American Federation of Government Employees and the National Association of Government Employees) were making efforts to organize the military services.

Marshall's statement approving unionization of the military was made in response to questions by Senator Orrin Hatch, a Utah Republican, and went unnoticed by the press and at the White House, but not by the group of senators who were at that time backing legislation that would outlaw any efforts to organize military personnel.

Senator Hatch, a conservative Republican lawyer from Salt Lake City, expected Marshall to be a supporter of the AFL–CIO's major goals, particularly the repeal of Section 14 (B) of the National Labor Relations Act, which was the major barrier to compulsory unionism. A total of twenty states had passed right-to-work laws to outlaw compulsory unionism, and the AFL–CIO had been trying to get that law repealed for nearly thirty years.

Also, Hatch and other conservatives expected Marshall to favor retention of the Davis–Bacon Act, which requires that contractors performing federal construction or federal-aided programs of more than $2,000 be required to pay their workers no less than "the prevailing wage" in the area as set by the Secretary of Labor. Critics contended that Davis–Bacon actually boosted construction costs above the prevailing wage levels in many areas, made federal projects more expensive, and added to inflation.

Ray Marshall told Hatch that he not only favored retention of Davis–Bacon, but he favored tighter enforcement of the law. Marshall also favored collective bargaining rights for public employees and the right to strike or have binding arbitration.

Hatch and other conservatives had anticipated that Marshall, enthusiastically endorsed by the AFL–CIO, would take these pro-labor positions, but they did not anticipate his support of unionization of the military services.

Moves by the racket-ridden International Brotherhood of Teamsters to organize police and fire departments and the military services had caused a sharp reaction among liberals as well as conservatives in Congress. Even AFL–CIO President George Meany himself had backed away from support of a military union in the face of the specter of the corruption-ridden Teamsters union's having control of personnel in the nation's military services.

In 1976 Senator John McClellan, the Arkansas Democrat who had exposed the Teamsters' corruption, had been joined by twenty other Senators on a bill that would outlaw unionization of the military services. Although most of the group were ultraconservative Democrats and Republicans, there were a few middle-of-the-road Democrats who joined in the sponsorship, including Senator Lawton Chiles, a Florida Democrat, and Senator Robert Taft, a Republican from Ohio. Even liberal Democrats, such as Senator John Culver and Dick Clark, both of Iowa, declared their opposition to the principle of a union organizing United States military services.

Although the AFL–CIO did not favor passage of the legislation to outlaw organizing of the military services, an AFL–CIO spokesman told this reporter that Meany had expressed opposition to organization of either the police or military services on grounds of "an inherent conflict of interest." The spokesman said that Meany's initial opposition to efforts to unionize the Army came in a press conference statement during the Vietnam War, when some pacifist groups were seeking that approach to end U.S. military involvement in the controversial war.

The AFL–CIO spokesman said that Meany had reiterated his opposition to unionizing the military in 1976 when answering a question from a White House Fellows group. The question was posed as a result of wide publicity given to the comments of Clyde M. Webber, then national president of the American Federation of Government Employees (AFGE), who had initiated a study on the feasibility of unionizing the military.

Although the AFGE is a member of the AFL–CIO, it would not necessarily be bound by Meany's views. Indeed, in 1976 the AFGE changed its constitution to permit it to organize military personnel in addition to the civilian defense department employees who held membership in AFGE. Webber and the new AFGE president, Kenneth T. Blaylock, both said they had doubts about the advisability of organizing the military services and were opposed to any right to strike. They said their moves gave military personnel an alternative to joining the corruption-ridden Teamsters union.

The furor over the Teamsters' organizing of the military services had been stirred by reports to Congress that the head of the Teamsters organizing department had made a speech before the U.S. War College in the fall of 1975 in which he called for unionization of the military services by the Teamsters union. He was reported to have told the War College audience that Teamsters organization of the military was as inevitable as Teamsters organization of the nation's police departments.

Norman Goldstein, head of the International Teamsters organizing department, refused to answer questions on the controversial speech he had given before the War College. The Teamsters' press office refused to answer questions on the speech but stated that the Executive Board of the Teamsters had taken no official action to appropriate funds for organizing the military services. The spokesman also denied there was any concerted drive to organize law enforcement officers, even though organization was known to have taken place in some cities from Maine to California, from Washington to Florida.

Months after Goldstein's speech stirred an uproar in Congress in opposition to unionization of the military, Teamsters President Frank Fitzsimmons agreed to be interviewed by this reporter. In the face of protests, Fitzsimmons declared his personal opposition to organizing the military services.

"The Teamsters will not organize the military services as long as I have any breath in my body," Fitzsimmons declared in his effort to end the criticism being heaped on him and his union.

The blustering Teamsters boss expressed outrage at reports that the Teamsters was one of several unions with plans to organize the military, and claimed to have "no idea" where officials of the AFGE and others got the idea that his union was involved. "I have never discussed such a plan with anybody, and have never heard such a plan discussed," Fitzsimmons said. "If it were brought up, I would oppose it."

However, Fitzsimmons told this reporter that in the more than two months since the controversy arose he had not had time to check reports on whether Goldstein, as head of his organizing department, had told the War College that Teamsters organization of the military services as "inevitable."

But in that same conversation Fitzsimmons confirmed the Teamsters national policy to organize city police, sheriffs' offices and other law enforcement agencies into Teamsters locals. Earlier, the Teamsters press office had denied that such a nationwide drive was taking place even though a close associate of Fitzsimmons from a Michigan local had traveled from coast to coast and had more than two hundred local units organizing local police, state police and sheriffs' offices.

It was against this background that Hatch asked Marshall for expansion of his views on collective bargaining for federal employees.

"There has been some consideration of a union in the armed forces," Hatch said. "What are your views with regard to a unionized military?"

"Well, I have not thought much about the unionized military," Dr. Marshall responded. Hatch followed up:

"I think you should. What kind of view would you have?"

"I think there is probably some merit to it," Marshall responded and then qualified his statement. "I would not permit strikes in the military, obviously."

"You might be amenable to have a military union?" a surprised Senator Hatch followed.

"I might be amenable to having a military union where you have got some kind of representation by the soldiers in making the rules that govern their working conditions," Marshall expanded his view. But again he qualified: "Now, I would not be in favor of strikes."

"Would you mean except with those we have today?" Senator Hatch said with reference to illegal strikes by police, firemen and military services in other countries that are barred from strikes by law.

"I am not sure what we have today," Marshall responded in missing the point. "My point is—and I believe in the military and certainly in peacetime and not in combat situation—there are circumstances where a military commander would benefit out of what the people are worried about and what the problems are and that kind of mechanism might be good business for the military."

"Would you have an outside collective bargaining agent?" Senator Hatch pushed, and when Marshall responded that he "had not thought that out as yet," Hatch followed:

"You think it is a possibility?"

"It is a possibility," Marshall said. "If you want me to think it out, I will."

Hatch had heard all he needed to determine that Dr. F. Ray

Marshall, despite all his fine academic credentials as a Professor of Economics at the University of Texas and despite a host of widely acclaimed publications on labor–management relations and the problems of minority groups, did not understand what George Meany meant about the "inherent conflict of interest" in the unionization of the military or police.

On January 19, 1977, Senator Hatch announced his opposition to the confirmation of Marshall as Secretary of Labor and called attention to Marshall's support of a right to strike by certain types of public employees, and his favorable attitude toward unionism in the military.

"Mr. Marshall went so far as to indicate that he believed there was a rightful place for unionism in armed services, but that he had not clearly thought out all of the parameters of such a proposal," Hatch said.

The Utah Senator said that he "found Mr. Marshall to be honest, sincere, and quite candid" in response to some very difficult and controversial labor questions. "Also, on the plus side, is his demonstrated intellectual capacity to carry forth the duties of his high office in a satisfactory manner."

Hatch inserted the transcript of his questioning of Marshall into the *Congressional Record,* and the passage indicating support of military unions caused an immediate furor. Within a matter of hours, Hatch was contacted by more than twenty members of the Senate. Liberals as well as conservatives expressed their great concern.

"I recognized that Mr. Marshall had views on support of compulsory unionism, construction site picketing and consumer boycotts of agricultural products that were at odds with my own beliefs," Hatch told this reporter. "I did not anticipate that he would openly support such a far-out proposition as that of unionizing the military services."

The White House was caught off guard, and Press Secretary Jody Powell called back after consultation to say Marshall had not cleared his views on unionization of the military services with the White House. "You can quote me that I believe President Carter would be opposed to unionizing the military services," Powell said. "I don't remember that we said anything on that subject in the campaign."

Powell said that the White House had not known of Marshall's testimony on the unionization of the military services until they started receiving calls the day after Senator Hatch had placed the transcript in the *Congressional Record.* Later, Powell said that he read Marshall's testimony and found it was not a firm support for unionization of the military but was "highly conjectural."

Hatch said that he and Senator Paul Laxalt, a conservative Republican from Nevada, were distributing a "dear colleague" letter to try to block Senate confirmation of Marshall unless he came out flatly against unionization of the military.

Hatch said that he could not support Marshall, even if he came out against unionizing the military, because "his positions are naive acceptance of the trade union handbook on a broad range of issues that would give more power to the unions at a time when they already have more than enough power to properly represent their members."

The Utah Senator said he would join with more than twenty-five other senators in reintroducing legislation that would make it illegal for anyone even to try to organize the Army, Navy, Air Force or Marine personnel.

"I know that officials of the AFGE are nice and reasonable people under most circumstances, but this does not change the principle that collective bargaining and a union-dominated grievance procedure is inconsistent with the discipline required in a military organization," Hatch said.

"I don't believe it is necessary to emphasize the totally impossible situation that would be created if a corrupt union or a union with pacifist leadership would gain control of the military."

It took a great deal of scurrying around for the Carter White House and the supporters of Marshall to get him over the confirmation barrier he had created for himself.

Senator Jake Javits, the senior Republican on the Senate Labor Committee, took the lead in explaining that Marshall "may not have used precisely the words he intended to use" in describing his views on collective bargaining for U.S. military forces.

"Both my colleagues and I were disturbed by the answer which Dr. Marshall gave, since in his answer he did not precisely define his terms," Javits said and inserted into the record a letter of "clarification" Marshall had written to Chairman Harrison A. Williams, Jr., of New Jersey.

In that letter Marshall wrote of his understanding that "military organizations require strong discipline and adherence to a single line of authority" and that to function effectively "the military services cannot allow their members many of the options that are available to members of unions."

"In my remarks at my confirmation hearing, I said that I would not be in favor of military strikes or military unions per se," Marshall explained. "My remarks were directed more toward the institution of certain practices that might improve the military. I do believe that the peacetime military can benefit from improved communication procedures whereby commanders are made aware of the problems affecting personnel."

Senator Javits termed Marshall's explanation as "credible and . . . understandable," but Senator John McClellan said that the letter did not convince him "that Dr. Marshall is seriously against and would vigorously oppose the unionizing of our Armed Forces."

In announcing that he would vote against confirmation of Marshall, McClellan said that he had no doubts about his integrity, his character or his general qualifications but felt strongly "that the unionizing of the military would be dangerous to the national interest and that it cannot be tolerated without impairment to the national sovereignty."

To bolster the case for Marshall, Senator Javits introduced a letter from Marshall in which he assured the Senate that he would follow up aggressively on investigations of corruption and mismanagement in the multibillion-dollar Teamsters' Central States pension fund. It was a case that had never been effectively investigated in the Nixon and Ford administrations, presumably because of the friendship and political ties of Frank Fitzsimmons with both Richard Nixon and Gerald R. Ford.

Ray Marshall was finally confirmed by the Senate as Labor Secretary by a 74 to 20 vote with six members not voting. But many of those who voted for confirmation were uneasy about his position on military unions and uncertain whether he would oppose with vigor any moves to organize the military services.

The twenty votes against the confirmation on January 26—six days after President Carter took office—made Marshall the second most controversial Cabinet nomination Carter sent through the Senate. The most controversial nomination was Griffin B. Bell as United States Attorney General, who was confirmed by a vote of 75 to 21.

CHAPTER FIVE

Griffin Bell—Carter's Crony at Justice

President Carter's announcement that Griffin B. Bell would be his Attorney General seemed to flout all of the experiences of the Watergate scandals and his campaign pledge to appoint the best qualified person "without regard to political considerations." To many of the Democrats who had supported Carter's candidacy with enthusiasm, it seemed too much like Richard Nixon's selection of his former law partner, John Mitchell, to be the Attorney General of the United States.

Although the Watergate scandals had pointed up many wrongs in the Nixon administration, the greatest abuse of power was in the politicizing of the Justice Department and the Federal Bureau of Investigation, which had hampered the investigations with obstructionist tactics and had made the White House–engineered cover-up possible for several months. And, in historical perspective, Nixon and Mitchell were not the first to mix a heavy measure of politics with the decisions on criminal prosecutions.

Candidate Carter had harped long and loud on his pledge to take politics out of the decisions on appointments to the Justice Department and to develop an even-handed justice to replace the favoritism of the Nixon and Ford years.

The announcement that President-elect Carter would name Griffin Bell, a long-time friend and political confidant, as Attorney General of the United States stirred a heated controversy over his role in the Carter political campaigns and his role as a legal adviser to a former segregationist Governor of Georgia, Ernest Vandiver, in 1959.

Griffin Bell had served nearly fifteen years as a United States Circuit Judge, an appointee of President John F. Kennedy, but his opinions as a member of that Fifth Circuit court came under a scorching attack from the Americans for Democratic Action (ADA), civil rights groups and legal scholars. They charged that there was a conflict of interest when Judge Bell failed to disqualify himself on cases involving litigations that he had a role in starting when he was a private lawyer in Atlanta.

Senator Edward W. Brooke, a Massachusetts Republican, led the fight on the civil rights issues stressing that Bell took segregationist positions as a lawyer, and as a United States Circuit Judge had ruled that the Georgia legislature had properly barred Julian Bond from a seat in the Georgia legislature.

"I fear that a double standard may be developing for nominees who appear before democratically controlled Congresses," Brooke told the Senate. "Our recent troubles with Watergate, conflicts of interest, impropriety in financial arrangements cry out for us to exercise great caution and great care in selecting attorneys general, judges [and] heads of regulatory agencies."

There had been five days of hearings from January 11 through January 18 on the Bell nomination, and Brooke said he could find no place in the hearings where the Democratic majority had explained why Judge Bell's actions did not constitute a violation of the Judicial Canons of Ethics. Judge Bell took part in a Fifth Circuit opinion dealing with the Atlanta plan after Bell had given counsel on the plan as a private lawyer.

Monroe Freedman, an acknowledged expert on legal ethics, testified that Judge Bell's participation in a case in which he had previously been involved as a lawyer was a clear violation of the Canons of Judicial Ethics and the Federal recusal laws, Brooke told the Senate.

Senator Donald W. Reigle of Michigan was the only Democrat on the Judiciary Committee who refused to vote for Bell's confirmation, because the nomination was not consistent with the stated campaign pledges and promises of President Carter.

He noted that Carter had pledged that political partisanship would have no role in the selection of the Attorney General in the wake of the Watergate scandals, which had centered on abuse and misuse of power in the Justice Department. Although Carter had praised Bell as "the best man" for the job and asserted that political support was not a factor, Senator Reigle said he had been at a loss "to find out what special and compelling reason warranted his being named."

"Rather than establishing clearly an unquestionable independence from the President, we instead find both the appearance and fact of a direct personal relationship," Reigle said. "Judge Bell was a financial contributor to the Carter presidential campaign—and assisted in the process of raising money from others. Further, his association with the President was close enough that Judge Bell was directly involved in constituting a list of prospective Attorney General nominees.

"And, of course, we have the well-known connection to the Kirbo law firm," Reigle said. "To many I have spoken with, this appointment, for this reason, has actually created some new cynicism."

Carter had campaigned on a slogan to put "the best" people in the Cabinet. Yet Reigle found Bell to have been "a courteous, workmanlike judge with a generally undistinguished record one way or the other" before he left the bench voluntarily in February 1976 to return to the practice of law with the Spaulding and King law firm in which his friend, Charles Kirbo, was a senior partner.

Senator Charles Percy, the Illinois Republican, also noted that Bell's association with Carter and Kirbo and his long-time role as an adviser for Georgia political candidates "could give the appearance of being inconsistent with the President's promise of an independent and nonpolitical Attorney General."

Senator John Heinz, a Pennsylvania Republican, noted that Carter had said he would do "as much as is humanly possible" to assure that the Attorney General was removed from the area of politics.

"I do not believe that this particular nominee [Bell] represents our best effort to remove the taint of politics and cronyism from the administration of justice," Senator Heinz said. He called the Senate's attention to a recent American Bar Association committee report on a study of federal law enforcement.

"The conclusions in this report address the specific task which we face today," Heinz said. "This Bar Association committee stated that removing partisan politics from the Attorney General's office 'is the essential precondition for restoration of public confidence in the administration of justice.'

"We can have no greater goal than restoring public faith in the system by which justice is administered in this nation," Heinz declared in emphasizing one of the major themes of Jimmy Carter's campaign for president.

Then the Pennsylvania Republican related the fact that Bell acknowledged a close personal and family tie with President Carter and a close tie with his law partner and friend, Charles Kirbo.

Without implying anything improper or insidious, Heinz said "it undeniably draws the Attorney General-designate closer to the President in a personal sense and closer to his circle of intimate political advisers."

Senator Heinz dealt with the claims of President Carter that Bell was not a political campaign adviser in the sense that Attorney General Herbert Brownell was to President Eisenhower, Attorney General Robert F. Kennedy was to President Kennedy, and John Mitchell was to President Nixon.

"Judge Bell has himself acknowledged on the record in the committee that he played an active role in President Carter's recent campaign—a more active role than I had been aware of prior to our hearings," Heinz said. He enumerated:

"First, he helped raise money prior to the Pennsylvania primary.

"Second, he wrote a campaign speech for Mr. Carter which the Democratic nominee subsequently delivered in Detroit.

"Third, he helped prepare another campaign address that President Carter delivered to the American Bar Association in Atlanta.

"Fourth, he prepared the questionnaire which President Carter used to interview prospective Vice-Presidential candidates.

"Fifth, he helped advise the President on the development of his position on amnesty during the campaign."

Heinz and other critics also noted that Bell had been in charge of John F. Kennedy's campaign for President in Georgia in 1960, which had set the stage for his appointment by Kennedy as a United States Circuit Judge.

"I think it may be appropriate to take a hard look at Judge Bell's close personal and political alliance with the President," Heinz declared. "Just as we would have a negative presumption against any nominee who came to us with a record of racism and racist statements, I think we must also have a similar negative presumption against any prospective Attorney General who comes to us with a close personal and political relationship with the President whom he is to serve."

Heinz declared that in addition "each of us must take a hard look at Judge Bell's record in resolving conflicts of interest and his sensitivity to this critical aspect of his job." Heinz explained that he wanted the next Attorney General to have strict standards and to be a chief law enforcement officer who could say "No" and make it stick.

"In too many instances, Judge Bell broke the spirit, if not the letter, of the canons and laws covering judicial ethics," Heinz said. "And on repeated instances, he has not demonstrated the sensitivity to conflict-of-interest questions that his new duties would demand of him."

Heinz found it "particularly troublesome" that Judge Bell belonged to the Biscayne Bay Yacht Club and at least two other clubs "that excluded Jews and Blacks from membership." He was receiving gift memberships from two of those three clubs while sitting on cases involving racial discrimination, and specifically one involving the yacht club, Heinz told the Senate.

"Judge Bell subsequently ruled in favor of the yacht club but did not disclose his memberships in the three clubs to the lawyers in the case before his sitting on the case." Heinz continued by noting that Dean Monroe Freedman of Hofstra had testified "that Judge Bell violated the canons [of ethics] and the Federal recusal statutes by sitting on this case." He added that Dean Freedman, a former chairman of the Federal Bar Association's Committee on Disciplinary Standards and Procedures, was the author of *Lawyer's Ethics in an Adversary System,* a book which won an award of distinction from the American Bar Association.

He explained that the free memberships that Judge Bell received from the white Piedmont Driving Club and the Capital City Club of Atlanta were worth about $2,000 a year, and that Judge Bell had failed to report them in forms required to be filed with the U.S. Judicial Conference.

Senator William Proxmire, a Wisconsin Democrat who had warmly supported Carter in the 1976 campaign, joined the opposition to Bell and said he could "subscribe wholeheartedly" to Senator Heinz's analysis of the Bell nomination.

"I opposed Judge Bell for this nomination [because] the Attorney General should not be a close friend or close associate of the President," Proxmire said. "Watergate most recently taught us that the immense power of the President can be corrupted and [it] made vivid the fact that the President of the United States could violate the law with serious consequences for our country.

"In all fairness, President Nixon was not the first President to play fast and loose with the law, and unfortunately, he will not be the last," Proxmire warned his Senate colleagues. "When anyone breaks a Federal law, the responsibility to act is the Attorney General's. This body should not have to review the President [Nixon] firing the Attorney General of the United States in the infamous Saturday night massacre to remind it of that.

"The Attorney General should be separate and apart," Proxmire declared in touching a nerve that bothered many of his Democratic colleagues who were privately critical of the selection of Bell but did not want to oppose the new Democratic president.

"He [the Attorney General] should not be a brother of the President, or an ex–law partner, or a campaign manager, or an old and close friend of any kind," Proxmire said. He mentioned some independent appointments: Attorney General Edward Levi, a law dean and a Democrat, who was named by President Ford; Homer Cummings, who was Franklin D. Roosevelt's Attorney General; and Harlan Stone, who served in President Coolidge's administration and prosecuted the Teapot Dome political crooks.

Also, Proxmire noted that he saw "nothing in [Bell's] record to show that he will be the kind of champion of civil rights that the principle law-enforcement official of the Federal Government must become."

Proxmire declared that for too long many of the laws dealing with equal justice have had no enforcement, and he was not convinced that Bell would actively enforce these laws.

Senator Robert Dole, the Kansas Republican, and Senator John Danforth, a freshman Republican from Missouri, expressed specific concern over Bell's statement in the Senate Judiciary hearings that he would remove Clarence Kelley as Director of the Federal Bureau of Investigation.

FBI Director Kelley, a former FBI agent and a former Kansas City Police Chief, had been appointed by President Ford to restore order in the wake of L. Patrick Gray's disastrous term as Acting Director of the FBI in the Watergate years. The Crime Control Act of 1976, under which Kelley was appointed, provided a fixed ten-year term to insulate the FBI from partisan political pressures. Gray's bending to the whims of the Nixon White House to the point of illegally destroying politically explosive evidence had demonstrated why the FBI director should serve for ten years unless removed "for cause."

Bell could cite no specific "cause" for removal of Kelley but said the legislative history was "not too clear on what 'cause' is."

Both Dole and Danforth said the maneuvers to force the removal of FBI Director Kelley appeared to be in violation of both the spirit and the letter of the Crime Control Act and at variance with Candidate Carter's pledge to make the Justice Department totally nonpolitical.

Dole quoted Candidate Carter's speech before the American Bar Association on August 12, 1976:

"As much as humanly possible, the Attorney General should be removed from politics and should enjoy the same independence and authority and should deserve as much confidence as did the special prosecutor during the last few weeks of the Watergate investigations."

The Kansas Republican said President Carter and Griffin Bell were "buddies" while Carter had campaigned "to end the buddy system in Washington." Dole also said that Washington lawyer Joe Rauh, of the liberal ADA, characterized Bell as "part of Governor Carter's political group."

Senator Lowell Weicker, the Connecticut Republican who served on the Senate Watergate committee, said he hated being "the skunk at the confirmation garden party" for Griffin Bell, because he had no personal antagonism toward the President or his nominee for Attorney General.

Senator Weicker, one of the earliest and most vociferous critics of Nixon and Mitchell in the Watergate investigation, dealt with his report on Watergate and the abuse and misuse of the office of Attorney General under John Mitchell and Richard Kleindienst.

He recalled that while Nixon was publicly saying it would be wrong for the White House to force political decisions on the Attorney General, a Nixon White House memo on effective methods of "insuring that political considerations" would be used in federal programs was directed to Mitchell.

"At one point it was even suggested that the Attorney General wield the power of his office to keep a Republican contender off the primary ballot in Florida," Weicker recalled. "That campaign role also included an extraordinary meeting in the Attorney General's [Mitchell's] very office, to review plans for bugging, mugging, burglary, prostitution and kidnapping.

"Another Attorney General [Kleindienst] was placed in the

awkward position of being asked [by a White House lawyer] immediately after the Watergate break-in to help get [Watergate burglar James W.] McCord out of jail before he was identified'' as an employee of the Nixon re-election committee, Weicker said, recalling that Kleindienst was later warned of White House concern about a too-aggressive FBI investigation, was asked to provide raw FBI Watergate files to the White House and was later used as a secret contact with the Senate Committee's investigation of Watergate.

''He [Kleindienst] later became the first Attorney General in history convicted of a crime for his false and misleading testimony about the ITT matter,'' Weicker noted in the hope of jarring the Senate Democrats into deciding that confirmation of a political crony as Attorney General could be courting disaster.

Chairman James O. Eastland, the veteran Democratic senator from Mississippi; Senator Strom Thurmond, a Republican from South Carolina; and Senator Herman Talmadge, the senior Democrat from Georgia, were among those who spoke enthusiastically of Judge Bell. They stressed that he was appointed to the Circuit Court by President John F. Kennedy, who judged him ''qualified.''

''Griffin Bell is a man of keen intelligence and high integrity,'' Senator Thurmond said. ''Almost all who have known him longest and best say he is a man with sensitivity toward civil rights and individual rights.''

He noted that the *Washington Post* had commented editorially that Griffin Bell should be confirmed as a ''man of substantial intelligence and staunch personal integrity.'' ''If the *Washington Post* makes a statement like this about the gentleman, a judge from Georgia, I consider that is considerable praise,'' Thurmond said.

Senator Talmadge declared that Bell ''is a man of impeccable character and integrity'' and defended his decisions on civil rights cases, which had been under attack from liberals and civil rights groups.

''He was a man of principle as Federal judge,'' Talmadge said in characterizing him as ''a voice of moderation.'' ''He will be a man of principle as Attorney General.''

Senator Talmadge noted that Representative Andrew Young, a Georgia Congressman who had been nominated by Carter as U.S. Ambassador to the United Nations, had expressed ''great confidence in Griffin Bell as Attorney General.'' Talmadge recalled that Andy Young had worked and marched with the late Martin Luther King, Jr., during the civil rights struggles of the 1960s.

Talmadge called attention to an editorial by Eugene Patterson, editor of the *St. Petersburg* (Florida) *Times,* that characterized Bell as "a pretty good man for a cleanup job that can lead to restoration of faith in the Justice Department."

Senator Edward Kennedy related that Bell had been President John F. Kennedy's choice for United States Circuit Judge and that Attorney General Robert Kennedy "was pleased" with the choice. He noted "one troublesome aspect of Judge Bell's record" in that "he did not exercise leadership in the development of civil rights laws at a time of critical and rapid change.

"Furthermore, before he became a judge, Judge Bell was closely associated with the Georgia Governor's resistance against desegregating that State's schools," Senator Kennedy said. He indicated he was persuaded that Griffin Bell had changed.

"If Judge Bell fulfills his own commitments and the pledges of President Carter, then he will have gone beyond the standards established by his critics," Kennedy said in rationalizing his decision to vote for President Carter's choice.

Senator Gaylord Nelson, a liberal Democrat from Wisconsin, said he was voting against Bell's confirmation because "I cannot properly defend two standards for Presidential appointments, one for Democrats and another for Republicans." He said that he was particularly concerned about Judge Bell's decision that barred Julian Bond from a seat in the Georgia House because of his endorsement of the criticism of U.S. policies in Vietnam and the American treatment of minorities at home.

Nelson noted that Judge Bell thought the Georgia House had a "rational basis for its decision." This decision was later reversed by the United States Supreme Court by a vote of 9 to 0. The Supreme Court pointed out that Bond was willing to take the loyalty oath and that the State of Georgia admitted that Bond's expression of admiration for those who opposed the war and resisted the draft would not have violated the selective service laws.

While Judge Bell told the Judiciary Committee that his opinion on the Bond case had been "a mistake," Nelson did not view the admission of error in the Bond case and other cases to be sufficient. "Mr. Bell did not address these issues in some casual, informal environment," Nelson told the Senate. "These cases were tried in formal judicial proceedings with arguments made and briefs filed. These decisions represented a carefully considered judgment on the merits.

"The question, in my mind, still remains—How, in the future, will Mr. Bell construe and interpret these constitutional rights when the occasion arises?"

Senator George McGovern, the Democratic candidate for president in 1972, also made reference to the Bond case. "We can forgive the mistake, but do not need to elevate the perpetrator [Judge Bell] to the highest law enforcement office in the land."

In announcing his decision to vote against confirmation, Senator McGovern said it was "painful" to vote against President Carter's choice: "In the long run, I am convinced that we will do the President the greatest service when we give him the benefit of our most critical judgment, not when we go along to serve our convenience or his. . . . We have an obligation to the President and to the American people to maintain the vigor and independence of the Congress so that the natural competition and disagreements between ourselves and the executive branch will increase the ingenuity and thoroughness of all concerned. We must help the President restore and renew public confidence in our system of government, and we will not set the new moral tone to which he aspires if we begin by abandoning the standards [we have sought] to establish."

On the final vote, there were only five Democrats who showed enough independence to oppose the confirmation of Bell, although there were many liberal Democrats who privately were critical of the selection because of Bell's political and personal ties with Carter and because of his questionable judicial record. Senator John Culver of Iowa joined with McGovern, Nelson, Proxmire, and Reigle to put their votes where their sentiments were.

Senator Jacob Javits, a senior New York Republican, said that on most nominations he felt inclined to go along with the president's personal choices, but he believed the post of Attorney General—the nation's chief law enforcement officer—required a more thorough scrutiny because of the power that resides in prosecution decisions.

Senator Harrison Schmitt, a freshman from New Mexico, said he had not made up his mind on Bell's confirmation until he heard the debates and then "reluctantly" concluded that "Mr. Bell's record does not demonstrate the required impartiality and adherence to ethical standards.

"I would much rather be positive in my actions as a Senator," Senator Schmitt said. "Nevertheless, the arguments against the nomination seem to be based solidly in fact, and seem to create fairly consistent patterns of activity by Mr. Bell that militate against his future performance as Attorney General."

Senator Schmitt said his "greatest concern" about the Bell nomination was that "it contributes to the appearance of a pattern of appointments which are contrary to President Carter's public statements.

"He stated publicly that Cabinet appointments will be removed from politics and independent of the White House in the performance of their statutory duties," Schmitt said. "They represent a pattern that is disturbingly reminiscent of portions of a recent Cabinet and White House staff which, by a lack of impartiality and ethics, put this great Nation through one of the most traumatic periods of our history."

Schmitt said "the new President has selected a White House staff composed largely of close associates from his home state and his recent political campaign.

"Although I voted to confirm Mr. Bert Lance, another close associate and friend of Mr. Carter, as Director of the Office of Management and Budget, I expressed great reservations about his experience to carry out his duties and responsibilities," the perceptive New Mexico Senator told his colleagues. "My reservations about Mr. Bell are much deeper and I cannot support his nomination."

Senator Charles M. Mathias, Jr., a moderate Maryland Republican who led the opposition to Bell, was able to rally only sixteen Republicans to oppose the Bell nomination despite the hearings that "raise some grave doubts as to whether [the public] can look to the Justice Department in the future as a citadel of justice." But it was significant that those voting against confirmation were largely in the liberal and moderate wing of the Republican party. They were Senators Javits, Percy, Weicker, Clifford Case (New Jersey), Heinz, Brooke, Richard Lugar (Indiana), John H. Chaffee (Rhode Island) and S. I. Hayakawa (California). Other Republicans voting against the Bell nomination were Senator Clifford Hansen and Malcolm Wallop, both of Wyoming; Senator Henry Bellmon of Oklahoma; and Senator Dole. They had little in common ideologically except that they viewed the Bell nomination as the breaking of a Carter pledge to keep partisan politics out of the Justice Department.

Even Senator Birch Bayh, the leader of the forces speaking for Bell, found things in Bell's record with which he disagreed.

Bayh noted that Bell, as a Federal Circuit Judge, had endorsed President Nixon's nomination of G. Harrold Carswell to the United States Supreme Court—a nomination that Bayh bitterly and successfully opposed.

He found "mistakes" in Judge Bell's work as counsel to Segregationist Governor Ernest Vandiver and declared Bell's opinion in the Julian Bond case was wrong. But, Senator Bayh said, he had given "substantial weight to [Bell's] pledges of strong enforcement of civil rights laws; protection of individual liberties, dedication to absolute integrity by public officials; monitoring of intelligence activities to prevent abuses; improving access to our judicial system for enforcement of important constitutional, consumer, and other individual rights. . . .

"Of course, we all have to face the fact that pledges are merely empty words unless they are accompanied by the personal qualities that will assure their realization," Bayh said in expressing his judgment that "his pledges are worthy of our confidences."

It was only a few months after the confirmation of Bell (by a vote of 75 to 21) that the firing of Republican United States Attorney David W. Marston and the handling of a Bert Lance investigation were to raise serious questions as to whether Bell was running a nonpartisan Justice Department.

There was joy in Hamilton Jordan's office at the White House when the confirmation of Griffin Bell was reported. The Bert Lance bank scandal and the Marston firing were months away. The success in getting Bell installed as Attorney General made President Carter and his Georgia White House crew confident that they had the clout to sell anything to Congress that Jimmy Carter believed in his heart was good for the nation.

CHAPTER SIX

Bert Lance— A Country Banker from Georgia

Even before Griffin Bell officially took over as Attorney General, Justice Department lawyers were making some decisions to accommodate the Georgia friends of President-elect Jimmy Carter. No evidence was produced that President-elect Carter had knowledge of the unusual steps that his banker friend, T. Bert Lance, took to clear up some long-standing problems over his "irregular banking practices" as president of the Calhoun First National Bank, at Calhoun, Georgia, and the National Bank of Georgia (NBG), in Atlanta.

The Office of the Comptroller of the Currency conducted investigations at the Calhoun First National, where Lance had reigned as president and chief executive officer. Auditors found that Lance and his family had overdrawn their accounts by at least $300,000. Bank examiners also found that Lance had used the interest-free funds of the Calhoun First National to pay some of the campaign expenses in his unsuccessful campaign for Governor of Georgia in 1974. By late 1975 the Comptroller's office regarded these alleged violations of banking laws and regulations as serious enough to refer the case to the Justice Department for possible criminal prosecution. At that time Lance had entered into an agreement with the Atlanta office of the Comptroller of the Currency to correct a number of irregularities, including some that were alleged violations of the law.

The problems with the Comptroller's office and the possibility of criminal prosecution by the Justice Department had been hanging over Bert Lance's head through the late months of 1975 and through 1976 as he helped his friend, Jimmy Carter, raise money for the presidential campaign. At the same time, he was helping Jimmy and Billy Carter with their personal business finances at the Carter peanut warehouse in Plains, Georgia. The National Bank of Georgia arranged a $6 million line of credit for the Carter warehouse in 1976 against the better judgment of some of the bank's officials.

When Carter won the election, it was immediately apparent that his long-time friend and financial benefactor would be in line for some high position in Washington, so Lance became active in clearing up his problems with the Comptroller's office and with the Justice Department. Lance contacted Donald Tarleton, Atlanta regional director for the Comptroller of the Currency, and Tarleton rescinded the potentially embarrassing disciplinary agreement between Lance and Calhoun First National Bank and the Comptroller's office.

Two days later, President-elect Carter announced that Bert Lance would be the Director of the Office of Management and Budget (OMB) in the incoming Carter administration. It was one of the most powerful positions in Washington, and with the close personal and political ties that Lance had with Jimmy Carter, it could be the second most powerful position in the federal government.

Lance and his lawyers had another equally serious hurdle to clear before he would be prepared to undergo the questioning in the confirmation process before the Senate Government Affairs committee. It was essential that they persuade John Stokes, Jr., the United States Attorney in Atlanta, to terminate the criminal investigation of practices at the Calhoun First National Bank. It would be embarrassing, or worse, if Senate investigators discovered that there was a pending criminal investigation of the banking practices of the man Jimmy Carter wanted to make the key man in his reorganization and economic planning for the nation.

United States Attorney Stokes, a Republican appointee, was interested in continuing as a prosecutor under Carter's announced nonpartisan administration of the Justice Department. Stokes cleared his action on the Lance bank matter with the criminal division in Washington, then headed by Assistant United States Attorney Richard Thornburg. Finding no objection, he terminated the criminal investigation of Lance in the first week of December 1976.

Those two actions by Tarleton and Stokes made it possible for Acting Comptroller of the Currency Robert Bloom to write a letter to the Senate Government Affairs Committee telling Chairman Abe Ribicoff of Connecticut and Senator Charles Percy, the ranking Republican from Illinois, that the agency reports "cleared" Lance of improper banking practices and that he was "well qualified" for the post of Director of the Office of Management and Budget.

The Senate Government Affairs Committee staff accepted from the Justice Department and Bloom the general reports that Lance had been cleared of charges of improprieties and irregularities. Meanwhile the artful Bert Lance made personal calls on Chairman Ribicoff, Senator Percy and other members of the Senate to smooth the way for his confirmation hearing. The confirmation hearing was a routine affair with the highly articulate self-styled "country banker" captivating the committee members.

Bert Lance volunteered no detailed explanation when Bloom's letter was placed in the record. Bloom noted only that a regularly scheduled audit in 1975 had "discovered that the bank (Calhoun First National) had permitted accounts maintained by the Lance for Governor Campaign in 1974 to be overdrawn."

"A full investigation into the facts of this matter was made by this Office, and it was our conclusion that no violation of 18 USC. 610 had occurred," Bloom wrote. "However, since such determination can only be made by the Department of Justice, the facts were referred to that Department and we understand that after consideration, the file was closed as not warranting further action.

"It has also been correctly reported in the press that the Calhoun bank allowed directors related to Mrs. Lance to overdraw their accounts for varying lengths of time in violation of good banking practices," Bloom wrote to Chairman Ribicoff.

"However, in response to criticism of this practice by our examiners, the amounts of all overdrafts were paid at standard rates of interest and the bank suffered no losses in connection therewith."

Bloom's letter gave no indication of the size of the overdrafts or the length that the Lance-related accounts were overdrawn, and said nothing of the rescinded agreement between Lance and the Comptroller of the Currency about the practices at the Calhoun bank.

The Acting Comptroller found only praise for Lance with regard to his tenure as president of the National Bank of Georgia. "Under his leadership the bank [NBG] has grown in deposit size from $224 million to $334 million and has emerged as an aggressive competitor in the Atlanta market."

Bloom's last glowing paragraph lulled the Senate Government Affairs Committee into a sense of complacency. Bloom wrote: "Mr Lance enjoys a very good reputation in the banking community and it is my opinion, based upon all the facts available to me, that Mr. Lance is well qualified to serve as the Director of the Office of Management and Budget."

Chairman Ribicoff inquired: "The press has reported that the decision to close your case was made the day before your nomination to the position of Director of the Office of Management and Budget was announced by President-elect Carter. Did you have any part whatsoever in the timing of the attorney's decision to close your case?"

"Absolutely not," Lance declared.

The Lance nomination was sent to the floor with a unanimous vote from the Senate Government Operations Committee and cleared the Senate on a voice vote. There was one dissenting voice, Senator William Proxmire, the independent-minded Wisconsin Democrat. He granted that Lance's record as "an eminently successful businessman" would be an important qualification, as would be the fact that "he is an old and trusted friend of the President of the United States.

"He has been the President's banker. He will now be his principal adviser on the budget. Why not?" Proxmire said and responded to his own question: "I will tell you why not. Mr. Lance simply has no experience or record of performance in what is in many ways the toughest job in the administration, except possibly for the President's."

Proxmire recited the wide range of experience required in federal government to be a full-time adviser to the President on budgetary matters involving more than $400 billion and covering everything from complicated social programs to complicated weapons systems.

"We need someone who has worked with Federal programs long enough to make mistakes and learn from those mistakes," Proxmire said. "We need someone who can give the President options and tell him what options will cost . . . someone who can listen to conflicting, expert advice and know enough to make a reasonable decision on it.

"What has been Mr. Lance's experience in the Federal Government?" Proxmire asked. "He has had none—zero, zip, zilch, not one year, not one week, not one day. He has shown impressive skill in operating a middle-size bank. He has been a candidate for Governor of Georgia. He headed the transportation department in Georgia. And what else?"

Commenting on Lance's "appallingly barren background," Proxmire said it should be remembered that "Mr. Lance will not be working for a President with great experience in the Federal Government." President Carter "comes to the White House as one of the most inexperienced Presidents in Federal government affairs in this century and probably one of the three or four least experienced in our 200-year history."

The Wisconsin Democrat, initially an enthusiastic supporter of Carter, noted that an inexperienced President should seek men of great experience as advisers. "He has surrounded himself with a White House staff that has two conspicuous distinctions. First, they are very young. And second, they have virtually no background, no record, no experience in Federal activities.

"The spirit, the will, the inspiration of the President may enable him to be a good President, despite the lack of experience in his top advisers." Proxmire said. "But, in my view the Lance appointment will handicap President Carter and this country seriously. The Lance nomination is a mistake."

The magnitude of "the mistake" of the Lance appointment was not apparent for several months, and by that time the gregarious Georgia banker had become recognized—for better or worse—as the most influential adviser on the White House staff. Lance was on a par with Georgia Lawyer Charles Kirbo, the one-man kitchen cabinet who continued as a senior partner in the King and Spaulding law firm in Atlanta while traveling to Washington every week or two to serve as an unofficial adviser to President Carter.

Even such long-time political associates as Presidential Assistant Hamilton Jordan and Press Secretary Jody Powell deferred to Big Bert Lance, who, as friend and political adviser to the President, had become the second most powerful man in Washington and by far the wealthiest member of the White House staff.

But, in late March, Philip Taubman, then an economic reporter for *Time*'s Washington bureau, spent a day with Bert Lance to get a feel for the personality and operating methods of this six-foot four-inch country banker who was such a power in the Carter plans to reorganize the government and the economy. Taubman was impressed with the confident manner with which Lance handled himself and the fact that he appeared unpretentious, but he also noticed more than a little touch of the wheeler-dealer in the former Georgia banker.

The twenty-nine-year-old reporter found Lance to be such a fascinating official that he decided to dig a bit deeper into the details of Lance's net worth of more than $2 million, which the Senate Government Affairs Committee had accepted as fact from Lance. The White House had issued a press release that Lance had debts totaling $650,000. Taubman checked with Senate Government Affairs Committee sources and was told Lance had debts of $5.3 million and assets of about $8 million, which included National Bank of Georgia stock.

There had been a sharp drop in the value of the stock of the NBG from $16 to below $13 a share. The way Phil Taubman figured it, that loss alone appeared to have wiped out most of the net worth Lance had reported in his financial statement in January. In a memorandum to *Time*'s Washington bureau chief, Hugh Sidey, Taubman spelled out his concern about Lance, his debts and the potential for conflicts of interest in his borrowing from other banks.

Sidey gave Taubman the okay to dig into the Lance finances even before he was aware of the details of the Comptroller of the Currency complaints against the Calhoun bank or the handling of the case at the Justice Department.

On a trip to Georgia, he found his misgivings about Lance's fiscal solvency confirmed in conversations with friends and acquaintances of Lance in various Georgia banks. Some of Lance's banker friends said they "couldn't understand how old Bert did it."

The bankers took consolation in the fact that they didn't have to solve Lance's financial problems in the face of the falling value of the NBG stock. A few of them volunteered with a chuckle that they couldn't understand how Lance had gained the image of a conservative banker when his reputation in the banking community in Georgia was that of a free-wheeling operator who prospered on taking chances.

It was just as Taubman had suspected, and the confirmation came much easier than he had expected. There were many more unexplored leads that he could have followed, but Taubman felt compelled to write his first story because of the constant fear of magazine editors that if they hold it for further developments, they will be scooped by the daily press or by the opposition magazines.

Although the New York editors of *Time* were eager for the story, when it was written they axed more than half of it with a claim of "a space problem." Taubman was disappointed with the cuts but happy that the editors were pleased. Even before it ran, he was planning to write further stories using the material cut from the first article and including supplements from further investigations.

Abruptly there was a lack of interest in a second story, or in further aggressive prodding into the financial affairs of the second most powerful man in Washington. But Taubman's first story, which appeared in the May 23, 1977, issue of *Time*, gave the press, the public and several federal agencies the first indication that President Carter's friend and Budget Director might be over his head in debts.

That Taubman story caught the attention of Stanley Sporkin, chief of enforcement at the Securities and Exchange Commission, and the staff members of the Senate Government Affairs Committee and the Senate and House Banking Committees. Lance had promised to sell his NBG stock by the end of the year, and that would be a financial disaster for the second most powerful figure in the Carter administration, as Taubman saw it. The Taubman story also punched the first big hole in the image of Bert Lance as the sound voice of conservatism in the Carter White House, where he was pictured as a force for sound fiscal policies and a balanced budget by 1981.

From that point on Bert Lance was on a downhill slide. Within a few weeks other publications became skeptical of Lance and then aggressive in pulling out the various pieces of his outrageous record of overdrafts, his questionable use of an NBG airplane, his use of the same bank stock as collateral for two different loans and miscellaneous other wheeling and dealing, which brought the *New York Times* and columnists William Safire and Tom Wicker into the critics' corner.

Initially, the big issue was whether Lance could sell his NBG stock and remain solvent, and on July 12, 1977, President Carter asked the Senate Government Affairs Committee to waive the deadline—the end of the year—on Lance's sale of the bank stock.

He said the deadline on the large Lance holdings had contributed to the sharp decline in the stock's price.

Amid editorial demands for a full investigation of Lance's financial dealings, the Senate Government Affairs Committee prepared for a hearing that was largely limited to the issue of whether Lance should be given an extension of the deadline to sell 207,000 shares of the National Bank of Georgia stock. Lance said a forced sale would have cost him $1.5 million. Chairman Ribicoff and Senator Percy were inclined to be sympathetic with his plight.

Chairman Ribicoff and his committee members accepted Lance's testimony at face value and exonerated him with comments that they saw nothing improper in his business or personal finances. Although they tentatively decided to abandon the investigation, the unanswered questions and contradictions in Lance's testimony drew a withering fire of criticism from newspapers and columnists.

Lance's explanation of his finances disclosed that he was incurring annual debt interest of $373,000, which he was paying on a $3.4 million loan from the First National Bank of Chicago in connection with his purchase of the NBG stock. Questions were raised about "conflict of interest." How can the Director of the Budget be so deeply indebted to any financial institution that has a large stake in U.S. fiscal policies? There were also unanswered questions about the circumstances under which Lance received that $3.4 million personal loan a month after the National Bank of Georgia deposited funds in a noninterest-bearing account in First National of Chicago.

Currency Comptroller John Heimann, brought into the government in July by Treasury Secretary Michael Blumenthal, launched his own "inquiry into certain matters relating to T. Bertram Lance and various financial institutions." The controversies that were the subject of sharply critical comments involved a half-dozen or more banks that were under the jurisdiction of Heimann's agency, and he intended to know about the facts so he would be in a position to report about them to his boss, Secretary Blumenthal, or to the Senate Government Affairs Committee or President Carter.

It was the voluminous report of more than 400 pages dated August 18, 1977, spelling out the details of the Lance family overdrafts of more than $400,000, that pulled President Carter into the controversy over his high-rolling banker friend.

After the issuance of the Heimann report, President Carter faced the press in the Old Executive Office Building and characterized Lance as "a man of complete integrity" and a man in whom he had "complete confidence." Carter's comments were justifiable only as loyal defense of a friend. From a standpoint of President Carter's claims of an administration of higher ethical standards, it was "an outrageous display of ignorance or arrogance," Senator Proxmire said.

CHAPTER SEVEN

Lies and Loyalty for Lance

It was not reasonable to expect that a busy President Carter would take the time to read and digest the details of the 403-page report by the Comptroller of the Currency on the inquiry into the financial affairs of Bert Lance. Presidents are too busy to devote their time to a personal analysis of the questions of ethical propriety and illegality such as those involved in the complicated overdraft of $400,000 by Lance and his family and associates at Calhoun First National Bank. Also, that voluminous report raised other complicated questions about the propriety of the National Bank of Georgia's interest-free deposits at Manufacturers Hanover Trust Company, New York, and the First National Bank of Chicago in a period in which those banks were making personal multimillion-dollar loans to Lance for his purchase of stock in the NBG.

Most presidents would have had some highly competent and trusted aide draw up a brief analysis of Lance's personal finances and fifty-four loans totaling $12.3 million that Lance, his relatives and business associates had obtained from twenty-three different banks. However, President Carter, who received the report on August 17, told his August 18 press conference that he had personally read the bulky report.

In his press conference, the President, who said he would never lie or mislead the American people, declared that the report of Currency Comptroller John Heimann confirmed his own view that Lance had done nothing wrong or illegal and that his old chum was "a man of complete integrity."

"I have reviewed the report of the Comptroller . . . both personally and also with the White House Legal Counsel Bob Lipshutz, and my faith in the character and competence of Bert Lance has been reconfirmed,'' Carter told the August 18, 1977, press conference to the amazement of those who had read the report. ''I see no other conclusion that can be drawn from any objective analysis of these findings.''

In terms reminiscent of President Richard Nixon's earlier efforts to put Watergate behind him by stressing the thoroughness of the investigation, President Carter commented: ''It's obvious that few individuals in government or out of government have ever undergone such an extensive and detailed investigation of their personal and business affairs by the Comptroller's Office, by the Justice Department, and twice by the Senate Committee.

''This process has not been an easy one for Bert,'' President Carter told the press, ''Nor for those who are close to him. . . . What is important is that Bert Lance is a man of competence, of honesty, and that his services to his country can and should continue.

''Bert Lance enjoys my complete confidence and support,'' President Carter said. ''I'm proud to have him as a part of my administration.''

Then turning to his Budget Director, President Carter said warmly, ''Bert, I'm proud of you.'' It was as if he believed that the Lance ordeal was ended because Jimmy Carter, President, had willed that it be ended.

Senate investigators, including Chairman Ribicoff and Senator Percy, both of whom had been supportive of Lance, could hardly believe what they had heard. Certainly the Heimann report had concluded that there were no grounds for criminal indictment of Bert Lance on the basis of evidence pulled together in a hurried inquiry of a few weeks. However, that report spelled out a wide range of minor and major violations of the banking laws and regulations, and Heimann's cover letter had noted that his agency could not initiate criminal prosecutions, that those decisons could be made only at the Justice Department.

''We do not believe,'' Heimann wrote, ''the information developed to date in the inquiry warrants the prosecution of any individual.'' Any discerning public official would see this comment as a warning that the investigation was not complete.

Heimann, in his summary, stated that Lance had made large borrowings from banking institutions which had a correspondent relationship with banks in which Lance was an officer and director, and he raised questions about the legality and ethical propriety of such arrangements.

Also, Heimann's four-page summary said that the Calhoun First National Bank from 1972 to 1974 permitted officers, directors, some employees and their families to overdraw checking accounts in substantial amounts for considerable periods of time. He stated that these "unsound banking practices" were in violation of the Financial Institutions Supervisory Act of 1966.

Furthermore, Heimann's summary included the fact that "Mr. Lance did not file with the banks of which he was an officer certain reports of outside business interests and personal borrowing and of borrowing by his affiliates as required by statute or regulation in the years covered in this inquiry."

Now, if President Carter had read no more than the summary of the 403-page report he was at least on notice that Bert Lance's actions were here alleged to have violated the laws that dealt with the banking industry, and that there were ongoing investigations that could mean more trouble in the future. Thus we cannot avoid the conclusion either that President Carter had stated falsely (or incorrectly) that he had read the report when he had not, or that he had read it too quickly to understand what he had read. The only other alternative was that he read it and understood it and was engaging in a willful effort to mislead the press and the public on the affairs of his banker friend.

Senator Ribicoff and Senator Percy, who now did not support President Carter on the Lance matter, saw immediately that there was serious trouble ahead. On the same day that President Carter told the press that the report had "reconfirmed" his belief in the "integrity" of Bert Lance, Chairman Ribicoff and Senator Percy issued a press release noting that Heimann's letter had "identified three areas of inquiry which have not yet been completed."

"We have asked the Comptroller that these areas of inquiry be completed and that a full report on these areas be provided to the Committee prior to September 7 [a date they had set for a new hearing]," the press release said. "Mr. Lance has been asked to appear . . . on September 8."

The Heimann report with its attachments and its comments on law violations and unethical banking practices provided the raw material for an avalanche of news stories, opinion columns and editorials critical of Lance and equally critical of President Carter for his unequivocal defense of his Budget Director.

A *New York Times* editorial criticized Carter for his "rush to judgment" in clearing Lance and said the issues surrounding the whole Lance controversy could not be sensibly appraised until all questions had been answered. *New York Times* columnist Tom Wicker said the Heimann report raised questions about Lance's competence for his job, and whether Lance's personal conduct met the high standards Carter had pledged for members of his administration.

The question was also being raised as to whether Jimmy Carter was really competent to analyze and handle great problems of the nation when he had failed so badly in his analysis of the Bert Lance affair. Had loyalty to an old friend and political supporter blinded President Carter to the fact that condoning Lance's wheeling and dealing was hurting his image with some of his most ardent supporters?

Press coverage centered on determining whether there was political favoritism by the Justice Department in its decision to terminate prematurely the criminal investigation of Bert Lance in December 1976, and in the decision of Donald Tarleton, regional director of the Comptroller's office, to rescind a disciplinary order involving the Calhoun First National Bank.

The Senate Government Affairs Committee chairman was particularly irritated by those decisions and the January letter from Acting Comptroller Robert Bloom that gave Lance "a clean bill of health." Chairman Ribicoff and Senator Percy felt that Bloom had deceived them and that Lance had been less than forthright in his financial statements and his responses to questions. Because they had relied on Bloom's letter and Lance's assurances, both had been embarrassed and subjected to considerable editorial criticism. They were determined not to be misled again when the hearings resumed.

Shocked at what their investigators were producing, Senators Ribicoff and Percy went to the White House to urge President Carter to seek Lance's resignation. When the President refused to ask for Lance's resignation, they said they would send the information to the Justice Department. Senator Percy suggested that President Carter name a Special Prosecutor to conduct the investigation, since this investigation involved a close personal friend and political adviser.

Chairman Ribicoff and Senator Percy said that Lance should voluntarily resign if President Carter did not make the suggestion.

Lance refused to resign, and President Carter was adamant even as Senator Proxmire was stating that his Senate Banking Committee would probe all of the circumstances of the manner in which Lance received a "clean bill of health" from the Justice Department and the Comptroller of the Currency in the face of gross irregularities in his overdrafts. On the House Banking Committee, Representative Fernand J. St Germaine, a Rhode Island Democrat, had his subcommittee investigators digging deeply into the Lance investigation.

Robert Bloom, who hoped for promotion to Deputy Comptroller of the Currency by the Carter administration, testified he had believed that his letter obscuring the seriousness of Lance's banking irregularities might win him career advancement. He said it had been "a mistake" to take part in the whitewash of Lance's record with his misleading letter to the committee.

Currency Comptroller Heimann, a Carter appointee, took issue with Carter's and Lance's assertion that the report had "cleared" Lance of wrongdoing. He said the report was not intended to clear anybody of improprieties but was a factual report stating that Lance and his wife had received $3.5 million in loans or refinancing over a thirteen-year period from the Calhoun First National Bank.

Heimann said that Lance and his family members had abused their influential position in the Calhoun bank by overdrawing their accounts to enhance their personal gain. Heimann said that if he had been privy to the facts that Bloom had in January, he would not have written a letter to the Senate Government Affairs Committee saying Lance was "well qualified." He said that Lance's patterns of overdrafts represented "serious violations" of the federal law that prohibits banking executives from borrowing more than $5,000 from their own banks, except on mortgages or loans for education.

John W. Stokes, Jr., a former United States Attorney, said he acted in good faith in closing out the criminal investigation of Lance in December 1976 but charged that Carter administration officials had withheld a lengthy derogatory FBI report on Lance's background from the Senate Government Affairs Committee.

Glenna Stone, an attorney in Stokes's office, said that Stokes was wrong to close out the investigation and testified that Stokes, a Republican, had expressed some hope that he would be retained as United States Attorney by the Carter administration for a long enough period to qualify for a pension.

White House Press Secretary Jody Powell admitted that he, Hamilton Jordan and White House Counsel Robert Lipshutz had seen the FBI report on Lance, but declared that they did not believe it "reflected adversely" on Lance's qualifications to be Budget Director. They said they did not pass the report or the information in the report along to President Carter because of assurances from the Comptroller's office that such banking practices were common in small-town banks.

A report by the Internal Revenue Service inspection office, assigned to conduct an investigation of the Comptroller's office personnel, stated that Attorneys John L. Moore, Jr., and Sidney O. Smith, Jr., of the Carter transition team had knowledge of Lance's problems in connection with preparing him for Senate confirmation. Moore had indicated to the Internal Revenue investigators that President-elect Carter had some knowledge of the Lance problems.

Senator Percy made public the testimony of federal bank examiner Charles F. Stuart, Jr., in which he recalled that Lance had advised Regional Director Tarleton on how to handle the issue of restrictions against his bank in case of a pre-nomination probe into Lance's background by the FBI. Tarleton testified he could not recall the discussion with Lance, or having told Stuart about it.

Feeling besieged and desperate, Press Secretary Powell called a number of Washington reporters, including Loye Miller of the *Chicago Sun-Times,* to relay information that Senator Percy had improperly used an aircraft owned by Bell & Howell during his 1972 re-election campaign. That vindictive effort to discredit Senator Percy as a critic of Bert Lance backfired and discredited Powell on two counts:

1. He was irresponsible because he "leaked" information that was not true. He later admitted that he had not checked it out before trying to smear Lance's major critic.
2. He angrily lashed out at "the enemy" of the Carter White House with an attack on an issue that was unrelated.

Powell came under a withering bipartisan attack by Chairman Ribicoff, Senator John Heinz and Senator Robert Packwood of Oregon for this action, which they considered reminiscent of the Nixon White House tactics at the time of Watergate. As the chorus of critics grew, Powell admitted he was "wrong" but denied that it was a vindictive effort to discredit Senator Percy because of his aggressiveness against Lance.

"It was just dumb," Powell told the press, and President

Carter, he said, agreed with him. So did his best friends in the White House press corps.

Presidential Assistant Margaret (Midge) Costanze became the first person on the White House staff to call for Lance's resignation. That break with the White House group was to be the start of her downfall. Her freedom to dissent (calling for the ouster of one of the Georgians) was not favorably received, and Ham Jordan and Jody Powell never forgave her. Nor did they appreciate the fact that witnesses from Treasury Secretary Michael Blumenthal's department—Heimann and the IRS investigators—were supplying some of the most damaging testimony against Bert Lance.

Lance had not even taken the witness stand when Senate Democratic Leader Robert C. Byrd suggested that Lance resign because he had been destroyed as an effective Budget Director. He declared that the damage to President Carter was not irreparable, but if Lance remained in office it might be.

When Bert Lance took the stand, accompanied by the suave Washington lawyer Clark Clifford, he read a lengthy statement using his own artful explanation of his banking practices. Because he was highly articulate and maintained a calm demeanor while his defenders on the Senate Government Affairs squabbled with Chairman Ribicoff and Senator Percy, Lance was able to dominate the televised hearings by avoiding the direct questions and filibustering on side issues that he insisted on explaining in detail.

Although it was a stellar performance, the hard facts were still there—his banking practices were violations of banking laws and regulations. Chairman Ribicoff confronted him directly with evidence that a bank examiner as early as 1971 had told him that his overdrafts violated the banking laws which limited loans to a bank officer. Lance argued that he did not recall it that way.

Senator Percy questioned him on the propriety of using the same shares of stock in the National Bank of Georgia as collateral for two different bank loans. The Chairman, Senator Percy and other committee members expressed their view that Lance had misled them and the staff about his financial problems at the Calhoun First National Bank. Lance said that he had tried to be frank, but neither the committee members nor the staff had "asked the right questions."

As Lance continued to spar with the Senate Government Affairs Committee members, on September 16, 1977, President Carter met at the White House with a group of editors and news directors. He declared that Lance had "enhanced his position" with his testimony.

President Carter also volunteered assurances to the group of editors that there had been "absolutely zero slippage" in the operation of the Office of Management and Budget as a result of the Lance investigation.

John McCormally, an ardent early supporter of Jimmy Carter for President in 1976, was worried about his *Burlington* (Iowa) *Hawkeye*'s continued support of Carter if Lance was retained: "We are very well aware of your concern for the need for fairness to Mr. Lance, and you're respected for that by the people who support you most," McCormally said. "Those same people are most concerned about the success of your presidency."

McCormally asked President Carter if he had considered the problem that would be presented if the alternative was one that was "not altogether fair to Mr. Lance, but which is necessary for the larger concerns of the presidency."

"That's something I'll have to balance," President Carter responded, ignoring the clear import of Heimann's report. "I don't know of anything illegal that Bert Lance has done. I don't know of any unethical conduct on his behalf."

President Carter indicated that he had read the FBI report on Lance, which had been withheld from the Senate Government Affairs Committee. "I wish that every one of you could read the FBI report which has been the subject of many references," President Carter said, indicating that he believed the editors would find nothing derogatory in the report. He said that among the people in the Justice Department and the Comptroller's Office "all . . . six men were unanimously almost effusive in their recommendation of Bert.

"But now their testimony under the pressure of Senate interrogation is a little bit different," President Carter continued. Then he almost reversed his criticism of the witnesses with the comment, "Obviously, a lot of new questions have been raised."

A New England editor declared that in his area "we don't engage in overdrafts" and bluntly asked President Carter, "When you were a businessman in Georgia, did you ever become involved in overdrafts?"

"Well, I can't say that I depended on overdrafts to run my business, but as I have said in one regular news conference . . . yes, I've had overdrafts."

He explained that it was "a fairly common practice" in small-town banks for the banker to permit a small overdraft in one account when a depositor has several substantial accounts. "That's not considered to be an illegal or an unethical act." The President gave the following example: He might have $50,000 or $100,000 in a peanut warehouse account, but if his wife happened to write a $25 check to buy a dress from the personal account and it bounced, "they would not send for the sheriff."

"I don't excuse overdrafts," President Carter said. "You know, it's obvious that I would rather my own life had been completely free of any overdraft. . . . But I still don't believe that it's an unethical or illegal thing in the banking circles in which I've had to operate."

No editor faced President Carter with the direct question of whether he approved or disapproved of the more than $400,000 in overdrafts by Lance, his family and his business associates over extended periods of time, or whether he accepted the conclusion that such a pattern constituted a violation of the federal banking laws.

President Carter was not dealing with the hard facts but was mainly concerned with generalities in stopping the political damage to his own public image. He acknowledged that Lance had been hurt by the early testimony against him but said he believed that his Budget Director had "certainly enhanced his position" since taking the stand in his own defense.

The days that followed President Carter's meeting with the news editors were filled with new demands for Lance's resignation. The comments of the committee members about the need for a further criminal investigation made it imperative that the Justice Department launch its own investigation before momentum developed to name a special prosecutor in view of Lance's close ties with President Carter and Attorney General Griffin Bell.

Attorney General Bell turned the job over to Deputy Attorney General Peter F. Flaherty and Assistant Attorney General Benjamin Civiletti, head of the Criminal Division. Bell said the reason for disqualifying himself from an investigation of Lance was his ownership of a large block of stock in the National Bank of Georgia. He saw no conflict resulting from his personal ties with Lance or with President Carter.

Critics noted that Flaherty was an early supporter of Carter as Mayor of Pittsburgh and had helped Carter win a crucial primary in Pennsylvania. Civilleti, a Baltimore lawyer, was recommended for his position by Atlanta lawyer Charles Kirbo, the number one unofficial adviser to President Carter. It was noted by some critics that it was not unlike the situation where objectivity was expected from Attorney General Richard Kleindienst and Acting FBI Director L. Patrick Gray in the Watergate affair.

Although the investigation appeared to be stacked with Carter partisans, the Justice Department had to consider that the Comptroller of the Currency and IRS investigations were continuing, as was a related investigation under Stanley Sporkin, chief of enforcement at the Securities and Exchange Commission. Also, the Senate and House Banking Committees and the Senate Government Affairs Committee were poised for effective oversight.

On September 21, 1977, President Carter opened his press conference by reading Bert Lance's letter of resignation. In that letter Lance recalled that he had told President Carter that there were some things of great importance to him:

"First, it was and is important that my name and reputation be cleared for me, my wife, my children, my grandchildren, and those who have trust and faith in me; and, I believe that this has been done. As I said at the Senate hearings, my conscience is clear.

"Second, it was and is important for me to be able to say that people should be willing to make the necessary sacrifices and be willing to serve their government and country. This I can still say, and say proudly."

Lance wrote the President that his only intention in coming to Washington had been "to make a contribution to this country and to you." Because of the various investigations, Lance said, he found it impossible to continue.

In response to questions, President Carter said he "did not ask for Bert's resignation." "I thought Bert did a superb job Thursday, Friday and Saturday in answering all of the questions that had been leveled about him and against him.

"Monday morning about 6 o'clock, Bert came to my office and we spent about 45 minutes going over all the present questions that still remained . . . the prospects for the future," President Carter explained. "I told Bert I thought he had exonerated himself completely . . . and asked him to make his own decision about what his choice would be."

President Carter related that on Monday afternoon Lance told him he had decided it would be best to resign, but he wanted to talk to his wife again and to his attorney, Clark Clifford. A delay in the press conference until 5 P.M. Tuesday was necessary because Clifford was in Detroit.

"I think he's [Lance] made a very unselfish and wise judgment," President Carter said.

In response to a question dealing with the President's early knowledge of Lance's difficulty, Carter said he had heard from Lance "last fall," before he had named him OMB Director, "that there had been questions about the Calhoun National Bank and overdrafts." "My understanding at the time was that the overdraft question referred to his 1974 campaign debt," President Carter said.

On December 1, 1976, President Carter related, "I was called from Atlanta and told that the matter had been resolved by the Comptroller's Office and by the Justice Department. On that date was the first time that either Bert or I knew that the Justice Department had been involved at all. And my understanding then was that it was an oversight and, had the oversight not occurred, that the Justice Department would have resolved the issue long before."

The continued praise for Lance surprised the reporters. One asked, "Mr. President, you've spoken so highly of Mr. Lance again this afternoon. I wonder if you feel that he was unfairly drummed out of the Government?"

"That's a difficult question for me to answer," the President replied. He went on to explain that some of the charges against Lance "were greatly exaggerated; some of them were actually untrue."

While contending that some of the reporting was "unfair," he expressed the belief that most of it had been fair. "I think his [Lance's] honor and integrity have been proven," President Carter said. He characterized Lance's resignation as "a courageous and also a patriotic gesture."

Another reporter referred to the fact that President Carter had campaigned on a platform of high ethical standards and had pledged that he would not tolerate impropriety or even the appearance of impropriety.

"I think now a lot of people are looking at your standards against the Bert Lance case. I'd like to ask you whether you, today, still feel that Mr. Lance has avoided the appearance of impropriety or whether a new standard is now in operation?"

President Carter bristled. "The standards were high at the beginning, the standards are still high, and the standards have been high in the service of Bert Lance.

"There has been not even one allegation that I have ever heard of that Bert Lance did not perform his duties as Director of OMB in a superlative way," said President Carter. "Even those allegations that were made about his life several years ago, in my opinion, have been proven false and without foundation. So, I don't think that any blame should accrue to Bert Lance for having acted improperly or having lowered the standards of our government."

Another questioner followed up. "Mr. Lance, by his own admission—I think this isn't in doubt—overdrew his checking accounts by thousands of dollars on a regular basis. He flew on corporate planes for what appear to be political and, perhaps, personal reasons. What I think many of us are interested in, sir, is your justification for reaffirming your belief in his integrity, given the positions you took as a candidate."

The President responded that Lance's many accusers had made their charges before the Senate Government Affairs Committee and that Lance "answered them adequately."

Another reporter asked President Carter "about your repeated statement that Mr. Lance never did anything illegal."

"The Comptroller of the Currency reported that Mr. Lance's overdraft loans of more than $5,000 violated the banking laws, and Mr. Lance, I think, conceded that his failure to report loans to [the] board of directors [of] two banks he ran also was an infraction of the banking statutes. . . . How did you justify this with your statement that he never broke any laws?"

"Well," the President responded coolly, "My assessment is that you are trying to succeed where the Senate committee failed.

"There was no judgment made that Bert Lance did anything illegal," President Carter insisted.

"The only Comptroller's report that I saw specifically said that he had done nothing illegal. I think he's adequately explained his position. I have no information to add to what Bert has already revealed to the Senators and to the public."

"Do you think that you have been, if only slightly, less than fully prudent and diligent because of [personal and friendly] feelings toward Mr. Lance in the way you read some of these things?" asked Judy Woodruff of NBC News.

"No," President Carter responded. "I don't think I've been remiss . . . even looking at it from this retrospective point of view.

. . . I don't think there's any feeling on my part that my friendship with him distorted my point of view in assessing his competence."

Another reporter asked, "If Mr. Lance had not decided to resign, were you prepared to have him stay or would you have tried to persuade him to resign?"

"I can't answer that question because it's . . . hypothetical," President Carter responded. "I have always trusted Bert Lance to do the proper and the unselfish thing. And my guess is that he was much more concerned about me and my administration and the reputation of the Government and the diversion of our attention to his case away from things that were important for the people."

In keeping with his stated faith in Bert Lance, President Carter permitted him to keep his White House pass, and the White House press secretary made special arrangements with the State Department for Bert Lance to continue to travel on a diplomatic passport until after *New York Times* columnist William Safire wrote a critical column about it.

Far from being treated as an exile in politics, Bert Lance was regarded "as a sort of folk hero" by Democratic National Chairman John White, who used Lance's connection with the business community for political fundraising activities.

Not until a few months before Lance's indictment in May 1979 did President Carter, Ham Jordan and Jody Powell exhibit any sensitivity about continued social and political association with Bert Lance. At that time, the focus was on the multimillion-dollar loans that Carter's warehouse had received during Jimmy Carter's long campaign for the Democratic presidential nomination in 1975 and 1976.

Several columnists, including Safire, now thought they saw the reason why Jimmy Carter felt compelled to express loyalty to Bert Lance.

CHAPTER EIGHT

Ham Jordan— Blue Denim Machiavelli

When Bert Lance resigned as Director of OMB, President Carter was forced to lean more and more heavily upon William Hamilton McWhorter Jordan, a thirty-three-year-old political strategist from Albany, Georgia. There was no doubt in the Carter White House or, for that matter, among political experts in Washington, that Ham Jordan was a brilliant political strategist. He had been responsible for the development of the seventy-page political strategy memorandum that correctly charted the course for Jimmy Carter to win the Democratic nomination and the election.

While Jordan was a hard-working young man of unusual intelligence and total dedication to President Carter, he had serious weaknesses in the area of management and practical business experience. Jordan, as a Special Assistant to President Carter, avoided the designation of White House Chief of Staff because that was the title carried by H. R. (Bob) Haldeman in the notorious Nixon years, but he was the natural leader of the so-called Georgia Mafia that included Press Secretary Jody Powell, White House Counsel Robert Lipshutz, White House Congressional Liaison Frank Moore, and Communications Director Gerald Rafshoon.

When Bert Lance was in the White House, even Jordan deferred to the millionaire Georgia banker because of his personal relationship with President Carter and his reputation as a man with connections who knew how to get things done. Bert Lance was an articulate, gregarious operator who quickly won a following in

Congress. He was admired for the competence and confidence he brought to his job. He gave assurances that he was a conservative in fiscal affairs who wouldn't let the "inexperienced liberals" run off with the Carter White House. Bert Lance, who leased a plush home in Georgetown, knew how to mix socializing in Washington with the detailed homework on budget problems and the government reorganization plans that were so dear to President Carter's heart.

By contrast, Jordan was almost a recluse from the normal Washington political whirl. He avoided nearly all formal social functions and took seriously President Carter's pledge to end the era of the imperial presidency so linked in the public mind with Watergate, Richard Nixon, Bob Haldeman, John Ehrlichman and Chuck Colson. Whether out of ignorance or by design, Jordan simply did not reply to formal invitations, nor did he show up after his office had indicated he would be present.

This obsession with maintaining a populist image for the Carter White House was carried to the point of wearing blue jeans to the office, rarely putting on a tie, operating with casualness with regard to his own time and allowing easy accessibility to President Carter for all of the top aides. Although it was laudable that Jordan was seeking to avoid the tough and arrogant control that Bob Haldeman had exerted on the Nixon White House, his effort to be just "one of the spokes" in the White House wheel resulted in organizational chaos. Jordan made no effort to cultivate the leaders of Congress and did not return the calls of even the chairmen and ranking Republican members of important committees.

Jordan's neglect of routine civility with regard to Congress started in the transition period between the November election and the Carter inauguration on January 20, 1977. Jordan and Jack Watson, an able young Atlanta lawyer from Charles Kirbo's law firm, were in charge of staffing the agencies and the White House with Jimmy Carter's team and helping in the job of selecting a Cabinet.

It was an overwhelming job under the best circumstances, and tension developed between Jordan and Watson that added to the chaos. Jordan emphasized the need to select people who had been early Carter supporters. He was fighting the desire of Cabinet officers who wished to make their selections on the basis of personal views on qualifications.

Jordan was thinking, like Haldeman before him, in terms of the 1980 election, and with that in mind, wished to demonstrate that Jimmy Carter did not forget his early supporters. Cabinet officers were arguing in terms of surrounding themselves with qualified people who would do the job, be loyal to them, and not peddle tales to a political mentor in the White House as in the Haldeman years.

Although he gave a lot of time and attention to taking care of the early Carter supporters, Jordan lost most of the in-fighting struggles with such skilled Washington operators as Secretary of Health, Education and Welfare Joseph Califano; Defense Secretary Harold Brown; Secretary of State Cy Vance; and Secretary of the Treasury Michael Blumenthal. Even in the various agencies where Jordan was successful to some degree, there was a resentment at the heavy-handed manner in which he pushed his selections. Rightly or wrongly, he was criticized privately by some Cabinet officials and their subcabinet appointees as "another Haldeman" and as a "blue-denim Machiavelli."

Caught up in these internal political struggles and the job of staffing the White House, Jordan let calls from important congressmen go without response and without an effective effort at even determining the reason for the "important" and occasionally "urgent" calls from Capitol Hill.

Adding to Jordan's problem was President-elect Carter's much heralded Talent Inventory Program (TIP), announced on television, which resulted in a flood of 34,000 applications for top administration jobs to help the new President restore competency and integrity to Washington. It was a mistake that the Nixon administration had made in the month after the 1968 election, when Nixon had proclaimed he was seeking help in finding the best brains in the nation to run the government. The flood of names and qualifications inundated the personnel operations of the transition team. After a brief effort to be responsive to the recommendations, the Nixon personnel team abandoned the struggle and sent out routine rejections that infuriated many early supporters.

In essence, the same thing happened to Mr. Carter's famous TIP project. One of those who wrote to President Carter volunteering his services was Arthur M. Schlesinger, Jr., the Pulitzer Prize–winning Harvard historian who had worked in the Kennedy White House. According to Dom Bonafede of the *National Journal,* Schlesinger received only a postcard from Carter headquarters rejecting his services. Although Jordan may have had no direct responsibility for such bungling, he was the most visible of Mr.

Carter's political advisers. He received the blame for everything that went wrong. Because he was busy cultivating the image of an easygoing, wisecracking "rube," Democratic Senators and Congressmen referred to him caustically as "Hannibal Jerkin."

Although Jordan and Carter insisted that he was not a chief of staff in the Haldeman sense but was one of seven senior presidential aides, it was apparent at an early point that he was "first among equals" and to some degree controlled the flow of paper and people to the Oval Office. The result, in the view of many of the people on the White House staff, was a chaotic lack of priorities on important programs and an overemphasis on political matters and those things in which Jordan was willing to take an active interest. Even on the subjects in which he was interested, there was only rarely an effective analysis and follow-through.

One of the first Carter pledges to fall victim to Ham Jordan's erratic thinking on government organization was the White House ombudsman office. President Carter had assigned the ombudsman function to Joseph Aragon, an intelligent thirty-five-year-old White House lawyer who had been an early Carter supporter in Los Angeles. Aragon possessed a Bachelor of Science degree from the University of California at Los Angeles and a law degree from the University of Southern California. He had experience in dealing with low-income housing programs, in directing voter registration for the Democratic National Committee in California and in the Washington office of the American Bar Association. It was this broad experience that could have made him an excellent presidential ombudsman.

It was to be Joe Aragon's job to listen to the public's complaints about the failure of various executive departments and agencies, to analyze the facts on allegations of mismanagement or corruption, and make reports directly to the President. Since the ombudsman's job is to bring a nonpolitical and objective analysis to a problem of government operation or personnel management, it is generally accepted that he should have no policy or political responsibilities that might interfere with his objectivity. The theory behind this is that no person can be totally objective when he reviews the government policies he helped to create or has approved the specific individuals for government positions.

From the outset, Aragon's ombudsman functions were encroached upon and cut back by President Carter and Jordan. First, he was assigned duties related to the energy crisis. Before he had concluded those energy assignments, there were a host of other policy and political chores.

Apparently without giving consideration to the inherent compromise involved, Ham Jordan, with the approval of President Carter, put the ombudsman in charge of community service agencies and gave him liaison functions with the Spanish-speaking community. Whether either or both understood the need for the ombudsman to be free of policy and political responsibilities, it was impossible to fathom.

Despite this confusion of assignments, Aragon patiently tried to perform the nonpolitical ombudsman function as the watchdog for the President over the whole White House. He busied himself with efforts to prod the Defense Department to get an equitable solution to the Ernest Fitzgerald case, called attention to questionable conduct on the part of a potential appointee at the Justice Department and made inquiries into questionable actions by White House personnel.

Jordan, like Bob Haldeman in the Nixon administration, was reported to be cool to the idea of having an independent ombudsman making inquiries around the White House. He directed limitations on the range of Aragon's inquiries.

A Senate Government Affairs Subcommittee, chaired by Senator John Glenn, the Ohio Democrat, had looked with high favor on Carter's announcement of a White House ombudsman. Senator Glenn and his staff looked with disfavor upon the report that Jordan was changing Aragon's assignment to eliminate the ombudsman function. The subcommittee investigators were unable to determine if any of Aragon's ombudsman responsibilities had been assigned to someone else. Nor could they learn whether Jordan had made the change in Aragon's role on his own or if those steps were taken with the suggestion or approval of President Carter.

Chairman Glenn and his subcommittee staff complained that the abandonment of the White House ombudsman function was breaking one of the pledges of the President—to make government more responsive to the people by providing a central office to which they could bring complaints and frustrations in dealing with the various government agencies. They told this reporter that Carter had pledged to make government more intelligible, to reduce paperwork and to cut red tape in government in order better to serve the people. By abolishing the ombudsman the President was silencing his own voice to respond to the people, Senator Glenn's staff argued.

By the first week of September 1977 Congressional critics were commenting privately that President Carter and the White House staff could have used an independent ombudsman to keep them informed about the seriousness of the problems of the questionable borrowing by Bert Lance. President Carter and his White House staff were unprepared for the sharp reaction to the Comptroller of the Currency's report on Lance's go-go banking operations. Either because he had no objective ombudsman to turn to or because of his own dependence upon Lance, President Carter blundered with misstatements on the Lance affair that were embarrassing to those who tried to defend him and support him. It was not unlike Richard Nixon's effort to "put Watergate behind us" without answering the tough questions about his two trusted advisers—Haldeman and Ehrlichman.

It was possible that neither Jordan nor President Carter would have wanted to hear the facts that a truly independent ombudsman would have told them. Those facts might have included President Carter's own dealings with the National Bank of Georgia when Lance was the bank's president. His dealings included construction and crop loans for the Carter warehouse of more than $4.5 million in 1975 and 1976—the period when Jimmy Carter and his family were trying to finance the political campaign for the Democratic nomination. Also, the President had acknowledged that he had received political and personal transportation, courtesy of Bert Lance, in a plane owned by the National Bank of Georgia.

A truly sensitive ombudsman would have warned President Carter to stay clear of any personal judgments on Bert Lance because of these financial ties as well as the personal friendship that would make any conclusions suspect.

When Lance left the White House in late September 1977, the mantle of Number One White House adviser fell on the shoulders of Ham Jordan, whose private life style was the talk of Washington political and social circles. While he shunned the formal Washington parties, the private partying of this handsome former football player eventually led to separation from his wife, Nancy.

On January 9, 1978, White House Press Secretary Jody Powell released a brief statement from Nancy Jordan disclosing that she and Hamilton "have decided to separate."

"We know that our families and our friends will understand

and respect our mutual decision,'' Nancy Jordan stated. She revealed that the couple had met with President and Mrs. Carter on the previous Sunday to tell them of the decision ''before they read about it in the newspapers.''

Donnie Radcliffe of the *Washington Post* reported that Nancy ''declined to comment on whether the Carters had tried to dissuade them or what had brought on the separation.'' The couple had been married since January 24, 1970, and had no children. They had worked together for Jimmy Carter in his campaign for governor of Georgia, but the strain of Washington public and social life had destroyed their marriage.

President Carter, while preaching a strict moral and ethical code for the nation, was tolerant of members of his staff and family who were consistently falling below the strict born-again Christian standards that he had set for himself.

Within a few weeks after the Jordans' announced separation, the number one assistant to President Carter was involved in an unpleasant little incident at Sarsfield's Bar, considered a favorite hangout for Carter White House staffers.

Jordan went to Sarsfield's after leaving the White House the night of January 27 and had an exchange of words with a young woman. That incident was the subject of reams of news copy, which was largely the result of White House overreaction to a gossip column item in the *Washington Post*.

Rudy Maxa, writing in the February 19 issue of the *Washington Post Magazine,* related that Jordan was drinking at Sarsfield's, behaved somewhat offensively toward the young woman, and after an angry exchange of insults, had spit his drink on the bosom of her dress. Maxa's source was obviously the young woman or her woman companion.

If the facts were not true, a simple denial by Jordan or the White House would have taken care of the accusation by the anonymous accuser—or it could have been ignored.

However, an angry Jody Powell and an even angrier Hamilton Jordan responded with an investigation by White House lawyer Michael Cardozo. They released a thirty-three-page rebuttal complete with statements from the bartender and witnesses who did not see or hear what was said. It also contained statements as to Jordan's character and his general demeanor by one of Jordan's friends who said he left before the incident took place.

The thirty-three-page statement was issued by the White

House press office for the single purpose of trying to establish that Hamilton Jordan, top White House assistant to President Carter, did not spit his drink down the bosom of the young lady. It was the contention of Jordan and Powell that Jordan was drinking his usual drink—Amaretto and cream—and (1) it would not have been likely to make Jordan drunk, and (2) it surely would have left a noticeable smudge on the young lady's dress that was not noticed before the young lady departed.

A *Washington Post* gossip item from an anonymous source was not a news item worth attention, but a thirty-three-page statement from the White House press office dealing with the details of the pub-crawling exploits of the Number One Boy to a Born Again President was news and grist for political columnists such as Art Buchwald, William Safire and David Broder.

Charles McDowell, Washington humor columnist for the *Richmond Times-Dispatch,* was impressed that the White House press release contained a twenty-four-page transcript of the interrogation of bartender Daniel V. Marshall III by Michael H. Cardozo V, the senior associate counsel to the President of the United States.

"What I enjoyed most is the transcript of the interrogation of the bartender," McDowell wrote. With regional pride McDowell noted that Marshall was "a young Virginian." "McLean was his home until he moved into Washington to be a professional bartender. He has a good eye, a good ear and great pride in his work."

He quoted Marshall's response to Cardozo's questions: "I have been tending bar in Washington for seven years. I am known as one of the more competent bartenders in Washington as far as amount of product I can put over the bar and the type of clientele that I handle. I have a very nice clientele, and the ability to do that is you watch everything that goes on, and you certainly watch things when you have celebrities sitting in front of you.

"Dustin Hoffman, Clint Eastwood, I am not particularly awed by these people. Redd Foxx did give me a lift because I thought he was so funny. Shirley MacLaine, those people . . . nobody runs up to them and says anything. On the other hand when Tip O'Neill [Speaker of the House] comes in—he likes our cheeseburgers—it's a tremendous commotion."

Marshall was reiterating a point he had made earlier about the difference in a Washington bar where patrons aren't impressed by a Johnny Bench, but "they run right up to the politicians."

On the night in question, Marshall related, "They were getting pretty pushy in there. It was getting crowded and there were other girls coming up to Hamilton and 'woo-woo,' you know what I mean? Three or four of them just basically hanging around and just hoping he would turn around and say something to them or whatever . . ."

Marshall related that he was uneasy about two of the girls before they joined the crowd around Jordan. "And I think Hamilton said something . . . to the point where enough's enough and I don't want to talk to you anymore, and I think one of the girls got insulted. I don't think, I know she got insulted. And she said something to him and he said something back, but there was no spitting of drinks or throwing of drinks or anything."

Following this statement, establishing that Hamilton Jordan had an angry exchange and that he did not see any spitting of drinks, Marshall added that he did not see Jordan get slapped. If he did get slapped, it was because somebody stood up in his line of sight at that crucial point.

The bartender said he saw no "improper behavior" by Jordan, while he declared that the two girls "were being jerks and had too much to drink . . . they were being a pain in the fanny."

Bartender Marshall said that in his professional opinion the women were not ladies and stated his qualifications. "You know I am basically a Southerner from Virginia and understand, having gone to Randolph-Macon and the University of Virginia, what Southern ladies are all about."

McDowell, as well as the more serious political columnists, picked out the lack of objectivity in the witnesses questioned by White House Counsel Cardozo. It was noted that Rich Evans, owner of the bar and the employer of bartender Marshall, had worked with Cardozo as an advance man in the Carter campaign and that Evans continued as a part-time advance man on some of President Carter's trips.

Bill Safire treated the incident with the same type of humor as McDowell and noted that President Carter was reported to be pushing Jordan to take over increasing foreign policy responsibilities. Others used the Sarsfield's Bar incident as a reason for going back and pulling together the gross conduct attributed to Jordan, including his action at a formal dinner in which he was reported to have peered down the bosom of the wife of the Egyptian Ambassador and commented about the twin Egyptian pyramids in a manner that offended the woman.

"In both instances, Jordan affirms that he was not the guilty party," wrote *Washington Post* political pundit David Broder in a largely sympathetic column about Jordan's problems in dealing with the White House power. "The President and his associates in the White House take Jordan's word for it.

"[Jordan's] power has risen inside the White House even as his notoriety has grown, and he is today, beyond much challenge, the most important of the President's policy and political advisers," Broder wrote.

"Jordan has a right to live his own life," Broder continued. "But more than a year ago, Bob Strauss, who shares with Carter a paternal affection for Jordan, gave him some advice." Broder quoted Strauss as telling Jordan:

"You are living in a company town and if you're going to thumb your nose at the standards of this town, you better live like a saint. 'Cause if you do one thing wrong, they'll never let you forget it, and they'll hound you out of town, like you were the devil."

It was good advice from a Washington professional politician, and there were indications that Jordan was finally taking it to heart as President Carter ignored the congressional hints and editorial suggestions that Jordan's conduct was a blemish on the White House.

The *Washington Post* society page reported on April 13, 1978, that Jordan was attired in a navy suit, pink shirt and maroon tie when he appeared on a White House panel before the American Society of Newspaper Editors in the huge East Ballroom of the Washington Hilton Hotel. It was a packed house that heard the new Hamilton Jordan, Jody Powell and Midge Costanza, Special Assistant for women's affairs, talk about "Life Behind the Gates at 1600 Pennsylvania Avenue."

"One of the first questions asked was the one everyone was panting for: About Jordan's private life," Reporter Sally Quinn wrote in the *Washington Post*.

"Can't you wait a little longer?" Jordan quipped and added, "Jody wrote out my answer."

In a half-serious, half-facetious speech, Jordan said that in his first year in office "I was told by the press I would do well to go out. And I did that. I've had things happen that were not true. All I can say is that they were not true.

"Now I'm very reluctant to go to functions because my comments might be misinterpreted or blown up,'' he said with no effort to repeat the explanations on Sarsfield's Bar or the reports on his ''twin pyramids'' comment. ''I find it difficult to have a private life.''

Midge Costanza, already in trouble for her criticism of Bert Lance, stuck with the White House position in answering questions about the President's programs on minorities. Both Powell and Jordan reiterated their defense of Bert Lance. They said Lance was ''a friend,'' had been and always would be.

The visiting editors—entertained royally by the superficial questions and the equally superficial responses of the White House celebrities—laughed with gusto. They were polite guests who did not ask the tough questions that would have gone to the heart of the problem of White House competency. They raised no question about the clear evidence in the public domain indicating that Jordan was as ruthless as Bob Haldeman and as much of a political hatchetman as Chuck Colson of the Nixon White House.

CHAPTER NINE

The Marston Firing

Even as President Carter and Attorney General Griffin Bell were resisting Republican demands for a special prosecutor in the Bert Lance investigations, President Carter took the first step toward enmeshing himself in political tampering with a federal prosecutor.

On November 7, 1977—only a year after his election on pledges to rid the Justice Department of political influence—President Carter took a call in the Oval Office from Representative Joshua Eilberg, a senior Democrat from Philadelphia.

Congressman Eilberg, who was at that time under investigation on allegations of fraudulent activities related to government grant programs, told President Carter he wanted United States Attorney David W. Marston fired immediately. His complaint was that Marston, a Republican appointee of the Ford administration, was only prosecuting Democrats.

Without asking any questions about whether Representative Eilberg was involved in Marston's investigations, or even making further inquiry as to what unjustified prosecutions had been carried out by Marston, President Carter immediately had a call made to Attorney General Bell.

According to the later explanation of the Attorney General, President Carter's call reached him on his car telephone. The President suggested that he go to the nearest telephone to call back, because he feared the conversation might be overheard on the radio-line connection.

Bell stopped at the Brooks Brothers clothing store to return the urgent call, and later recalled the following conversation:

"What's the status of the U.S. Attorney in Philadelphia?" President Carter asked.

"I expect I'll be replacing him about the first of the year," the Attorney General responded.

"Well, I wish you'd hurry up. I'm getting a lot of complaints about you from Eilberg. . . . He claims that this man in Philadelphia [Marston] doesn't do anything but prosecute Democrats."

Bell replied, "They seem to tell me that, too." And the President prodded him again with the comment, "I wish you'd hurry."

Complying with the President's suggestion, and without making inquiry as to Representative Eilberg's motivation, Attorney General Bell took steps to hurry the exit of the offending Mr. Marston.

Marston received the first hint of political "pressure" to fire him when he attended a conference of United States attorneys in Washington later in November. According to Marston, Michael J. Egan, an Associate Attorney General operating out of Bell's office, said "we may have to move you sometime in the spring." Marston said that Egan explained that the pressure for the move came "from on high" and "because Eilberg called the President and said you've got to remove Marston."

Egan, a Georgia lawyer who still hoped to be able to retain Marston, suggested that the pressure for U.S. Attorney posts in Pennsylvania "might be relieved by replacing the two other Republican U.S. Attorneys in Harrisburg and Pittsburgh."

Marston said he did not mention at that time that Congressman Eilberg and Representative Dan Flood, also a Pennsylvania Democrat, were under investigation in connection with a $14.5 million federal grant for an addition to Philadelphia's Hahnemann Hospital. He said he did not want to create the impression that he would make such claims simply because a political figure was lobbying against him.

A few days after the conversation with Egan at the United States attorneys conference, Marston did mention the Hahnemann Hospital investigation and the targets of the probe to another Justice Department lawyer, Russell T. Baker, Jr., deputy to the then Assistant Attorney General Benjamin Civiletti, who was head of the Criminal Division in the Justice Department.

In addition to the work his office was doing in connection with the investigations of Congressman Eilberg and Flood on the Hahnemann Hospital, Marston had been moving aggressively against corrupt officials in local government. In June, former Pennsylvania House Speaker Herbert Fineman, a Democrat, was sentenced to a two-year prison term for obstruction of justice. The Democratic legislator had been charged with accepting more than $50,000 from four parents to influence their children's admission to professional schools and with trying to destroy school records to interfere with the investigation, the *Philadelphia Inquirer* reported.

The *Inquirer* noted that the key witness at Fineman's trial said he had been told that if the trial could be stalled until after the Democrats won the 1976 election, "it's going to be all over."

The *Philadelphia Inquirer* quoted the witness as saying, "They'll put guys [in the U.S. Attorney's office] who are favorable" to Democrats.

But, it wasn't only Democrats that Marston's office was prosecuting. In September 1977 they convicted one of the most powerful Republican politicians in Eastern Pennsylvania of extorting $6,400 from architects in exchange for building design contracts. Theodore S. Rubino, formerly the most influential Republican politician in Chester County, was sentenced to six months in jail. Marston was quoted by the *Inquirer* as commenting that he was pleased that Rubino had received jail time and that the judge who sentenced him had "accepted the principle that public officials who break the public trust should go to jail."

Marston's office had conducted investigations that led to indictment in October 1977 of Augustine Salvitti, executive director of the Philadelphia Redevelopment Authority, on charges of having accepted a $27,500 kickback in a cash settlement for the contract with the Authority, and James J. O'Neill, former Plumbers Union boss, on charges of accepting more than $100,000 in kickbacks and other illegal payments in the handling of loans from the union pension fund. Salvitti was a part of Philadelphia Mayor Frank I. Rizzo's organization, and O'Neill was a former Rizzo campaign manager. Neither of those cases had gone to trial at the time Attorney General Bell fired Marston.

The biggest Democratic target of the Marston investigations was former State Senator Henry J. (Buddy) Cianfrani, who for years had been a power in Democratic politics in Philadelphia and in the State Legislature in Harrisburg.

On January 3 or 4, 1978, Cianfrani entered pleas of guilty to a 106-count indictment charging obstruction of justice, bribery and mail fraud and a nolo contendere (no contest) plea to four charges of income tax evasion for the years 1973 through 1976.

United States Attorney Marston had said there would be a continuation of the investigation of others in connection with the $52,500 in bribes Cianfrani admitted receiving from parents of applicants to medical and veterinary schools to gain admittance for their children, when the *Philadelphia Inquirer* learned that Attorney General Bell planned to remove him.

On January 8 the *Inquirer* reported that Bell's decision to fire the aggressive Republican prosecutor was in response to political pressure from the Pennsylvania congressional delegation. It was reported that a panel of five Philadelphia lawyers had been named by the Justice Department to recommend Marston's successor.

Senator Richard Schweiker, the Pennsylvania Republican for whom Marston had worked as a legal aide, declared that the five-man panel "smells like a devious ploy to . . . hide from the public a raw political power play." Marston said he was "stunned" but told the *Inquirer,* "You certainly shouldn't be writing my obituary yet."

The *Inquirer* story identified Representative Eilberg as the "most vocal" of the complaining Philadelphia Democrats and reported that both Eilberg and Representative Flood were being investigated by Marston's office for irregularities in the financing and construction of the Hahnemann Hospital.

On January 9 the *Inquirer* reported that the White House had received 472 telephone calls and 84 telegrams supporting Marston, and on January 10 the *Inquirer* editorialized: "The administration of President Jimmy Carter, through the actions of Attorney General Griffin B. Bell, has struck a crippling blow to investigations of political corruption in Eastern Pennsylvania."

The editorial reviewed the background of Carter's promises to keep politics out of the Justice Department and declared that in removing Marston, "Mr. Bell, in effect, has allied the U.S. Justice Department and the Carter administration with the forces of government by graft and those forces' classic self-preservation weapon: to punish or to remove anyone who effectively combats political corruption."

The *Inquirer* commented further: "Bell did his damage in a surreptitious manner, secretly seeking to enlist the collaboration of five Philadelphia lawyers in private practice to make the replacement of Mr. Marston seem politically respectable."

The *Inquirer* stated that the investigations should continue under Marston and that the only way the Carter administration could regain confidence was "to declare, publicly and unequivocally, that Mr. Marston will remain in office for the remainder of his four-year term."

By the time President Carter held his press conference on January 12, the White House and Justice Department officials were on notice on all of those facts in the Marston case. There had been time for a President interested in high standards of integrity to consult with his Attorney General on any facts that were not clear.

As could have been anticipated, one of the first questioners asked about the plan to remove Marston that Mr. Carter had discussed with Congressman Eilberg in early November.

"Mr. President, you promised during the campaign to appoint U.S. attorneys strictly—without any consideration of political aspects or influence— . . . on the basis of merit." The reporter called attention to Mr. Carter's campaign promise and then asked bluntly: "Why are you removing the U.S. attorney in Philadelphia, David Marston, who on the surface seems to have a credible record, which includes the prosecution and conviction of a number of prominent Democrats?"

President Carter responded affirmatively about his intention "to make sure that all of the appointments that are made to Federal judgeships and also U.S. attorneys are made on the basis of merit.

"I think until each appointment is observed very carefully—who was in office compared to who is the replacement for that person in office—that it would be hard to criticize a particular instance," Mr. Carter said, cleverly seeking to avoid criticism until the blue-ribbon panel action.

He said he had "recently learned" about the U.S. attorney named Marston. "This is one of hundreds of U.S. attorneys in the country, and I was not familiar with the case until it became highly publicized," President Carter said, making no reference to his own political intervention at Representative Eilberg's insistence.

"The Attorney General is handling the investigation of the replacement of Mr. Marston," the President said in seeking to avoid any direct responsibility. "I think the focusing of attention on this case will certainly doubly inspire him to make a selection that will be admirable and a credit to him and to me, and I've not interfered in it at all."

President Carter was standing by the firing of Marston, which was in line with his promise to Representative Eilberg, and hoping that the replacement would have a laudable background. Again, President Carter sought to give the impression he had "not interfered" in it at all.

"Before I first heard about Mr. Marston, the Attorney General had already decided to replace him," was the President's technically accurate but deceptive comment.

"We have encouraged the Members of Congress, Democratic Members of Congress, not to be involved in trying to influence the Attorney General about who should be the new U.S. attorney there," President Carter added. He did not reveal his own role in relaying a demand for the removal of Marston by a congressman who was under criminal investigation by Marston's office.

The answer was reminiscent of Richard Nixon's technically accurate but evasive responses on the Watergate cover-up.

The questioner, deceived by Mr. Carter's careful evasion, moved to the question of whether Attorney General Bell felt that Marston "had done a good job" as a prosecutor.

"Well, I can't say that Mr. Marston has or has not done a good job," the President said, ignoring the record of solid prosecutions for fraud over a period of more than eighteen months. "He was appointed at the last minute under the previous administration." The President was repeating the Justice Department's efforts to disparage Marston's contribution by emphasizing his lack of experience. "He was not a practicing attorney [and] had never had any prosecuting experience. And the only criticism that I've heard about him was that he had a very heavy commitment to calling press conferences and so forth when he obtained evidence or when a grand jury took action in an indictment. I think this is not unique in the country."

President Carter had engaged in a clever repetition of the classic complaint of crooked politicians who contend that any comments on the seriousness of their crimes are unethical and improper. There was not one case of improper or unethical comments on prosecution by Marston, as was later acknowledged by the Justice Department and the White House.

After the effort to smear Marston with derogatory comments about his lack of experience and trial by press conference, President Carter claimed lack of knowledge of Marston's faults. "I've not discussed the case with the Attorney General and asked him specifically what was wrong with Marston. I don't know who he will recommend to me for replacement. But I can assure you that when the replacement is announced, that there will be an emphasis on the quality of the replacement—his qualifications compared to the incumbent. And I have absolute confidence that the Attorney General will do a good job in that respect."

In his concluding remarks Carter ignored the complaint of the *Inquirer* and other critics of the Marston firing who viewed the legal panel selection as a device for getting a lawyer with excellent paper credentials and one who would be more acceptable to the Democratic political machine in Philadelphia.

Later in the press conference, a reporter got back to the subject of Marston, noting that Marston was in the midst of an investigation involving two Democratic Congressmen from Pennsylvania. The reporter noted that there had been published records that at least one of those Congressmen [Eilberg] "Has sought to contact the White House or you yourself to, in effect, get Mr. Marston off their backs.

"I wonder if you are aware of any such contacts . . . and what your reaction to such a contact would be?" the reporter asked, putting President Carter squarely on the spot about the obvious impropriety of Eilberg's seeking to use political pressure to get Marston removed.

Again President Carter's response was an evasion—an evasion on the level of a Nixon comment of his role in the Watergate cover-up.

"The only contact I've had with any Congressman directly was . . ." Mr. Carter started slowly. "I think Congressman Eilberg called me and asked that we look into it. At that time, the Attorney General had already decided to make the change."

Up to that point, Mr. Carter's answer was technically correct but, in his following response regarding the sequence of events, he gave the impression that he had talked to Bell about the Marston replacement prior to the time Eilberg had called rather than in response to Eilberg's request. "When I talked to the Attorney General about it, before Eilberg had let his views be known on the telephone call, he said that the replacement would be made and that he hoped that the Democratic Congress members who had shown an interest in it would not be involved in trying to decide who would be the replacement."

Again, President Carter emphasized keeping members of Congress out of the selection of the replacement while avoiding the issue of the impropriety of Congressmen bringing political pressure to oust an effective prosecutor.

Mr. Carter concluded: "As far as any investigation of Members of Congress, however, I'm not familiar with that at all, and it was never mentioned to me." This was stated fully a week after there were stories and editorials in the Philadelphia papers and other papers, and a flood of calls and telephone calls to the White House protesting Marston's ouster.

"Could you tell me, sir," another reporter asked Mr. Carter, "what reason Mr. Eilberg gave for asking you to look into it and what do you mean by 'it'?"

"He wanted the replacement process to be expedited," the President answered directly in his first sentence, but then he continued in the evasive and equivocal manner that had marked his earlier answers. "The decision had already been made to replace Mr. Marston, and I think the Attorney General can answer your question better specifically. And my importunity to Mr. Eilberg was that it would be better if the Congress members would let the Attorney General make the selection [of the new U.S. attorney] on the basis of merit alone. And that was Mr. Eilberg's comment to me, that he had no interest in who would be the replacement at all, but he thought that because of the confusion there that the decision that the Attorney General had already made ought to be expedited. And I feel the same way. I have complete confidence that the replacement will be chosen on the basis of merit and not politics."

Later, a third questioner returned to the subject of Marston with the unanswered query: "It's still not clear to me why he's being removed in the first place. Could you expand on what you've said already a little bit?"

"Well, I think I've covered that at least as far as I am able to," President Carter responded. "I've never looked into Mr. Marston's qualifications . . . I depend upon the Attorney General to assess the quality and the performance of duty of the U.S. attorneys around the country." He declared that he had never asked Attorney General Bell "to delineate all the reasons." "My only involvement in it at all was to expedite the process," Mr. Carter said.

Although President Carter said he was unaware that Representative Eilberg was under investigation by the Justice Department, it was obvious that top people in the Criminal Division were aware that Eilberg—who had sought to expedite Marston's removal—was one of the targets of fraud probes. As late as January 17—five days after the first press conference—the White House issued a statement that it still had no information that Representative Eilberg was the target of a Marston investigation.

Congressmen visiting the President that week were told by

Mr. Carter that "the Attorney General as late as today [January 17] has been unable to even ascertain the existence of an investigation involving Democratic Congressmen in Philadelphia."

President Carter's statement said a lot about the ineffectiveness of the communications within the Department of Justice, or between Attorney General Bell and the White House, or perhaps both.

The Marston affair had become a national scandal by Monday, January 16, when Bell sent three of his aides to Philadelphia to meet with Marston and others and report back as to whether any corruption cases that were under investigation would be jeopardized by Marston's removal.

The then Deputy Attorney General Peter Flaherty, former Democratic mayor of Pittsburgh, told Bell it would be "making a serious mistake" to remove Marston. Flaherty told a press conference that he had told one of Bell's aides that "since Marston was doing a good job, he should be kept."

In the face of this advice, Bell, with President Carter's approval, went ahead with the Marston firing on January 20. He said that his Justice task force had assured him that the removal of Marston would not interfere with progress on any cases of corruption. He stuck by his position that pure politics had dictated the removal of Marston. "We have two parties," Bell explained. "The 'ins' are the Democrats. They can get in to complain easier than the other party can."

"I have nothing against Marston," Bell told a National Press Club audience. "He's a fine young man. But this is a political system in this country."

Bell's blue ribbon committee for the selection of Marston's successor was dissolved after one member quit and another was quoted by the *Inquirer* as saying that Carter's and Bell's plans to remove Marston had "the serious appearance of an obstruction of justice."

Senator John Heinz III, a Pennsylvania Republican, declared Bell's action "an immense breach of faith of President Carter's commitment to take politics out of the administration of justice."

On January 22 the *Inquirer* editorialized that the Carter administration's firing of Marston was "an outrage" and that Congress should conduct a full investigation of all circumstances.

"Mr. Carter has told the nation that he puts political expedience above concern for justice or for honest government," the editorial stated. "Mr. Carter has revealed his administration, and especially his Department of Justice, as shockingly hypocritical.

"He has also raised a real question of whether his administration has obstructed justice. That question now can be resolved only by the United States Congress."

At a press conference on January 30, President Carter was asked if he had "seen anything improper in the handling of the Marston affair."

"Have you learned any lessons from it and all of its ramifications, and do you contemplate any changes in procedures for appointing and removing U.S. attorneys?"

"I see nothing improper in the handling of the case," President Carter said, ignoring the implication of his own admitted role in asking Bell to expedite the firing. "I made a campaign commitment that any appointee to a position as U.S. attorney or a judgeship would be appointed on the basis of merit, and this campaign commitment will be carried out."

It was a clever effort to limit his commitment to take politics out of the Justice Department to a merit selection of the Democrat that he and Bell would select.

"But isn't it time to depoliticize the Justice Department?" another reporter, putting his finger on the evasion, asked. "How about an end to the political firing of . . . prosecutors wholly apart from seeing to it that the Democratic replacements are highly qualified?"

"I think we've moved strongly in that direction," President Carter responded. "In some instances, U.S. Senators have specifically come forward and advocated that a Republican U.S. attorney be kept in office. I remember once in particular in New York that [Senator] Pat Moynihan said to keep the Republicans in office, and we've done so."

Another reporter pressed Mr. Carter about inconsistencies between his January 12 denial that he knew any member of Congress was under investigation, and a later White House statement that he had been told about the investigation of Eilberg only a few minutes before going to the January 12 press conference.

The President said he saw no inconsistency in his assertion that he did not know of any investigation of any Congressman. "The only inkling I had at all that Mr. Eilberg was involved with an investigation was that [Congressional Liaison] Frank Moore mentioned, just as I was leaving my office to come over for the press conference, that [Eilberg's] name had been raised in connection with an investigation. I was not told at that time and had no idea that he was being investigated.''

The President was drawing the close distinction between having been told that Eilberg's name was a part of an investigation and not having been told specifically that Eilberg was the target of a probe.

Another questioner asked the President if he would favor House approval of ''an impartial investigator of the Marston matter'' as set forth in a resolution introduced by Representative Philip Crane, the conservative Illinois Republican.

''It is difficult for me to comment objectively on Congressman Crane,'' the President answered in a facetious manner that drew laughter.

''There is nothing about the Marston matter at all that causes me any regret, except the extraordinary publicity that's been brought to it,'' President Carter declared. ''I don't see, in retrospect, after careful examination of the issue, that anything improper was done.''

He declared again that there had not been an appointment of a U.S. attorney or a judge that was made ''other than strictly on the basis of merit.

''That was my commitment to the American people, and I have not violated it,'' President Carter said in another effort to limit the language of his commitment.

President Carter noted that the Senate Judiciary Committee was at that time conducting hearings into the nomination of Assistant Attorney General Civiletti to be Deputy Attorney General to replace Peter Flaherty, who had disagreed with the administration's removal of Marston.

''The Republican members of the Senate Judiciary are going to go into the Marston matter [as a part of the Civiletti hearings],'' President Carter said, indicating that the Senate Democrats did not intend to make an issue of the Marston affair in connection with Civiletti's nomination.

Another questioner noted that the Civiletti hearings had already produced evidence ''that there were some significant deletions in the Justice Department affidavits on the Marston case, bearing upon his competence and upon the nature of politics in Pennsylvania.

''This evidence of deletion has led to new charges of cover-up by some people high up in the Justice Department, or at the very least, some incompetence on the part of Justice Department people," the questioner said to Carter. "What is your assessment of how the Justice Department handled this?"

President Carter replied that he was "not dissatisfied" with the Justice Department concerning deletions of FBI comments that were highly favorable to Marston's leadership. "I didn't know anything about the information presented to the congressional committees," Mr. Carter said. "I think, in retrospect, it would have been better to go ahead and include the statement [favorable to Marston] of the FBI agent."

An internal Justice Department probe had already issued an unusual report clearing both President Carter and Attorney General Bell of obstruction of justice or improper conduct. The report was made by two of Bell's subordinates in the Justice Department—Solicitor General Wade McCree and Michael Shaheen, Jr., head of the department's office of professional responsibility.

The finding reported on January 24 that the Justice Department could find no evidence that either the President or Attorney General Bell knew that Representative Eilberg "might be of investigative interest" to the Justice Department at the time they complied with the congressman's request to "expedite" the removal of Marston.

On the face of it, that investigation was superficial and intended by the Carter administration to put the Marston affair behind it. It was reminiscent of President Nixon's first efforts to use the Justice Department to cover up the Watergate crimes with the pronouncement by two Nixon appointeees—Attorney General Richard Kleindienst and Acting FBI Director Pat Gray—on the thoroughness of the Watergate probes and the lack of any White House involvement in those obstructions of justice.

Like Watergate, the Marston affair was to continue to plague the Carter administration and specifically the nomination of Ben Civiletti to be Deputy Attorney General. Although President Carter and Attorney General Bell continued to speak of taking politics out of the Justice Department, the Marston case remained a constant challenge to the Carter administration for their self-serving comments about new higher ethical and moral standards.

CHAPTER TEN

Ben Civiletti

Benjamin R. Civiletti was recognized as a power from the time he was selected by Attorney General Griffin Bell to head the Criminal Division in the Justice Department. Bell had received the recommendation for Civiletti from none other than Charles Kirbo, who was Bell's former law partner in the Atlanta firm of King and Spaulding and a man recognized by nearly everyone as President Carter's most intimate nonofficial adviser.

Attorney General Bell related that Kirbo had worked with Ben Civiletti on the same side of a litigation when the King and Spaulding firm was working in a correspondent relationship with the Baltimore law firm of Venable, Baetjer and Howard. Bell said that Kirbo had been "most impressed" by Civiletti who headed the Baltimore law firm's litigation department, supervising the work of twenty trial lawyers.

That recommendation from Charles Kirbo carried more weight in the Carter administration than the fact that Ben Civiletti had been a treasurer in the successful campaign of Senator Paul Sarbanes in Maryland. There was no controversy as Civiletti was nominated, confirmed and sworn into office on March 4, 1977, as Assistant Attorney General in charge of the Criminal Division. He came into office too late to be involved in the initial controversy over the premature clearance and cover-up of Bert Lance's problems, but he was involved in controversial actions in connection with the Marston firing.

Although Civiletti was not directly involved in the decision to fire David Marston, the United States Attorney in Eastern Pennsylvania, he was head of the criminal division and responsible for keeping Attorney General Bell informed on various criminal investigations of significance.

In that capacity he had a conversation in November 1977 with

Robert T. Baker, Jr., one of his top deputies in the criminal division. Baker said in an affidavit that in that conversation with Civiletti he spoke of the Justice Department's investigation of Representative Joshua Eilberg and specifically recalled that he had told Civiletti the Eilberg case was "alive."

Civiletti told the Judiciary Committee, which was trying to piece together the vital sequence of events in the Eilberg case and the Marston dismissal, that he could not remember such a conversation with Baker on Eilberg. Civiletti's lack of memory on that crucial conversation brought an effective end to the efforts to trace knowledge of the Eilberg probe to Attorney General Griffin Bell. Bell could have been involved in a criminal obstruction of justice if it were established that he had knowledge that Eilberg was under investigation when he carried out Eilberg's political demand that Marston be fired.

Although Civiletti convinced Senator Eastland and the Democrats that he was telling the truth when he said he could not recall the conversation with Baker on the Eilberg case, he did not convince Senator Malcolm Wallop, an aggressive Wyoming Republican.

Wallop carried the weight of the questioning in the seventeen days of testimony to determine if Civiletti should be elevated from Assistant to Deputy Attorney General. That questioning covered the firing of Marston as well as other controversies on Civiletti's role in the investigations of the Korean bribery scandals, the plea bargaining with former Central Intelligence Agency Director Richard Helms and the "admitted neglect in handling" the investigation of Bert Lance.

Senator Wallop said he did not question Civiletti's prowess as a lawyer and was in fact "impressed by his skillful response and sharp legal mind.

"I do, however, question Mr. Civiletti's credibility," Senator Wallop said in his opposition to confirmation. "His seemingly selective memory has caused me to doubt his credibility insofar as his affidavit and testimony go on the Marston matter."

Then Senator Wallop detailed the specifics:

"Mr. Civiletti claims to have no recollection of a meeting with Mr. Baker on or around November 25 [1977], and has absolutely no recollection of Mr. Baker's having discussed with him an 'Eilberg case.'

"Mr. Baker's affidavit, testimony and personal notes all indicate that a meeting did in fact take place on November 25 at which time Mr. Baker informed Mr. Civiletti that the 'Eilberg case is alive'—to quote from his notes. Both Mr. Baker [still a subordinate to Civiletti] and Mr. Civiletti have dismissed this as an insignificant conflict which is simply incapable of resolution. They have downplayed the significance of their inconsistent 'recollections.' "

Senator Wallop declared that in his view, "we are presented with much more than a mere conflict in memories.

"We have a contemporaneous executed document—Mr. Baker's notes—which expressly states that on November 25, the date at the top of the document, Mr. Baker spoke to Mr. Civiletti about the Eilberg case being alive—a notation which is checkmarked by Mr. Baker." Senator Wallop explained. "That note is extremely telling, especially when read in light of all of the other evidence of an investigation concerning the Congressman [and] centering on Hahnemann Hospital." Wallop said that official reports were "circulating around the Department of Justice beginning in May of 1977 [and] developed in much more detail by November and in [still] greater depth by December.

"All of the pieces of this puzzle, when meshed together, tend to bolster the credibility of Mr. Baker's statement that he did tell Mr. Civiletti about an Eilberg case on November 25. In turn this raised a very serious question about Mr. Civiletti's credibility which lingers on and troubles me deeply," Senator Wallop summarized.

Added to his doubts about Civiletti's credibility were "doubts about Mr. Civiletti's sensitivity" in the handling of the Bert Lance investigation.

"His admitted neglect in handling . . . the Lance case has demonstrated this lack of sensitivity," Senator Wallop stated. "We know by his own testimony that he did not think it his duty to advise or counsel the President about the chilling effect that his [Carter's] continued visibility with Mr. Lance might have.

"We also know that he has been insensitive to the complaints of the three attorney panel who have been working on the Lance case," Wallop said.

Wallop stated flatly that "in the Lance investigation, conflict of interest exists at the top levels of the Department of Justice and the White House.

"The President is a close personal friend of Mr. Lance," Wallop detailed in his complaint. "The Attorney General [Bell] is a close personal friend of Mr. Lance. The Attorney General has excused or disqualified himself from the aspects of the case dealing with the [National] Bank of Georgia and the Calhoun First National Bank."

Wallop said he found Civiletti's testimony with regard to the conduct of the Lance investigation "particularly disturbing."

"From the time that Mr. Flaherty [former Deputy Attorney General] left the Justice Department [in January] until a few days ago [in late April], Mr. Civiletti has neither supervised nor participated in the Lance investigation," Senator Wallop specified in his complaint. "The three attorneys who were previously reporting to Mr. Flaherty were functioning virtually without supervision by Mr. Civiletti or anybody else in the Department. Yet, in view of the Attorney General's disqualification from this case, we know that it is Mr. Civiletti who is responsible for the Lance investigation."

Senator Wallop said that "to compound this problem" it "has been reported that the three attorney panel has complained about the President's visibility [continued praise of and political and social association] with Mr. Lance.

"The public displays of affection are certainly enough to prejudice a case—one way or the other—which the Attorney General has acknowledged in his testimony," Senator Wallop said. "Yet, Mr. Civiletti has testified that he has no legal duty to advise the President as to the chilling effect his actions might have on the administration of justice.

"Indeed, [Civiletti] refused to recognize a public, moral or private obligation in this matter, and the American people can only be left with the discomforting thought that the process of justice is reserved for the meek," Wallop said, making a point that many Republicans and some Democrats had made on Civiletti's fence-straddling effort to avoid actions or comments that might be resented by the Carter White House.

Senator Wallop declared that the investigation of Bert Lance and the investigation of the Marston matter required "an impartial, nonpartisan special prosecutor" by the "President's own standards."

Wallop pointed out that "the President, the Attorney General and Mr. Civiletti have all supported legislation which would trigger the appointment of a special prosecutor to investigate actions of misconduct in cases involving the President and the Cabinet among others."

The Wyoming Republican related that President Carter had endorsed the special prosecutor bill that passed the Senate, with the Presidential comment that such a special prosecutor is needed in certain cases "to eliminate the appearance of high level interference with sensitive investigations and prosecutions."

Wallop quoted President Carter as saying that in the wake of Watergate, "the American people must be assured that no one, regardless of position, is above the law."

In his detailed explanation, Wallop also quoted Attorney General Bell as having testified:

"If I can't make the Justice Department have the appearance of justice then I've failed. That's what bothers me so much about the Marston case. I felt like the Marston case set back a year what I have been trying to do, which was to restore the confidence of the American people."

Wallop declared that "the Marston matter and the Lance investigation are precisely the kind of situation" envisioned by the law as providing for the appointment of a temporary special prosecutor with no personal or political ties to the persons who are under investigation. The Wyoming Republican pleaded with Chairman Eastland and the Democratic majority to join him in asking Attorney General Bell to appoint special prosecutors who would have full authority for the investigation and prosecution of the Bert Lance financial manipulations and for Bell's firing of Marston.

Chairman Eastland, as expected, rejected Senator Wallop's suggestion. The conservative Mississippi Democrat held no brief for what he considered "the liberal Carter White House," but he liked Attorney General Griffin Bell and considered him his kind of guy. Also, Senator Eastland had given his word to the White House that he would support the Civiletti nomination and oppose a special prosecutor. He had been a man of his word in the Nixon administration, where he took verbal brickbats from the Democrats for his support of Richard Kleindienst for Attorney General in the face of testimony indicating that Kleindienst had been less than truthful. Also, Senator Eastland had stuck with the Nixon nomination of L. Patrick Gray to be Director of the FBI long after he had become convinced that Gray was "an incompetent political opportunist" who had aided in the White House efforts to obstruct the Watergate investigation.

It seemed certain if Jim Eastland would stick by a promise to the Nixon administration regarding Pat Gray until his nomination was belatedly withdrawn, that he would keep his word to Griffin Bell and President Carter to support Civiletti.

Wallop and Senator Charles Mathias, Jr., of Maryland had expected to persuade some of the liberal Democrats who had been most vocal in criticism of "conflict of interest" in the Nixon and Ford administrations. However, they were unable to stir any opposition on the Democratic side of the aisle, and only a sprinkling of support on the Republican side, where there was a natural reluctance to raise opposition to the man who was at that time in charge of the Justice Department's Criminal Division and now was nominated to become Deputy Attorney General—the more powerful number two post in the Justice Department.

The Justice Department and White House promised full cooperation with the investigation of the handling of the Marston firing, but when requests were made for various internal documents and witnesses from the Justice Department and White House, there was stalling, foot-dragging and finally refusal to produce the material unless the request came on a formal vote from the whole Judiciary Committee. All of Wallop's most controversial requests for key witnesses and documents were defeated by the Democratic majority.

Because the actions of Senator Wallop's requests were not met the delays were interminable, and the Carter White House through Press Secretary Jody Powell complained that the Republicans were delaying action on the Civiletti nomination.

In the third week of April 1978 the Democratic majority summarily pulled down the curtain to end the hearings on the Civiletti nomination before all of the witnesses had been called. The first vote was 10 to 2 agreeing that Benjamin Civiletti was qualified to serve as Deputy Attorney General. The committee then voted by a 15-to-2 margin to send the nomination to the floor for action, with several Republicans declaring they were not satisfied with Civiletti's performance but believed that the President was entitled to his own preference in Cabinet and subcabinet officers.

The Democratic staff members, in consultation with the Justice Department, wrote a report that declared that "it is clear Mr. Civiletti had nothing to do" with the firing of Marston. "It was not in his area of responsibility," the staff-written report stated.

"From all the evidence, it appears to the committee that there was no investigation of Congressman Eilberg at the time of the call to the President, and that Congressman Eilberg did not begin to be involved significantly in the investigation until December 19, 1977, well after the telephone conversation,'' the staff wrote in a factually inaccurate statement. It then concluded, ''There was no 'cover-up' of an investigation because there was no such investigation in existence during the time in question.''

When Senator Wallop got the printed copy of the report he was outraged, and he called several of his Republican colleagues from the committee to ask them why they had agreed to such a factually inaccurate report. Senator Orrin Hatch of Utah, Senator Strom Thurmond of South Carolina, Senator William Scott of Virginia and Senator Charles Mathias of Maryland said they had not seen the report, and would have objected to what they agreed was ''a whitewash'' of Civiletti as well as a gratuitous effort to put the majority of the committee on record to clear President Carter and Attorney General Bell of any possible obstruction of justice.

Then Senator Wallop and his Republican colleagues made contact with Democratic members of the Judiciary Committee and learned that none of them had approved the language of the report. The Committee Democrats, including Chairman Eastland, voted to recommend confirmation of Civiletti, but they wanted to be no party to a report that drew such sweeping conclusions.

Chairman Eastland told this reporter that only a part of the report was read to him on the telephone, and he had not caught the implications of some of the sweeping language when those parts were read to him. He said that the staff had written the report in consultation with the Justice Department.

In the days that followed, Senator Richard Schweiker, a Pennsylvania Republican, lambasted the report as a ''misleading whitewash.'' His Pennsylvania colleague, Senator John Heinz, declared that ''the conclusions in the report are clearly not sustained by the hearing record.

''There are numerous inconsistencies and the fact situations remain unsettled,'' Senator Heinz said. ''What is more alarming and even less palatable is the fact that the full committee did not see the report and was not given an opportunity to review or consider said conclusions.

''We have only the unsubstantiated opinion rendered by the staff of the committee,'' Senator Heinz said.

Senator William Scott, one of the Republicans who had voted to report the Civiletti nomination to the Senate floor, told the Senate that he ''would be ashamed to sign my name to such a whitewash as this report is.''

Senator Thurmond, one of the Republicans who had supported the Civiletti nomination, made a motion to send the report back to the committee with instructions to report back the nomination without the offending whitewash report.

There was no objection, even from Chairman Eastland, to a unanimous vote by the Senate to kill the Judiciary Committee staff report, which would have cleared President Carter and Attorney General Bell of any wrongdoing in the firing of Marston.

The Civiletti nomination was then reported back to the Senate floor without the offensive report, but the embarrassed Democratic leadership could find no Democratic members who wished to speak on behalf of the nomination after Senator Paul Sarbanes, Civiletti's long-time friend, made a brief but general statement on his knowledge of Civiletti since the time they met twenty years earlier as law clerks to federal judges in Baltimore.

Senator Sarbanes's laudatory comments were general as to Civiletti's "intelligence, integrity, experience and commitment to the rule of law," but he carefully avoided any mention of Civiletti's testimony or Civiletti's responsibility for the lack of diligent handling of the Lance investigation.

When Senator Wallop lashed into the Civiletti record and the Civiletti testimony, there was not one Democratic voice raised to dispute Wallop's facts. Senators Eastland and Kennedy did dispute his conclusions on the credibility of the man nominated to hold the second highest law enforcement post in the nation.

Wallop documented as devastating a bill of particulars as any Senator has spelled out against any nominee for a top Justice Department position in decades. Wallop characterized the hearings as "protracted, awkward, often hostile, always faced with a reluctant Department of Justice and a reluctant nominee who were unwilling to cooperate with the committee to determine the nature and extent of certain problems which had arisen . . . during the time Mr. Civiletti had been in charge of the Criminal Division."

Senator Wallop commented that the Democratic members of the committee were rarely present during his questioning of Civiletti and other key witnesses, and he noted that the last half of the Civiletti hearing record was not yet printed and available for examination by Judiciary Committee members and other members of the Senate.

The Wyoming Republican charged that the investigation was ended against his wishes, before he had an opportunity to question important witnesses, and despite the fact that the Justice Department and White House had refused to supply witnesses and documents.

The Wyoming Republican reiterated his charges that he doubted Civiletti's credibility because of his "selective memory."

Faced with a torrent of public criticism and speculation that a whitewash might be ahead, Attorney General Bell had nominated an experienced, tough federal prosecutor named Peter Vaira. Vaira, who headed the Justice Department's organized crime strike force in Chicago for more than a decade, was not a lawyer who could be pushed around by the Teamsters union or the organized crime bosses, and he certainly wasn't going to be influenced by either Democratic or Republican pressures from Washington. In addition, Bell made public statements assuring Vaira a free hand in following up the Marston investigations.

By the time Wallop was making his protest against Civiletti's role in the Marston firing, cover-up and other actions, it was already apparent that the massive evidence was going to require the indictment of Congressman Eilberg and Congressman Flood on criminal charges of fraud and misuse of their offices for personal financial gain. It was evident that even the House of Representatives, traditionally reluctant to criticize its members, would also have an investigation and a public report on the criminal conduct of both Pennsylvania Democrats.

Representative Joshua Eilberg was defeated for reelection in 1978, and on February 24, 1979, he entered a plea of guilty to federal charges that he had illegally taken money for helping his former law firm gain a $14 million federal grant for Philadelphia Hospital. United States District Judge Raymond J. Broderick fined Eilberg $10,000 and sentenced him to three to five years probation. A few weeks later, Eilberg was disbarred by the Pennsylvania Supreme Court for the felony conviction, which also bars him from ever again holding federal office.

Although Representative Daniel J. Flood won reelection in Wilkes Barre despite pending federal charges of conspiracy, bribery and perjury, his lawyers and doctors in November, 1979, pictured him as a shattered man, unable to stand trial because of a deteriorated mental capacity caused by a combination of drug addiction and illness. The 75-year-old Congressman announced his retirement from Congress on January 31, 1980, because of his deteriorated health. The pending indictment charged Flood with taking $65,000 in bribes from several businessmen in return for help in obtaining federal grants.

Senator Wallop declared that continuation of Marston's investigations of Democratic corruption in Pennsylvania under pressure from Congress and the press did not blot out the need for an investigation of Marston's firing.

Only the appointment of a special prosecutor could bring the needed objectivity to a probe into whether the highest officials had been involved in a criminal obstruction of justice, Wallop argued. It could not be done properly by anyone then in the Department of Justice, because they were appointees of President Carter or Bell or were subordinates of Civiletti.

Wallop recalled that Attorney General Bell had opened the great metal doors of the Justice Department after years of being closed to protesters. It was "a symbolic act welcomed all over America—welcomed by me," Wallop said.

The Wyoming Senator said that the Justice Department's strong partisanship, and the refusal to provide information and witnesses had been one of the "major disappointments" of his time in the Senate. He declared this disappointment was "not because there was a political man fired, as I think that is well within the rights of a President when he takes office, but because of all the other circumstances and events surrounding his ouster.

"It was not just Marston; it was not just Lance," Wallop told the Senate. "It was also the Korean influence-buying investigation, the fact that we could never get an answer as to whether or not there was a connection between the President's sudden change of pace in the Korean withdrawal and the simultaneous announcement that Tongsun Park would come to this country under a different set of circumstances."

Wallop declared that the Justice Department had engaged in case settlements in a broad range of cases involving high-level officials and prominent political figures that would preclude an objective review by Bell or any of his subordinates.

"I do not think that [Civiletti's] confirmation by the Senate will in any way diminish the public's perception of a double standard of justice," Wallop said, realizing that a Democratic power play would assure confirmation of Civiletti.

Senator Lowell Weicker, a member of the Senate Watergate investigating committee and a severe critic of the Nixon Justice Department, praised Wallop's analysis of the Civiletti nomination, particularly his warning against "the danger of a double standard of justice."

He recalled that it was "only a few short years back" during the Watergate hearings that everybody understood that there "had to be equality of justice under law."

"Here it is 1978," Senator Weicker said, "and here in its lowest and most clear-cut form is the example of what we talk about when we talk about a double standard of justice."

He declared that when one removes specific names and party labels and actions on the Marston matter, it is comparable to the Watergate cover-up. Weicker reviewed testimony by the members of a team of top FBI supervisors who had recommended prosecution. Civiletti had initially agreed with their recommendations but had abandoned them when Attorney General Bell opposed the prosecutions.

"What makes Mr. Civiletti's involvement in this whole affair as culpable as that of the Attorney General, if not more so, is that he was intimately involved with all aspects of the case, and with the reasoning that dictated the tactics of this particular [FBI investigation] task force," Senator Weicker declared. "And, indeed, he agreed with those tactics and that reasoning, and he agreed with those indictments. Yet, when the slightest pressure came from above, he did not have the guts to stand up to it, either in the sense of his job security or his politics or, most important, in the sense of the facts of the case."

"What we need is less politics and more justice," Weicker said. "We will not get that with Mr. Civiletti. He is less interested in doing what is right than doing what his boss wishes. . . . If we want to have an Attorney General whose instinct is to go with the tide, then we need as his Deputy a person to stand strong against the wave which would erode the structure of the country. Mr. Civiletti has already proven he is not such a person.

"I do not believe in Mitchell justice, I do not believe in Bell justice," Weicker said. "I do not believe in Civiletti justice. I believe in the American system of justice."

Senator Weicker noted, "the emptiness of this [Senate] chamber," adding: "It was not so when the names of Mitchell and Kleindienst and [Robert] Mardian and others were before us.

"Then [in 1973 and 1974] there was a high standard that was to be applied to those [Justice Department] positions and to the power which those positions represented," Weicker said in chiding the Democrats for their lack of attention to the evidence of politics in the Carter administration's Department of Justice. "Believe me, the politics of a few years back in the Justice Department . . . had nothing on the politics of the Justice Department of today under Griffin Bell and Benjamin Civiletti."

He declared that he was "not naive" enough to believe he could stop the confirmation of Civiletti against the "wheeling and dealing" of the Carter administration, which had assured approval. And, Senator Weicker declared, the narrowness of President Carter's victory meant that Mr. Carter might have been elected on the basis of people's belief in his campaign promise that a U.S. attorney would not be chosen on the basis of politics, but rather on the basis of legal qualifications.

No Democrat rose to answer the charges leveled against Civiletti by Senator Wallop, Weicker and others. No Democrat tried to defend the faulty "whitewash" report that the Justice Department and the committee staff had tried to push off as an official Judiciary Committee finding on the Marston matter.

The Democratic majority on May 9, 1978, voted as a block in support of the Civiletti nomination, and they were joined by a few Republicans who were unmoved by the arguments of Senator Wallop and Senator Weicker or were unconcerned about politics as usual in the Justice Department. There were seventy-seven votes in favor of confirmation of Civiletti, and only twenty-two Senators —all Republicans—willing to register a protest against the man who was to be the nation's Number Two Prosecutor.

The Lance case and the Marston affair were not the only problems that the Justice Department would face where there would be cries of political tampering and demands for the naming of a special prosecutor. Two of those problems involved investigations of the activities of First Brother Billy Carter. Problems emerging in connection with the operation of the Georgia State Energy Office when Jimmy Carter was governor gave some indication of why the Carter White House might be eager to have politically responsive lawyers in the top jobs at the Justice Department.

CHAPTER ELEVEN

Energy Policies and Politics

On the same day (May 9, 1978) that the Senate Democrats pushed through the confirmation of Benjamin Civiletti as Deputy Attorney General, they confirmed Mr. Carter's nomination of an oil company lawyer-lobbyist as General Counsel for the Department of Energy.

The nomination of Lynn R. Coleman, a thirty-eight-year-old lawyer from a prominent Houston law firm, was opposed by twenty members of the Senate who claimed the nomination violated President Carter's pledge to end the "revolving door" approach to filling positions in the government regulatory agencies. Most of the opposition to Coleman came from Democrats, led by Senator William Proxmire and Senator Howard Metzenbaum.

Proxmire and Metzenbaum found no fault with the professional credentials of the brilliant young Texas lawyer, who had served as a law clerk to United States Circuit Judge John R. Brown before joining the law firm of Vinson and Elkins. But they noted that the Vinson and Elkins law firm, in which John B. Connally was a senior partner, represented major oil interests. Coleman had personally represented many of the major companies and had lobbied for those oil interests in the Senate and House as well as before the Federal Power Commission and Federal Energy Administration—predecessors to the Department of Energy.

In testimony before the Senate Committee on Energy and Natural Resources, Senator Proxmire presented Mr. Coleman's successful representation of a dozen oil companies, including such major ones as the Continental Oil Company and Union Oil Company.

"In fact, Mr. Coleman's former superior at Vinson and Elkins —Rush Moody—is currently representing Continental Oil Company before the Department of Energy's Office of Administrative Review, Proxmire told the Senate Committee. "I submit that it would be extremely difficult for any former industry lobbyist to carry out the duties of General Counsel for the Energy Department. If Mr. Coleman fails to disqualify himself even from relatively minor cases such as the one I have just mentioned, then he is in a conflict of interest position.

"If he does disqualify himself, as he must, then his participation in the duties of his office is necessarily limited and his effectiveness is compromised," Proxmire said, setting forth a reasoning that was pursued to a large degree by Senator Metzenbaum and James R. Flug, director and counsel of Energy Action Educational Foundation.

Proxmire said he would "be the first to acknowledge that there are obviously times when the federal government needs expert advice" available "only from industry representatives," adding: "I frankly doubt that getting industry opinion and advice is much of a problem."

He related that in 1974 the Federal Energy Office Administrator, William Simon, acknowledged that 102 former oil industry employees had been hired as part of the government's chief energy operation following the Arab oil embargo. Senator Proxmire said he hoped that President Carter "would be able to turn over a new leaf" in staffing the newly created Department of Energy and made reference to Mr. Carter's "campaign commitment" to "eliminate 'revolving door' exchanges between industry and government.

"I am sorry to say that the Coleman nomination gives me cause to doubt that we will," Senator Proxmire said on November 9, 1977.

The assurances of Coleman that he would not let his past association with the Houston law firm color his judgments as chief counsel did not satisfy Senator Proxmire, Senator Metzenbaum and other critics of the principle of appointing an oil industry lobbyist as General Counsel for the Department of Energy.

They were not persuaded by a letter from White House Counsel Robert Lipshutz assuring them that President Carter had reviewed the problem and was satisfied by Coleman's commitments to disqualify himself on matters involving the Vinson and Elkins law firm or in any case in which the law firm of his wife, Sylvia deLeon, might appear to present a conflict of interest.

The White House Counsel wrote that Ms. deLeon was on a salary as a lawyer in the Washington law firm of Akin, Gump, Hauer and Feld and did not receive a share of the firm's profits as a partner. He noted that Ms. deLeon agreed not to work on any matter requiring her to appear before the Department of Energy or to have any written or oral contact with the Department of Energy.

"It is my opinion that the steps you have agreed to take to insulate yourself from conflicts of interest which might otherwise arise as a result of your past association with Vinson and Elkins are appropriate and sufficient," Lipshutz wrote Coleman.

Senator Metzenbaum expressed skepticism. "When Mr. Coleman makes a decision on whether or not to prosecute a case, will he forget his ties to the companies and people he had known in the industry? Will those people have more access to Mr. Coleman's time than does a Ralph Nader, an environmental spokesman, a labor leader, an agricultural spokesman, or a Lee White of the Consumer Federation of America?

"When a committee is asked to review a nomination, as we are doing here, we are forced to rely on the nominee's past history," Senator Metzenbaum said. "In my review of Mr. Coleman's record, I have found no example where he has worked explicitly on behalf of the public or consumer interest without regard to his own personal income.

"By approving the nomination of Lynn Coleman as General Counsel, we would, in fact, be placing a major lobbyist for the oil industry in a key government position," Senator Metzenbaum declared. He was not persuaded by the bipartisan support that Coleman received from the Texas Senators—Republican John Tower and Democrat Lloyd Bentsen.

Senators Tower and Bentsen declared that their personal knowledge of the "integrity" and "competence" of Lynn Coleman convinced them that he would not let his past representation of the oil industry influence his decisions.

"He [Coleman] is prepared to serve at a substantial personal sacrifice, and he has willingly complied with a stringent series of procedures that eliminate even the suspicion of conflict of interest," Senator Bentsen said.

Senator Tower related that Coleman had been the 1972 political campaign manager for his opponent in the Texas Gulf Coast area, and facetiously commented that this "suggests a major flaw in Lynn's political judgment.'' But, he declared seriously, the fact that he and Coleman ''had been on different sides in Texas political battles'' did not detract from Coleman's ''broad knowledge and experience in energy law.''

Both Tower and Bentsen stressed Coleman's specialty in ''energy law'' and avoided reference to his representation of ''oil interests,'' which had been the rhetoric of the critics.

''I cannot think of a better way to get this new agency off the ground,'' Tower said, endorsing the Texas lawyer who had been a campaign manager for his political opponent.

Consumer advocate Ralph Nader viewed this bipartisan support from the Texas Senators as a bad omen, and James Flug declared that the Coleman appointment ''looks like the epitome of a revolving door appointment on the face of it.''

Noting that he would probably have to deal with Coleman if he was confirmed, Flug said he does not quarrel with the fact that he was well qualified as an honor graduate (Order of the Coif) at the University of Texas, that he ''is a nice guy'' and that ''we think he will be more progressive than most people who come out of law firms like Vinson and Elkins.''

He rejected reports ''that someone at the highest level of the Department was characterizing the opposition as being McCarthyist [guilt by association]—the implication being that people were against him because he was a partner of John Connally's or just because he came from a law firm that represented the oil industry.''

Flug declared that while Coleman may disqualify himself on matters that directly involve the Vinson and Elkins law firm, he would be making legal rulings day after day on a thousand matters that would involve the same issues that lawyers for Vinson and Elkins may be pursuing.

In addition to the inherent problem of ''conflict of interest'' and the appearance of such conflicts, Flug argued that if Coleman was going to reverse himself on positions he had advocated for the oil interest, it would be a potential public embarrassment.

Flug recalled President Carter's campaign statements. ''In his presentation to the platform committee, the first item on his agenda was an open and honest government, and one of the subcategories . . . was [elimination of] the sweetheart arrangement between the federal regulatory agencies and the regulated industries . . . and the revolving door between them should be closed.

''Is there any possibility, whatsoever, that the 215 million

Americans can ever have confidence that an oil and gas company lawyer will be impartial and objective in spite of the highest standards of integrity, character and the strongest legal document that might be executed by him prior to assuming office?" Flug summed up his opposition.

Although many Democrats complained privately about the appearance of conflict in the Coleman nomination, a majority of them fell in line with the demands of the Carter White House. The nomination was approved by a 75-to-20 vote, but the Carter White House still had another controversial nomination to the Energy Department that had been pending since January 1978.

The nomination of a young Georgia woman, Omi G. Walden, to the $50,000-a-year post of Assistant Secretary of Energy for Conservation and Solar Application was sent to the Senate in January despite the skepticism of Senator Henry M. Jackson, Chairman of the Senate Energy and Natural Resources Committee, about her qualifications for such an important post in the Department of Energy.

The major qualification of the thirty-one-year-old journalism school graduate was her service in Georgia state government posts as an appointee of former Governor Jimmy Carter. On the face of it, that hardly seemed to be "the best" qualification for the job of supervising the vital energy conservation and solar development, which would constitute a major portion of the multibillion-dollar annual budget of the Department of Energy.

Omi Walden had certainly gone up the ladder quickly since her graduation in 1968 with an A.B. degree in journalism from the University of Georgia. From 1968 through 1969, she was assistant director for public relations for the Georgia Port Authority in Savannah. From 1970 through 1973 she was director of public relations for a federal model cities program in her home town of Alma (population 3,700), the county seat of Bacon County in southeast Georgia.

In 1973 the then Governor Carter appointed her as a coordinator of Federal–State Relations and Policy Advisor in the Governor's Office of Planning and Budget. In that capacity she was the liaison person with Lewis C. Spruill, director of the Georgia state energy office. Spruill's office handled the allocation of the state's emergency fuel set-aside program from 1973 following the Arab oil embargo.

She served in that capacity through Carter's term as Governor and continued when the new Governor, George Busbee, succeeded Carter. Governor Busbee abolished the old Georgia state energy office in 1976, because of federal government complaints of political favoritism, improprieties and possible criminal conduct in the allocation of fuel in the set-aside program under Carter's administration in Georgia.

Governor Busbee accepted Spruill's resignation after receiving these reports of favoritism and irregularities and named Omi Walden as Director of the Georgia Office of Energy Resources.

Ms. Walden had served as Director of the Georgia Office of Energy Resources from August 1976 until the late fall of 1977, when the Carter White House decided to bring her to Washington to help in the "moral equivalent of war" on the nation's massive energy problems.

Understandably, Chairman Jackson and his committee staff were skeptical about what professional qualifications this attractive young woman, if confirmed, had to take on one of the most trying assignments in federal government. After the nomination was formally sent to the Senate in January 1978, they became even more skeptical as news stories started appearing exposing the extent of corruption and maladministration in Jimmy Carter's energy program in Georgia. Such stories didn't quite square with Carter's campaign utterances, in which he claimed great honesty and efficiency in the manner in which he had managed and reorganized the various regulatory functions in state government.

Certainly there was no indication that Governor Carter had any direct role in the free-wheeling activities of Lew Spruill, the former oil company executive he had appointed to direct allocations of the emergency fuel set-aside program in Georgia.

But there was sufficient sensitivity, in the wake of the inadequate investigation of the Bert Lance nomination, to try to examine thoroughly the specific relationship of Omi Walden to the scandals that permeated the administration of the fuel set-aside program in Georgia. The new Department of Energy was continuing an investigation into the relationship between Lew Spruill and the old Federal Energy Administration (FEA) regional director, Kenneth Dupuy on the one hand, and William (Billy) Corey, a flamboyant, free-wheeling Georgia oilman, on the other.

Corey, who operated a string of wholesale and retail gasoline stations, had been a social friend of both Dupuy and Spruill in the period when Corey's stations were receiving millions of gallons of fuel from the Georgia "emergency" set-aside program without establishing that an "emergency" did exist within the federal and state laws and regulations.

There were factors in the investigation that could be a personal political embarrassment to President Carter. His son, James Earl (Chip) Carter was given a job by Spruill at the personal request of the then Governor Carter. It was a low-level job with no possible decision making, but it was brazen political patronage with the help of the errant Lew Spruill.

In January 1978 *Federal Times* reporter Sheila Hershow wrote the first stories raising the question of whether Douglas Robinson, a lawyer for the Ford administration's energy agency, had engaged in a cover-up of the Georgia fuel emergency scandal by limiting an agency investigation as to the relations between Corey and FEA regional director Kenneth Dupuy and by stopping an investigation of Spruill, the Carter appointee.

In December 1977 CBS investigative reporter Charles C. Thompson II came across some even more devastating information indicating that Spruill's operation of the Georgia energy program had resulted in "emergency" allocations of up to 25,000 gallons of gasoline a month to Billy Carter's service station in Plains, Georgia.

Thompson also learned, and then verified, that Roy Cross, Executive Director of the Georgia State Independent Oilmens Association, had talked with Lew Spruill and Billy Carter relative to the emergency set-aside fuel that went to Billy's service station.

Cross related that Spruill had told him that he "kept Billy Carter in business [in 1974 and 1975] with the set-aside program." Cross also told CBS reporters that Billy Carter in a speech before the Georgia State Independent Oilmens Association had commented that "Lew Spruill kept me alive" with allocations from the set-aside program.

Thompson wanted to do a CBS News series on the operations of the Georgia energy office when Jimmy Carter was governor, specifically pointing out that Billy Carter's gas station in Plains—by then a national institution—had received questionable allocations without the solid justification of an "emergency" that was required in most state programs. In theory, that was the law in Georgia.

CBS superiors in Washington rejected the story, because "Billy Carter isn't a national news story." Thompson resigned at

CBS and went to work on the project for the *St. Petersburg* (Florida) *Times*. With Patrick Tyler, another experienced investigative reporter, he combed the records of the Georgia State Energy Office to corroborate the verbal accounts of favoritism in allocations to Billy Carter, Billy Corey and others who were reported to have benefited from special treatment by Spruill.

Digging through thousands of documents, they were able to establish that Billy Carter and Billy Corey had indeed been allocated "emergency" fuel with no proof or with inadequate documentation of an "emergency."

In late February, a few weeks after the nomination of Omi Walden had been announced, Thompson and Tyler were able to demonstrate to editor Eugene Patterson that they had a story that merited a top line display in the Sunday *St. Petersburg Times*. The headline read: "Emergency Gas Boosted Billy Carter's Business." The punchy and well documented story started with this lead and an Atlanta dateline:

"While his brother stumped political paths from the Georgia governor's mansion to the White House, Billy Carter kept a two-pump gas station 'alive'—and very profitable—with the help of up to 25,000 gallons of emergency state gasoline a month, oil company and Georgia Energy Office records show."

Thompson and Tyler related that while the President's brother paid for the emergency gasoline, the gasoline was sold to those with an "emergency" for several cents a gallon less than the normal supplies. "The guaranteed volume allowed Carter to turn his station—known as a "country dog" to Georgia fuel dealers—into a farm-belt gold mine whose earnings skyrocketed to a reported $100,000 a year after Carter-mania tourist traffic provided it with a six-fold increase in business."

That story noted: "The federal energy regulations, that created the emergency gasoline supplies in all 50 states, strictly forbade treating the 'hardship' fuel as a windfall stockpile for commercial service stations.

"Moreover, a U.S. Energy Department official in Atlanta said that retail service stations did not qualify for emergency gasoline, but the official, Otis D. Phillips, acknowledged that the federal guidelines were widely ignored in Georgia and elsewhere."

Those hard-hitting stories in the *St. Petersburg Times* were widely ignored by the nation's press or were picked up with inadequate documentation to establish the depth of corroboration

Thompson and Tyler had established for their story. Those stories included damaging admissions by Billy Carter that the fuel had been delivered.

Carter admitted that he had received the "emergency" fuel on a regular basis, admitted that he did not have any hardship, and admitted to not establishing the "emergency" required to be eligible for the set-aside fuel. But he insisted that it was "above board" and quipped, "Hell, if I've done anything illegal, I wouldn't try to hide it, I'd brag about it."

But the Energy Department investigators did not ignore the *St. Petersburg Times* stories, nor did they ignore the probing questions that Thompson and Tyler had been asking concerning the closing of the investigation of Lew Spruill and the status of the investigation of Ken Dupuy.

Nor did the Department of Energy ignore the implications of one of the stories indicating that the allocations of set-aside fuel to Billy Carter had continued in late 1976 and early 1977, when Omi Walden directed the Georgia energy office.

Fearful of being found negligent in the handling of the Georgia energy investigation in 1976 and 1977, the Department of Energy investigators notified the Senate Committee on Energy and Natural Resources that they were engaged in the investigation and reexamination of Ms. Walden's knowledge of the questionable allocations to Billy Corey, Billy Carter and others, as well as her knowledge of, or participation in, the premature termination of those investigations.

Omi Walden had a fine line to tread. On the one hand, her experience with the Georgia energy program was her only claim as background for becoming an Assistant Secretary of Energy. However, it was essential that she had no role in the operation of the Georgia energy office or in the questionable decisions that were under an active criminal investigation.

Frustrated with the long delays on her nomination, Ms. Walden told the *St. Petersburg Times* that she was about fed up and might ask that her name be withdrawn. She said that, in addition to the Energy Department, the White House Counsel Robert Lipshutz was also conducting an inquiry.

In the same period Representative John E. Moss and Representative John Dingell, both Democrats, showed an additional interest when they were told in early March that the Department of Energy had sent the investigation to Justice for study for criminal action.

Moss and Dingell did not see how Attorney General Bell or any of his subordinates could make an objective decision on criminal prosecution if it involved the officials and operation of the Georgia Energy Office at the time Jimmy Carter was governor. If anything was to be learned from the Watergate affair, it was that this type of case called for a special prosecutor.

On March 4, 1978, the two Democratic Congressmen wrote to Attorney General Bell as chairmen of two important House subcommittees. Dingell, as chairman of the Subcommittee on Energy and Power, and Moss, as chairman of the Subcommittee on Oversight and Investigations, explained that for some months they had "been concerned about the conduct of the Georgia State Set-Aside investigation."

"The investigation basically involves allegations that the Director of the Georgia State Energy Office, an appointee of the then Governor Carter, gave unwarranted and highly advantageous gasoline allocations from the State Set-Aside program to select and favored jobbers and dealers," they wrote, emphasizing that a Carter appointee was involved. This favoritism worked "to the detriment of others who were not so well connected politically with the Director and his associates.

"Some of these allocations, we have been told, were in return for a variety of alleged favors," they said, but did not repeat the published reports that Billy Corey had financed a "love nest" apartment for a few energy officials.

"For two and a half years the investigation dragged on in the Department of Energy until March [1978] when the Department finally made a criminal referral of the case to the Department of Justice," Moss and Dingell explained that "a new dimension of this case" had surfaced when reporters for the *St. Petersburg Times* had come across files disclosing that "Billy Carter, the President's brother, allegedly was a recipient of large volumes of the State Set-Aside gasoline.

"Department of Energy officials told the Subcommittee staff that they missed the Carter involvement because they failed to audit his suppliers in the initial audit, although the information was in the files of the Georgia Energy Office," the congressmen informed the Attorney General, indicating negligence in the initial probes.

"Because of these circumstances and others, serious questions arise as to whether the U.S. Attorney in Atlanta can investigate and prosecute this case without severely eroding the nation's public confidence in the integrity of its government and its governmental processes.'' Moss and Dingell spelled out the reason for believing that U.S. Attorney William Harper, a legal aide to Governor Carter in 1974 and 1975, should not be given the responsibility:

''Certainly, the appointment of an independent prosecutor not associated with any parochial [Georgia] interest would go a long way toward erasing the public's perception of simply 'politics as usual and the good old boys.' '' And they added, ''We are sure you share our concern about this problem of public confidence.''

They suggested that ''the independence and integrity of the process [of selecting a special prosecutor] could be further strengthened by having the decision on the selection of a particular independent prosecutor made by a Justice Department official who has had no previous association, personal or otherwise, with the parties allegedly involved in the Georgia State Set-Aside case.'' It was as diplomatic a way as possible to tell Bell to stay out of the decision because of his past social and political association with Jimmy and Billy Carter.

Moss and Dingell asked to be kept informed and expected an early reply on a problem that carried potential political dynamite, but there was no reply for weeks as the Justice Department wrestled with the Lance case, the Marston affair, and the questions raised by the controversial Civiletti nomination.

When Bell finally answered in May, he flatly rejected the suggestion of a special prosecutor. He said that he had examined the facts of the criminal investigation and that Billy Carter was not and could not be a target of the federal probe. Elimination of Billy Carter as a target took the investigation out of the area for an appointment of a special prosecutor, Bell said, disregarding the fact that it was an investigation that centered on the operations of a Georgia government agency when Jimmy Carter was Governor.

Moss and Dingell protested publicly that the Carter White House and Justice Department were insensitive to problems of conflict of interest and were breaking their campaign pledges about keeping politics out of the Justice Department.

Senator Jackson, Chairman of the Senate Energy and Natural Resources Committee, privately suggested to the White House they they should withdraw the Omi Walden nomination and send up the name of someone with superior qualifications. He warned that an aggressive Republican push on the Omi Walden hearing could result in full national attention on the operation of the Energy program when Jimmy Carter was Governor and on the allocations of "emergency" gasoline to Billy Carter's service station.

The word came back to Chairman Jackson and the staff from Hamilton Jordan's White House office that "Omi Walden is a must" and that the name would not be withdrawn.

On June 29, 1978, the Omi Walden nomination hearing was held, but there was scant newspaper coverage. A letter from recently confirmed Deputy Attorney General Civiletti gave Ms. Walden the kind of clearance she needed. Civiletti said that on April 20, 1978, the FBI had reopened their background inquiry on Ms. Walden as a result of a letter signed by Senator Jackson and Senator Cliff Hansen, the ranking Republican member of the committee. On May 24, 1978, FBI Director William Webster had written a letter to the White House, making three points. Civiletti repeated those points to the committee:

"First, that the Department of Energy's criminal referral focuses on possible criminal violations by individuals within the Georgia State Energy Office during the Lewis Spruill administration during the period of January 1974 to approximately June of 1976.

"Second, Director Webster's letter and the Department of Energy's referral indicate that Omi Gail Walden had no responsibility for the Georgia State Energy Office during the period in question and further that [under] Walden's directorship of the Office of Energy Resources of the State of Georgia . . . prior discrepancies and irregularities were corrected.

"Third, Director Webster reports that there is no evidence that . . . Walden is or is likely to be included as a subject of the criminal investigation."

He added that the Public Integrity Section of the Criminal Division had advised him that there were no allegations and no evidence "that the skewed pattern of fuel distribution of the Georgia State Energy Office continued under . . . Walden or that she received any gifts or payments from oil companies."

In her letter to Chairman Jackson, Ms. Walden admitted that she had approved two deliveries of fuel to Billy Carter's service station. She explained that she was unaware at that time that the certification letter from an Americus, Georgia, distributor stated that part of the 16,000 gallons was for Billy Carter's Service Station.

Chairman Jackson remained skeptical of her professional qualifications, and Staff Director and Counsel Grenville Garside questioned her closely about the circumstances of her approval of Billy Carter's "emergency" allocations in 1977. She simply did not know about those allocations in 1977 that Billy Carter had admitted he had received.

Senator Jackson, at odds with the Carter White House on energy policy and on military posture, did not want to be viewed as an obstructionist, even though Omi Walden was not "the best" that Candidate Carter had promised. Late in the afternoon of July 26, 1978, Senate Majority Leader Robert Byrd of West Virginia had the nomination confirmed with a voice vote and with no discussion of Ms. Walden's qualifications for the $50,000-a-year subcabinet post. It was done so quietly that the *New York Times* did not have a line on the confirmation.

Charley Thompson, who had joined an ABC investigative news team, was finally able to get on television with the story of Billy Carter, his emergency allocations of fuel and the general chaos and corruption in the energy program when Jimmy Carter was Governor. On camera, Charley Thompson and the ABC News crew were able to ask Billy Carter what the "emergency" had been that resulted in his receiving as much as 25,000 gallons of gasoline a month from Lew Spruill.

"There wasn't any emergency," the First Brother answered with a grin.

"Where did the gasoline come from?" Billy Carter was asked. He brought down the house with his nonresponsive answer, "On a truck."

Billy Carter was still a comic character, and in some ways a welcome relief from the serious and pious President, whose self-serving rhetoric stressed his continuing search for "integrity," "high standards," "efficiency" and a high degree of competency. The comic relief of Billy Carter's colorful antics was reaching the point where it could become a serious embarrassment to the Carter administration, but no one—not even President Carter—appeared to have the courage to silence the First Brother.

But Billy Carter was no more an embarrassment to the administration than were the broken promises connected with the people retained and the new people appointed to the Department of Energy. It was a far cry from Jimmy Carter's campaign slogan, "Why Not the Best?"

CHAPTER TWELVE

Conflicts for a Commodity Regulator

The Bert Lance affair should have alerted the Carter White House and the Congress to the problems that can arise from sloppy, superficial or hurried consideration of the financial affairs of a nominee for high public office. The lengthy delays on the nomination of Omi Walden to be Assistant Secretary of Energy and the long-pending nomination of Robert Mendelsohn to be Assistant Secretary of Interior for policy, budget and administration were indications that Chairman Henry Jackson and his Senate Energy and Natural Resources Committee staff were alert to the responsibility of learning the details of potential conflicts of interest before confirmation to government positions.

Since the fall of 1977, Senator Abraham Ribicoff and Senator Charles Percy, Chairman and ranking Republican on the Senate Government Affairs Committee, had been warning of the dangers of the pro forma confirmation processes that had been used in the initial confirmation of Bert Lance as Director of the Office of Management and Budget.

Senator Ribicoff admitted "a mistake" in the hurried confirmation of Lance but noted that such laxity was more the rule than the exception in the overwhelming majority of high-level presidential appointments. Even before his own error was so dramatically demonstrated in September 1977, he and Senator Percy had approved a report that was critical of the general performance of regulatory agencies and had emphasized the superficiality of the investigations of those named to the regulatory agencies by various Democratic and Republican presidents.

The Connecticut Democrat said it was a "rare" case when a Senate committee carried out any more than superficial investigations of the men the President nominates for Cabinet posts, subcabinet jobs, and the regulatory agencies. Ribicoff was concerned that, barring some serious flaw, the President should have rather broad discretion in his Cabinet choices. This was not true of those nominated to the various independent regulatory agencies, where the people named are responsible for looking out for the public interest against the powerful industry and political lobbying groups.

While it was anticipated that President Carter's administration might bend its ethical standards to accommodate old political friends and supporters from Georgia, it was expected that the White House legal counsel was doing a thorough job of investigating possible conflicts of interest and clearing them with President Carter so that the highest standards would be maintained.

However, in the summer of 1978 the hurried confirmation of David G. Gartner, a former aide to Senator Hubert H. Humphrey, as a member of the Commodity Futures Trading Commission (CFTC) embarrassed the White House and the Senate Agriculture Committee. Although both President Carter and Vice President Mondale later implored Gartner to resign because of the "image of impropriety" resulting from a $72,000 gift he had accepted from a multimillionaire commodity firm executive, the former Senate aide successfully defied President Carter and his personal friend, Vice President Mondale.

Both President Carter and Vice President Mondale declared that they did not know that Gartner had accepted a gift of $72,000 in Archer Daniels Midland (ADM) stock from Dwayne Andreas, or else they would not have approved his nomination to the five-member CFTC.

The President's belated requests for David Gartner's resignation from the CFTC came at a press conference on June 26, 1978, more than a month after the nomination was rushed through the Senate Agriculture Committee and floor action. The President's resignation demand came in the wake of criticism from Democrats and Republicans who charged that there would be an obvious "conflict of interest" if Gartner was one of the five regulators of the $900-billion-a-year commodity trading industry.

Vice President Mondale made his belated request for Gartner's resignation in answer to questions in a meeting with editors of the Associated Press and United Press International.

The *New York Times,* the Scripps-Howard newspapers, and the *Minneapolis Tribune* had been sharp in their criticism of President Carter for making the nomination, and of Gartner for his stubborn refusal to leave the $50,000-a-year post.

Democratic critics were humiliated that President Carter's demand for Gartner's resignation had no influence on the former Humphrey aide, while Republicans gleefully commented that it was just another example of President Carter's ineffectiveness.

Close examination of the handling of the Gartner nomination demonstrated a lack of communication at the White House and in the office of Vice President Mondale, plus a woeful lack of concern over evidence indicating "conflicts of interest" by a nominee. In this case the White House was dealing with a long-time Senate employee who for fourteen years had been one of Senator Hubert Humphrey's key aides in dealing with agricultural problems and with the Senate Agriculture Committee.

The Senate Agriculture Committee, chaired by Senator Herman Talmadge, a veteran Georgia Democrat, was notorious for its lack of investigations of corruption and mismanagement at the Department of Agriculture or of the potential "conflicts of interest" of Presidential nominees. It was impossible to determine whether this was because of the dominance of the Agriculture Committee by Chairman Talmadge, who had a relaxed attitude toward his personal and political finances, or whether it was the general laxity of all the committee members.

It was common knowledge that the Agriculture Committee did not conduct tough or comprehensive investigations and did not put most witnesses under oath even when there was conflicting testimony indicating perjury. Chairman Talmadge was a "live and let live politician" of the old Southern school. In addition, the senior Georgia senator was not interested in ruffling the feathers of the Carter administration, for some of his own personal financial problems were then under investigation by the Federal Bureau of Investigation.

Senator Humphrey died of cancer at his home in Waverly, Minnesota, on January 13, 1978. David Gartner, as a long-time aide and personal friend of the family, was present in Minnesota at the time the sixty-six-year-old Democratic wheelhorse died. Muriel

Humphrey was appointed to serve the two years remaining of her husband's term. She indicated that she would keep Gartner as her administrative assistant.

However, in February Dave Gartner, ready to try to strike out on his own, had contacted Vice President Mondale and the White House staff to state his interest in the next vacancy on the Commodity Futures Trading Commission, which regulated the $900 billion-a-year commodity market. Gartner's credentials were good. As a press aide, legislative aide and administrative assistant to a senior Minnesota Senator, he had worked extensively on agricultural problems and legislation that directly dealt with trading in wheat, corn, soybeans, and sugar produced and marketed in agricultural states of the Upper Midwest.

The negotiations were handled with extreme quiet at first. Then authoritative reports were printed that Gartner was in line to succeed Vice Chairman John Rainboldt in the summer and that President Carter would move him to the chairmanship when the controversial CFTC Chairman, William Bagley, bowed out in the fall of 1978.

Weeks before the Gartner nomination was officially announced by the White House, there were reports that Vice President Mondale and Senator Muriel Humphrey were actively pushing him for appointment to the CFTC. When the nomination was officially announced by President Carter on May 10, it was reported and accepted that the forty-year-old former Senate aide was in line to be the next chairman of the Commodity Futures Trading Commission.

Information on the $72,000 stock gift from Andreas and Andreas's daughter, Sandra McMurtrie, was not included in the material sent to President Carter, nor was it discussed with Vice President Mondale and his staff before the Gartner nomination was sent to the Senate. Just a few days prior to the Senate hearing, Gartner informed Senator Mondale's staff of the gift of $72,000 worth of stock in one of the largest agricultural commodity trading firms in the nation and in the world.

Believing that this might be a sensitive and controversial matter, Mondale's staff members said they did not want to make a judgment and suggested that the proper people to make a judgment were in the office of White House Counsel Robert Lipshutz.

In Lipshutz's office the Archer Daniels Midland Company stock gift to Gartner was examined by Michael Cardoza. Apparently without taking it up with Lipshutz or with President Carter, Cardoza made the decision that the gift did not create a conflict of interest or even the appearance of a conflict of interest.

When Gartner told the Senate Agriculture Committee staff of the $72,000 stock gift to his children, he informed them that it had already "cleared" with the White House counsel's office. He delivered a memorandum of explanation as to why the gift of stock in one of the largest commodity houses from one of the wealthiest commodity dealers did not constitute a potential conflict of interest.

Agriculture Committee Counsel staff members were noncommittal but concerned as they took steps to protect themselves against any negligence. Senator Talmadge instructed the staff to have letters hand-delivered to the offices of the Senators on the Senate Agriculture Committee and to attach the White House letter about the stock gifts from Andreas and also Gartner's memorandum of explanation.

Those letters contained no warning of the possible "conflicts of interest" and no indication of the value of the stock gift.

When the Agriculture Committee opened its hearings on the Gartner nomination the morning of May 17, there were only a few Senators present as Chairman Talmadge welcomed Gartner and his family. The Chairman raised no question about any possible impropriety or apparent conflict of interest, and Gartner explained that his children had received the ADM stock in 1975, 1976 and 1977 when he was employed as Administrative Assistant to Senator Hubert Humphrey, an influential senior member of the Agriculture Committee and a long-time close personal and political friend of Andreas.

Senator Dick Clark, an Iowa Democrat whose legislation had created the CFTC, went out of his way to note that it was understandable why such a wealthy and generous commodity trader and processor, who had business interests in Iowa, would make a gift of $72,000 in stock to a family friend. Senator Clark's statement was particularly strange, because he had been an outspoken critic of conflicts of interest in the Nixon and Ford administrations and only three months earlier had issued a statement commending the General Accounting Office (GAO) for a report stating that the CFTC "is beset with serious [management] problems," including "the problem of 'revolving door' personnel transfers between the Commission and the [commodity] trade."

Chairman Talmadge, himself under investigation on charges of unethical financial dealings, praised Gartner's qualifications and offered no objections on the several questions later raised by critics of the nomination.

First, there was the question of whether the gift from Andreas, who had business before Senator Humphrey's office, violated the Senate's ethical standards. Gifts of more than $100 from any person with business before the Senate were taboo for Senators and key staffers. Full disclosure of all gifts from anyone but relatives was required. That question was not even submitted to the Senate Ethics Committee staff at the time of the May 17, 1978, hearing.

Second, did the acceptance of such a substantial gift as $72,000 worth of stock from a person prominent in the regulated industry, even if it was for his children, establish a conflict of interest or the appearance of a conflict of interest that would violate Mr. Carter's much-heralded higher ethical standards?

Third, did the holding of $72,000 worth of stock in ADM, one of the firms directly influenced by CFTC rules and regulations, establish a conflict of interest that might jeopardize Gartner's objectivity as a member of the CFTC?

Senator Robert Dole, the Kansas Republican who was an outspoken critic of Bert Lance and other Carter administration appointments, engaged in only mild and friendly questioning of Gartner on the ADM stock gift. Then he lavished praise on Gartner, saying that in the past, when Gartner worked for Senator Hubert Humphrey, he had been "cooperative, helpful and totally objective."

Senator Dole, as the senior Republican on the Agriculture Committee, would have been expected to take the lead in raising every possible question concerning the ethics of the nomination. Whether he was influenced by his personal association with Gartner as a Senate staffer or by other considerations was not clear. The Kansas Republican, President Ford's vice presidential running mate in the 1976 campaign, was already involved in campaign fund raising for 1980. Tim Wyngaard and James P. Herzog, staff reporters for the Scripps-Howard Washington bureau, later established through Federal Election Commission records that business associates and relatives of Dwayne Andreas had given $6,000 to Campaign America, the group that financed Dole's political travels.

The contributions to Dole's campaign took place in the months just prior to the Senate Agriculture Committee's action on the

Gartner nomination, but Dole denied that there was any relationship between the political gifts from friends and relatives of Andreas and his support of Dave Gartner.

The Agriculture Committee staff had done no investigative work on the ADM stock gifts to Gartner's children and made no effort to challenge the facts or the conclusions.

Senator Henry L. Bellmon, an Oklahoma Republican, became aware of the size of the gift of ADM stock during Gartner's testimony, and with only that knowledge raised a question of whether Gartner's children could retain the ADM stock even in a "blind trust" without creating the appearance of a conflict of interest.

"The danger of conflict really troubles me," Senator Bellmon said. "I'm afraid of the precedent we might set."

Gartner immediately suggested that if Senator Bellmon was seriously troubled, he would contact the trustee of the "blind trust" and have the ADM stock sold that day.

Senator Bellmon, pleased to have won an agreement, said that if the ADM stock was sold he would raise no objection. He later told this reporter and others that he was still troubled but did not want to appear to be a partisan critic when other members of the committee were expressing such strong approval of Gartner and were raising no ethical questions.

There were no witnesses in opposition to Gartner, because there had been no notice of the hearing or of the controversial $72,000 stock gift. The committee voted unanimously to send the nomination to the floor of the Senate, subject to Gartner's complying with Senator Bellmon's request that the ADM stock be sold.

Normally, the Senate protects itself against precipitate action by letting the nomination lay over for several days while hearings are printed and reports written and distributed so that all one hundred members of the Senate will have the opportunity to raise any informed objection. However, those familiar with the rules of the Senate know that in rare circumstances it is possible to cut through these standard procedures and get immediate action by "unanimous consent."

The Gartner hearing was over by noon, since he was the only witness. He took immediate steps to have the trust officer sell his children's ADM stock. Midway through the afternoon Gartner went to Senator Dole, the ranking Republican on the Agriculture Committee and the key to getting the "unanimous consent" for Senate confirmation that day without a roll call vote.

Gartner told Dole that he wanted his friend, Vice President Mondale, to swear him into office as a member of the CFTC; since Mondale was going out of town later that week, it was important that the Senate action on the confirmation be expedited. Gartner said that he had taken care of the sale of the ADM stock as requested by Senator Bellmon, so Senator Dole agreed "to accommodate Vice President Mondale" by talking to Senator Bellmon to arrange for the required "unanimous consent."

Dole told Senator Bellmon that Gartner had sold the ADM stock and asked if he had any objection to taking the nomination up that same afternoon. Senator Bellmon agreed to the hurry-up procedure "to accommodate Mondale."

The first time that most of the Senators knew about the gift of $72,000 worth of ADM stock to Gartner's children was when it appeared in the news accounts hours after the Gartner nomination swept through the Senate on "a unanimous consent" agreement. Because the Republicans and the independent-minded Democrats —usually most vocal on such matters—raised no fuss, the story was buried on the back pages or on the financial pages of most newspapers.

The nomination was given only routine coverage by most reporters because it was not much of a story when Democrats and Republicans were in unanimous agreement with President Carter's counsel that there was no appearance of conflict of interest that violated the new, higher post-Watergate standards of ethics.

Other Senate staff members, including some long-time friends and associates of Dave Gartner, read with amazement the stories that he had accepted a $72,000 gift of ADM stock for his children and that the Senate Agriculture Committee had approved the nomination so quickly. Those staff members called it to the attention of their bosses, and some made discreet calls to newspaper reporters and columnists suggesting that the Agriculture Committee record be read in order to understand the full import of all the questions raised by the ADM stock gift to the family of a man who was expected to be a fully objective regulator.

The whole Bobby Baker scandal in 1963 and 1964 had revolved about legal fees, other fees, and gifts that Secretary to the Democratic Majority Robert G. (Bobby) Baker had received from various people with business before the Congress.

After lengthy hearings and a lot of soul-searching because of the Bobby Baker scandal, the Senate and House passed tough new standards of conduct and disclosure rules that were to cover

United States Senators and all of the higher-paid members of their staffs. Bobby Baker was fired from his Senate job, castigated by the Senate, and later indicted and convicted on charges of larceny, embezzlement and income tax evasion.

These Senate Rules required that all Senators and key staff members make a full disclosure of all gifts of more than $50 from any person other than relatives. Although the gifts of stock in 1975, 1976 and 1977 were technically to Gartner's four children, there was no question that a $72,000 stock gift was of some substantial benefit to Gartner and his wife.

The number of copies of the Gartner hearing transcript were limited, so it took several days before reporters and Senators could run down the details to the point where they felt certain in dealing with the facts. At first they could not believe that a questionable $72,000 gift could pass through the White House counsel's office without some objection, nor could they believe that such a transaction could pass through the Senate without debate in the post-Watergate era.

Newspaper reporters started taking another look at the Gartner–Andreas relationship and wrote critical stories pointing out that Andreas was more than just a generous, wealthy personal friend of Gartner's family. He was a canny operator in the commodity trading field who mixed expertise in the corn, wheat and soybean markets with big political contributions to Democrats and Republicans.

Senator Hubert Humphrey had been the beneficiary of $94,000 worth of ADM stock given to a tax-exempt foundation created in Humphrey's name. From 1965 to 1974 a tax-exempt Andreas Foundation owned about 14 acres of the 18-acre Humphrey lakefront acreage at Waverly, Minnesota, the Scripps-Howard Washington bureau reported.

It was also noted that Andreas had been faced with federal charges in 1974 for allegedly making an illegal corporate contribution of $100,000 to Humphrey's 1968 presidential campaign. A United States District Judge in Minnesota dismissed the charge when Andreas contended he did not use corporate funds for the political contribution but had merely borrowed the money from his corporation.

A number of newspapers recalled that it was a secret $25,000 cash contribution from Andreas to the campaign of Richard Nixon that, unknown to Andreas, had helped to finance the Watergate break-in.

The Watergate hearings had established that Andreas made that mysterious $25,000 donation to the Nixon re-election campaign in April 1972—just before the deadline on secret giving. Andreas was also in 1972 financing Senator Humphrey's bid for the Democratic nomination but was concerned that his Minnesota friend might lose to Senator George McGovern of South Dakota. He wanted to hedge his political bets.

That $25,000 cash contribution from Andreas to the Nixon campaign was given to Kenneth Dahlberg in an envelope on a Miami golf course, and Dahlberg delivered it to Nixon's campaign finance chairman in Washington, D.C. Bob Woodward and Carl Bernstein of the *Washington Post* traced that so-called Dahlberg money to the Watergate burglars in late July. There was a question of whether the secret $25,000 had been given before the April 7 effective date of a more strict federal campaign law, or whether it had been given at the time Andreas put it in an envelope in a safety deposit box with an agreement when to give it. That question brought the investigators from the Federal Elections Office into the Nixon financing.

This story was considered one of the most significant of the exclusive stories that Woodward and Bernstein wrote, because it did get federal election office investigators into the Nixon campaign finances, and it put the pressure on the Nixon-dominated Justice Department to conduct more thorough investigations.

Noting the political giving by Andreas, Senator Orrin Hatch, a Utah Republican, declared that under the hiring policies of the CFTC Gartner's relations with such a big commodity dealer as Andreas would bar him from any lower-level staff position.

"I do not believe that, under present hiring policies of [the CFTC], Mr. Gartner even would be qualified to get a job," but his appointment to be a member of the powerful commission "was rushed through on the floor of the Senate about 5:40 P.M.

"The commission supervises more billions of dollars ($900 billion) in commodities than all the business combined that is done by the stock markets of the United States, including the New York Stock Exchange, the American Stock Exchange and the other stock exchanges in this country," Senator Hatch said.

"I had the temerity to criticize this appointment because I think it is wrong when a man would not qualify if he applied for a job with the commission [and is then] appointed to the commission [despite] such a blatant conflict of interest," Hatch declared.

"I cannot imagine anybody, whether he is a Democrat or a Republican, who is a member of the Senate and has an administrative assistant who had taken gifts from some big oil company, being able to sit on any power commission . . . which has to do with oil companies, without having all [kinds of] problems break loose on the floor of the Senate," Hatch told the Senate.

The Scripps-Howard newspapers chastized the Gartner appointment as "politics as usual," flying in the face of President Carter's pledge of higher ethical standards. A Scripps-Howard editorial said that the Gartner appointment to a key federal regulatory post "points up much that is tawdry about government in Washington—cronyism, corner-cutting, double standards.

"What we have here is the appointment to a top government post of someone personally beholden to a man with an overpowering interest in what that government agency does," the Scripps-Howard editorial board explained.

"In ordinary times that's called a potential conflict of interest," the Scripps-Howard editors said. "But not this time. In zip-bang fashion, the Senate Agriculture Committee OK'd Gartner, and he was confirmed that day by the full Senate without a murmur."

The Scripps-Howard editorial accused Vice President Mondale of pressuring his former Senate colleagues to whip the nomination through after Senator Dole explained his laxity by saying he was simply trying to accommodate a request for Mondale.

Vice President Mondale denied that he had requested the speedy confirmation but acknowledged that he had agreed to preside at the Gartner swearing-in ceremony. The Vice President's spokesman said Mondale relied upon Gartner to tell Senator Dole of Mondale's agreement to preside at the swearing in and that he was not personally aware of the gift of $72,000 in ADM stock to Gartner's children.

Senator Dole said Vice President Mondale did not personally request the speedy action by the Senate, but Dole had interpreted his conversation with Gartner to be a request for special action to accommodate the Vice President's schedule.

Regardless of who was responsible for the hasty action on the Gartner nomination, laxity in the Carter White House clearing process resulted in embarrassment to President Carter, Vice President Mondale, and the Senate Agriculture Committee members.

Chairman Herman Talmadge was the only person directly involved who was unconcerned about the charges of "politics as usual." He was at the time involved in the first stages of defending himself against charges of having illegally diverted Senate expense money into his personal bank account. Also he was trying to explain about the thousands of dollars in secret cash accounts that were the result of gratitude on the part of his Georgia constituents, who pressed these cash gifts into his hands for pocket money when he returned to campaign. The cash gifts were always in amounts of less than $25, he insisted in order to show he was under the amounts required by the Senate ethics code and the campaign financing laws. Over the years it had amounted to thousands of dollars, Senator Talmadge said, and he was not certain just how many thousand, because he had not made any effort to record the names of the donors or the amounts.

With those personal problems upon him in May, June and July of 1978, Senator Talmadge had no desire to get into comments on the ethical problems involving Gartner, beyond having his committee staff ask the Senate Ethics Committee if a gift from Andreas to Gartner's children had to be reported under the financial disclosure law in operation in 1975, 1976 and 1977.

The reply from the Ethics Committee stated that while Gartner, as a key Senate employee, would have been required to report a personal gift of $72,000, there was no clear requirement regarding gifts to children.

Besides the Scripps-Howard newspapers, other newspapers, including the *New York Times* and the *Minneapolis Tribune*, were critical of the Gartner appointment and Gartner's acceptance of the gifts, even if they were for his children.

The *Minneapolis Tribune*, sensitive to the fact that Senator Humphrey had died of cancer only a few months earlier, came down firmly against "public servants" accepting any "private favors."

"In the one sense, the gifts of Dwayne Andreas and his daughter to the David Gartner family were private, generous and otherwise unremarkable acts," the Minneapolis newspaper approached it gently. "The families were friends. Andreas' daughter had worked for Gartner [in Humphrey's office] in the 1960s. Over the years Gartner learned something about agriculture from Andreas, chairman of Archer Daniels Midland Co. Andreas had given financial help to Gartner's employer [Humphrey], too, so perhaps it was not surprising that the wealthy businessman and his daughter established trust funds totaling $72,000 for Gartner's children."

Then they hit firmly on the point that "because Gartner was a public servant, these were not just private acts among friends. His employer was Hubert Humphrey, Senator and Vice President, and he advised Humphrey on agricultural issues."

The *Minneapolis Tribune* in its June 12, 1978, edition noted that at the hearing Gartner had said he would sell the ADM stock and would disqualify himself from CFTC "activities affecting Andreas or his firm."

"That's fine," the editorial said. "The point, however, is that someone in Gartner's position should not have accepted the gifts in the first place. It's hard to believe that no one questioned their propriety when the gifts were made—between 1975 and 1977, when post-Watergate sensitivities were at a peak. If Hubert Humphrey knew about the gifts, he should have disapproved. If he did not know, Gartner should have told him."

The editorial concluded, "Either way, this is a sad example of a lesson still unlearned: Public servants cannot expect to inspire public trust when they accept private financial favors."

Gartner declared that he had told Senator Hubert Humphrey of the Andreas gift, and Senator Humphrey had approved the stock. Humphrey's widow, Senator Muriel Humphrey, defended Gartner and got off a stinging, bitter note of criticism for the Senate floor attack on the Gartner nomination.

Senator Howard Baker, the Republican Senate leader, led off with demands that Gartner be recalled before the committee to give further explanation of his financial dealings with Andreas and the things Gartner was doing on legislation that would be beneficial to Andreas's businesses. Under prodding from Majority Leader Robert Byrd of West Virginia, the Senate Agriculture Committee agreed to recall Gartner for further hearings even as Senator Dole was saying he "couldn't see what good it will do—Gartner's already been confirmed."

Dole said that by hindsight he considered the hurried action on the Gartner nomination to have been "a mistake." "It wasn't Gartner's fault, because the responsibility was in the White House and in the Senate Agriculture Committee," he said. It was an unusual and uncharacteristic attempt by Dole to absolve Gartner of blame and to take part of the blame on his own shoulders.

Vice President Mondale, who had been a supporter of Gartner's nomination, insisted that he had no knowledge of the $72,000 ADM stock gift. A Mondale spokesman was quoted as saying that Mondale would fire any staff member who accepted a large gift for himself or any member of his family from someone with business pending before his office.

Later, Mondale's press man said the Vice President was withdrawing his comments as to what he would do if one of his staff members accepted a gift, because he did not wish to make "a hypothetical" statement related to the Gartner affair.

House Agriculture Committee members were so outraged at the apparent conflict of interest in the Gartner appointment that they initiated steps to question Gartner. Representative Floyd J. Fithian, an Indiana Democrat, declared that Gartner won the appointment because of "laxity" in the White House and because of the "clubbiness" of the Senate Agriculture Committee members. Senator Muriel Humphrey's statement that Gartner had "served my husband loyally and effectively" could not, he declared, overcome the improprieties of the Andreas gifts to the Gartner children.

Representative Ed Jones, a Tennessee Democrat who headed a subcommittee with jurisdiction over the CFTC, arranged for five of his subcommittee members to meet privately to question Gartner about the gifts from and his connection with Andreas. After the meeting, Chairman Jones said he was still not satisfied with Gartner's nomination, and Representative Fithian declared that he was even more concerned about "the propriety of the appointment and confirmation of Mr. Gartner."

Representative Berkley Bedell, an Iowa Democrat, said the Carter White House had "blundered" in the naming of Gartner. "We just can't imagine why they would have gone ahead [following disclosure of the ADM stock gifts]. Gartner has no particularly great qualifications for the job, and there are plenty of [other] places where they could have put him."

"ADM and Dwayne Andreas have interests in what happens in the commodities market," Bedell said. "When supposedly there's an effort to clean up things, we just don't know why the devil they would do this."

Representative Fithian said he was as concerned about Gartner's long-time friendship with Andreas as he was about the gift of ADM stock, because of the financial interest that ADM could have in CFTC decisions made with regard to matters where ADM was not directly involved.

"There isn't any overriding reason why this guy ought to be a commissioner, let alone a possible chairman," Fithian said. "By raising enough of a ruckus, we might prevent him from becoming chairman and put the White House on notice that we are disturbed."

The House Agriculture Subcommittee members did write to the White House, spelled out their objections, and requested that President Carter ask for Gartner's immediate resignation.

However, at a White House Press Conference on June 14—more than a week after the House Democrats were protesting the nomination—President Carter said he did not believe the Gartner nomination constituted either a "conflict of interest or the appearances of conflict."

Ted Knapp of the Scripps-Howard Washington bureau asked the President how "in the light of your code of ethics pledge . . . do you justify appointing . . . David Gartner to the commission regulating commodities when he had accepted for his children $72,000 in stock from a major commodities dealer, Dwayne Andreas?"

The reporter had spelled out all of the relevant facts, in case President Carter had been too busy to study them personally, and concluded his two-part question, "Did you know these facts before you made the appointment?"

President Carter replied that he did not know of the $72,000 stock gift before making the appointment, and then placed the responsibility upon the Senate for clearing the nomination. "I believe the Senate Committee and the full Senate did have this information before they decided that Mr. Gartner was qualified. Also, he has pledged himself not to become involved at all in the consideration of any matter that [is] related to that particular company.

"So," the President continued, "although I didn't know about it before I submitted his name, we knew about this before the Senate committee and the Senate at large considered his appointment. It was approved overwhelmingly, as you know."

Mr. Carter avoided the direct question of whether this appointment met his higher standards. The reporter asked another direct question. "You believe it does not constitute a conflict of interest or the appearance of conflict?"

"That's correct," President Carter said. "I think that the circumstances and the facts have been made known thoroughly, so far as I'm able to tell. In spite of this . . . the Senate did approve his appointment."

However, the political furor did not die down. Criticism came from Democrats and Republicans. Republicans were examining

Gartner's admitted personal role in working out an amendment to a sugar bill that Andreas and ADM were lobbying through Congress. The amendment, introduced by Senator Humphrey, boosted sagging domestic sugar prices from 6 cents a pound to 13.5 cents a pound. Andreas and ADM were pushing the legislation because of the firm's $80 million investment in plants making corn fructose syrup, a direct competitor of sugar. This investment was endangered by low sugar prices.

Gartner explained that he and Humphrey were motivated in the sugar price dispute to aid sugar beet growers and processors in Minnesota and not to help Andreas or ADM.

There were reports that the President, alarmed at increasing criticism, had asked that Gartner resign, but that he had refused. Among the first questions at the June 26, 1978, Presidential press conference was a direct question as to whether the rumors were true. "And if so, what are you going to do about them?"

"I might say I don't know Mr. Gartner," the President started his reply to minimize any personal or political stake in this nominee. "He's one of the roughly 700 people that we recommended to the Congress to be appointed to positions of importance. In assessing the factors in this case during the last week or so, both I and my staff members, after consultation with the Vice President, who does know Mr. Gartner well, we have decided Mr. Gartner ought to resign.

"He has not committed a crime, he has not violated the law, but the image of impropriety, resulting from the acceptance by his children of a substantial gift, leads me to think that it would be better if he did resign," Mr. Carter said. "I understand that on Friday, Mr. Gartner called my staff members and said that he did not intend to resign."

Mr. Carter, the man who campaigned as a forceful leader, then said, "I do not have authority to remove Mr. Gartner from office once he has been confirmed by the Senate. But I think he should resign. The decision is now up to him."

"Mr. President," a questioner asked with incredulity, "so there's no further step that you feel you can take at this point?"

"No, except to encourage him to reconsider and resign," Mr. Carter replied softly.

Another reporter said that it was his impression that Mr. Carter had already assessed the Gartner case before his June 14 press conference and "saw nothing wrong with the circumstances surrounding all of this."

"What has caused you to change your mind?" the reporter asked. The President responded, "Well, I have looked into it much more thoroughly than I had before I came to the last press conference. The report I made last time was basically accurate. . . . I believe, though, [that] there is now an allegation of impropriety on his part with which I agree [and] that he should resign."

Although the regulatory agencies are independent of White House politics and pressure, Presidents from Roosevelt through Nixon had found ways to force resignations when the President believed "improprieties" were established. Presidents Truman, Eisenhower, Kennedy and Johnson exerted a variety of means to obtain resignations of members of regulatory agencies when there were appearances of conflict of interest.

Senator Howard Baker charged that the Gartner appointment to the CFTC "posed a serious, and in my view, insurmountable conflict of interest." He said, "I sincerely hope that [Gartner] will heed the advice of the President and others [including] requests from the House [and Senate]."

Gartner clung tenaciously to the position on the CFTC, defying President Carter and Vice President Mondale and again dramatically demonstrating the ineffectiveness of the Carter White House in the following areas:

1. The much-heralded tighter scrutiny of appointees for conflicts of interest had some large gaps in it.

2. Whether by clever political design or by gross laxity, major conflict problems went undetected until such time as they constituted a major political embarrassment.

3. President Carter's White House did not have the competent personnel with the ethical sensitivity to recognize the problems even after a major political storm.

4. When the "improprieties" were finally analyzed and acknowledged in crisis conditions, President Carter could not deal with them effectively.

The Gartner appointment to the CFTC was not the last case, or the most publicized, to raise serious questions about the competency of the Carter White House staff.

CHAPTER THIRTEEN

GSA Scandals—Problems Solomon Couldn't Solve

In the summer of 1978 the problem-plagued Carter administration was presented with a rare opportunity to demonstrate that it had the will and the competence to clean up corruption. In the General Services Administration (GSA) a Carter appointee, GSA Administrator Joel W. (Jay) Solomon, had on his own initiative hired an experienced lawyer-investigator, Vincent Alto, and they were shaking up the $5-billion-a-year agency for the first time in its thirty-year history.

Jay Solomon's cleanup of corruption and mismanagement at GSA was already generating enough headlines to make the voters forget about the Bert Lance bank overdrafts, the questionable political firing of prosecutor Marston, and the admitted White House bungling on the nomination of David Gartner to the CFTC. The Republican Nixon and Ford administrations had controlled nominations and promotions in the top jobs of the agency for eight years prior to the time Solomon was named to head the agency in 1977.

Solomon, a Chattanooga, Tennessee, businessman, had no special qualifications for the type of investigations involving the massive corruption and mismanagement that had surfaced periodically in the politics-plagued government purchasing agency. The indications of serious and pervasive frauds became apparent in his first months as administrator of the GSA. It also became obvious before he was in that job a year that he was going to have to bring in an experienced and independent investigator from the outside if he expected to make any real progress against the combination of lethargy and skillful cover-up that permeated the old-line bureaucracy. Solomon gave orders to get to the bottom of the complaints of scandals. Either nothing happened, or he got back reports that serious irregularities in the bidding procedures could be explained as accepted practices in GSA.

In May 1978 Solomon hired Vincent Alto, a former prosecutor with the organized crime strike force in the Justice Department, to take on the much-needed internal investigations of fraud and irregularities in the personnel practices of the GSA. There seemed to be a tradition within the GSA that the honest employees who complained to their superiors about waste or dishonesty were placed in jobs with few duties or were fired through personnel office manipulations comparable to what the Air Force had used in its unsuccessful efforts to get rid of Air Force cost analyst A. Ernest Fitzgerald.

Solomon and Alto were combing through past newspaper accounts of scandals in the GSA to get a grasp of whether past investigations had been thorough or had been swept under the rug with the firing or transfers of a few low-level clerks. Solomon found an eager and reliable friend in Ronald Kessler, one of the most able and tenacious investigative reporters on the *Washington Post*'s staff.

One of the scandals that Kessler had been digging into, even before Alto was hired, was the story of Robert J. Lowery, a forty-three-year-old painting contractor, who said he had paid off GSA officials with cash, call girls, vacation trips and free painting work on the GSA officials' homes.

"You paid off or you didn't get the jobs," Lowery told Kessler as he had told investigators for the FBI and the GSA months earlier. After going along with the corruption for several years, Lowery found the rigging of payoffs to be both time-consuming and expensive. He explained that to cover-up for nonexistent projects and kickbacks, it was necessary to use phony checks and nonexistent people.

As a small operator, Lowery said his dishonest payments to GSA officials to get contracts were costing him $1,500 a month. Lowery told Kessler that as early as 1975 he was making his complaints to the GSA, the FBI and anyone else who would listen. He said that companies being paid for work for GSA were in many cases not doing the work or putting on one coat of paint when the GSA was paying for two or three.

Some of his 1976 complaints were written reports, as long as three single-spaced pages, to members of Congress, the GAO, the Justice Department, the GSA and the *Washington Post*.

On June 22, 1978, Alto told a Senate Governmental Affairs Subcommittee that GSA employees, through a variety of criminal schemes, were stealing more than $66 million a year for themselves and the private business firms that contracted with GSA. He declared that if loss from noncriminal negligence was included the total loss would exceed $100 million a year. The GSA special counsel said that in only one month of investigating he had been able to establish that the criminal activities included the negotiation of "sweetheart" contracts with certain select companies, false certification for work that was never done and supplies that were not delivered.

Chairman Lawton Chiles, a Florida Democrat, expressed shock at finding that a firm linked with dealings with organized crime was paid by GSA to install a security system in government buildings. He outlined the widespread misuse of government credit cards, for example, the ludicrous situation in which the government paid to have one vehicle washed four times in one day.

Senator Chiles was particularly distressed "that recent GSA surveys show clear indications that, right in the middle of a whole series of nationwide criminal investigations, there are some employees who are so arrogant or so relaxed, that they are carrying on under the noses of the FBI." Alto said that it was a result of long-time neglect in failing to follow through on complaints of past frauds and thievery.

Alto declared that the continuation of such widespread frauds was indicative of either criminal culpability or gross negligence among some of the top officials of GSA who failed to understand the thievery or failed to take effective action to stop it.

Chairman Chiles put the frauds and thievery in perspective: "We are talking about a situation which has occurred during a time in which taxpayers have essentially mutinied and told public officials that they have had quite enough waste and overspending. . . . We are also talking about tens and dozens of GSA and other federal employees who are nothing better than common thieves, and who have systematically looted the public treasury of millions of dollars."

Alto said he was at that time investigating GSA plans to sell 80 million pounds of surplus lithium hydroxide at less than half the market price without competitive bidding. He said the plans to sell the lithium hydroxide to two specific firms had been stopped pending study of an auditor's report that estimated that taxpayers would lose $45 million on the sale.

Alto told the Senate subcommittee members that "very frankly, prior to these investigations, there were no checks and balances" to stop the stealing. He said that GSA Administrator Jay Solomon had been working to establish a checking system to cut or reduce the corruption and noted that Solomon had already instituted an effective system of inspection on maintenance and repair work to make certain that the government was receiving the goods and services it paid for.

Jay Solomon may have been inexperienced in big government, but he was a breath of fresh air at GSA. His instinctive reaction to evidence of corruption and mismanagement was to move swiftly to correct it. He hired Alto, a man experienced in criminal investigation and federal prosecutions to spearhead his drive. It appeared that Jay Solomon and Vincent Alto exemplified the type of swift, direct action that was needed against crooked and negligent government employees to save millions of dollars.

There would have been a political bonanza in simply doing what was right in following up the evidence of crime without fear, favoritism or ideological bent. Those responsible for the most recent frauds were appointees of the Republican administrations of Richard Nixon and Gerald Ford, so there was only slight likelihood that current prosecutable crimes would go back to the Democratic administrations of John F. Kennedy and Lyndon B. Johnson.

And even if a few Democrats were caught in the cleanup, that was not likely to deter the nonpartisan fight against corruption that Jimmy Carter had promised. There seemed to be every reason for the Carter White House to back Jay Solomon and Vincent Alto all the way in a dramatic cleanup at GSA, which could have eliminated to some degree the bad taste of the all-out defense of Bert Lance and the political firing of David Marston.

In late July Solomon went to the White House to explain that he was going to fire Robert T. Griffin, the Deputy Administrator of GSA. Griffin was interfering with efforts to reorganize the purchasing procedures and to shift personnel whom Solomon suspected of either corruption or serious mismanagement. Solomon recognized that dismissing Griffin was a serious step, because Griffin had been pushed by House Speaker Thomas (Tip) O'Neill for the administrator's job at the time he was appointed.

Griffin, one of the top officials of the GSA for more than seventeen years, had been forced to settle for the $50,000-a-year number two job in the agency. It had been an uncomfortable arrangement from the outset, and the tension had increased when Solomon hired Vincent Alto as an investigator to get to the bottom of the agency's problems.

House Speaker O'Neill, learning that the job of his long-time friend was in jeopardy, contacted President Carter and was assured that he would be kept abreast of any developments. Only a few hours before Solomon announced the dismissal of Griffin, Carter's congressional liaison, Frank Moore, told Speaker O'Neill that he would be informed before any final action was taken.

Solomon's announcement of the dismissal of Griffin on July 28 brought a roar of outrage from O'Neill, who immediately met with President Carter at the White House. An hour later President Carter met with Griffin, showered him with praise for his thirty-five years of government service and promised to find him another job "worthy of his talents." Without making any inquiry of GSA special investigator Alto, President Carter assigned Vice President Mondale to the task of finding an "appropriate" position for O'Neill's friend.

On August 2 O'Neill blamed Congressional Liaison Moore for misleading him about the manner in which the Griffin case would be handled and declared that Moore would be barred from his Capitol offices—a drastic and probably unprecedented action for a House leader to take against the congressional liaison for a President of his own political party.

On August 3 the White House announced that Griffin was to be appointed to a $50,000-a-year job as a "senior assistant" to Robert S. Strauss, President Carter's special trade representative.

Apparently, neither President Carter, Vice President Mondale nor any of their top aides gave a thought to the fact that Griffin, long a top executive at GSA, might have at least "chain of command" responsibility for some of the massive fraud and mismanagement that was being characterized as "the biggest money scandal in the history of the federal government." Intent on pacifying House Speaker O'Neill, they had failed to make even a routine inquiry of Vincent Alto to determine if Griffin's actions or his negligence might be a part of Alto's investigations. In failing to take even routine precautions they had laid themselves open to embarrassment by taking Griffin into the White House itself.

Any investigation by the GSA, Congress or the Justice Department that focused on Griffin would be an immediate reflection upon Carter's White House. The President and his aides had compounded their problems by failing to carry out a thorough examination of Griffin's career. They should have required certification that he was blameless in the frauds and mismanagement that were all around him.

Republican National Chairman Bill Brock criticized Carter's creation of another $50,000 White House job as "a political payoff" and an unjustified response to the "temper tantrum" by O'Neill. The *Washington Post* and other newspapers commented that "Mr. O'Neill is guilty of shabby behavior in taking advantage of the President's current political weakness to holler up a storm over this firing . . . to do a favor for a friend.

"Our principal criticism of Mr. Carter's performance in the matter does not concern who notified whom [or] when, but rather the fact that the President let himself be bullied into assigning the Vice President—no less—to find the displaced Mr. Griffin a comparable well-paying job," the *Post* commented.

"Mr. Griffin's contemptuous behavior toward the head of GSA—Carter appointee Jay Solomon—was clearly based on his close relationship to Speaker O'Neill," the *Washington Post* stated. "It is too bad, finally, that Mr. Carter did not persist in indicating to him and his patron, Mr. O'Neill, that their arrogant assumptions were misplaced."

The *Post* stated: "The President's alleged crime in O'Neill's eyes was to have supported Mr. Solomon in his determination to clean up the scandal-plagued agency." It quoted Solomon as telling the Senate subcommittee a month earlier, "I am sick and tired of 'business as usual' at GSA."

The *Post* noted that "Mr. Griffin had not been accused of wrongdoing or incompetence" but that he personified "business as usual," at GSA.

"Although Mr. Solomon, a Tennessee developer and Carter fund-raiser, took office in May 1977, many GSA managers apparently thought until last week that Mr. Griffin was really running things—and nothing much had to be changed."

The *Washington Post,* other newspapers and columnists

called attention to the fact that Solomon had taken forceful steps to reinstate several GSA employees who had been discharged, downgraded or otherwise punished after persistent complaining that there was evidence of crimes and mismanagement. The *Post* stated that "Solomon has made it clear that whistleblowers in the agency will not be punished or downgraded, as they have been in the past." It noted that the forcefulness of Solomon and Alto should be a pattern for "comparable forcefulness" by the White House that would get White House relations with Congress "back on a healthy course."

In August Alto drafted an internal memorandum charging that the ousted Deputy Administrator Griffin had attempted to undermine efforts to crack down on corruption and had harassed employees who would not go along. Alto related in the memorandum that in 1975 and 1976 Griffin tried to get GSA investigator William Clinkscales to conduct a "bootleg investigation" with no official records kept. Clinkscales informed Alto that when he refused, Griffin had brought pressure on GSA personnel officer Al Petrillo to transfer Clinkscales to an undesirable post in Fort Worth, Texas.

According to *Time* magazine, Petrillo confirmed for Alto that he had initiated the order to transfer Clinkscales, then had second thoughts about the transfer, which he felt violated GSA personnel rules. Petrillo said that Griffin retaliated by starting a campaign of harassment against Petrillo that lasted for several months. Alto's memo stated that Petrillo related he was stripped of his authority and warned that "his situation would get worse." In December 1976 Petrillo told Alto that he resigned and filed a grievance with the Civil Service Commission.

Alto's memorandum said that Griffin next offered Petrillo a lower-paying job in the GSA's Federal Supply Service, which indicated an attempt to persuade Petrillo to drop the Civil Service Commission grievance. Although Petrillo accepted the lower-paying post, he refused to cancel his grievance.

Alto related that Petrillo had told him that "not a single piece of paper crossed my desk for eight months" and that a Civil Service administrative judge dismissed his grievance against Griffin after GSA lawyers filed 150 objections to his charges. In the months just prior to the discharge of Griffin, Solomon named Petrillo personnel officer for the National Archives.

Time quoted Griffin as denying he had engaged in any pressures relative to Clinkscales or Petrillo. "I never pressured anybody," Griffin was quoted as saying. "There was no effort by me to drive anybody out of any agency at any time."

In late August Solomon announced that he had reinstated two GSA employees who had been fired after complaining about what they believed were illegal and improper GSA contract awards to a New Jersey manufacturer that for years had been a major supplier of metal desks, filing cabinets and bookcases. Art Metal, a Newark manufacturing firm, had been identified a month earlier as the firm that sells almost exclusively to GSA, repeatedly winning contracts by bidding low and then providing furniture that failed to meet government specification standards.

The employees reinstated by Solomon were Robert J. Tucker, an employee of GSA's regional office in Boston, and Robert F. Sullivan, a GSA investigator who provided the *Boston Globe* with the GSA audit report corroborating Tucker's claims that construction contract awards were permeated with collusion, fraud and favoritism.

Solomon also restored Petrillo and another demoted GSA official to their original seniority and pay levels. The other official was Wilton F. Shearing, a GSA construction engineer who was removed as a supervisor for the construction of a federal building in Honolulu after complaining that the contractor had received excessive payments.

Solomon's direct intervention on behalf of whistleblowers appeared to be precisely in line with what candidate Carter had promised the American people, and it was coupled with criminal investigations of at least 50 GSA officials and the major shifting of personnel to break up the old bureaucratic cliques.

Solomon was summoned to the White House for a meeting with the President and Deputy Attorney General Civiletti on September 4, 1978. At that meeting it was reported that the only point of dissatisfaction on President Carter's part was a desire for the prosecution of "even bigger fish" who had been responsible for thievery and mismanagement at GSA.

To demonstrate the President's personal interest, the White House announced that President Carter had appointed his friend and political confidant, Charles Kirbo, to monitor the GSA probe. Deputy White House Press Secretary Rex Granum explained Kirbo's role: "He will be advising the President on it, indicating the importance the President places on the matter." Granum explained further that Kirbo "will be talking to Justice people . . . and presumably will be receiving information from Justice on the investigations."

Again, President Carter's well-intentioned steps were not well thought out or were garbled in the transmission. As a result, Atlanta attorney Kirbo did not understand his limitations as an unofficial adviser. Reached in Atlanta by the *Washington Post,* Kirbo said he had already talked with Attorney General Griffin Bell and other Justice Department officials about the several ongoing federal investigations of GSA corruption. He was also quoted as saying he had already talked with GSA Administrator Solomon.

When the *Washington Post* wrote stories that quoted unidentified Justice Department sources as questioning the propriety of a private citizen's monitoring federal investigations, the Carter White House and Kirbo clarified the situation. Kirbo would be given no information from federal grand juries, for that would be against the law. Attorney General Bell said it was his understanding "that Mr. Kirbo has been asked to counsel Jay Solomon on whatever needs to be done at GSA."

"This [Kirbo assignment] has nothing to do with Justice," Terrence B. Adamson, a special assistant to Bell was quoted as saying.

The *Washington Post* reported that one source told reporters that Carter had called a surprise meeting with Civiletti and Kirbo after reading in the Sunday *Post* that one GSA official under investigation had said he believed that under political pressure Carter might pardon GSA officials who broke the law.

President Carter had fumbled his way into a defensive posture, and even if his motivations in bringing Kirbo in were the purest, he appeared to be seeking to undercut Solomon and Alto. Two Republican Senators—Bob Dole of Kansas and William Roth of Delaware—called for a special prosecutor for the GSA probe to keep it free of White House influence. Dole charged that President Carter's naming of Kirbo had "undercut" the officials with the responsibility for the investigations. Senator Roth declared that circumstances dictated that a special prosecutor should be appointed.

"Self investigation doesn't work," Roth said. "Charles Kirbo is closely identified with the executive branch he is investigating."

Then, to add to the problem for Carter, the Gannett News Service reported that ousted Deputy Administrator Griffin's office files were missing and were the object of a search by Alto's office. Peter Mollica, a former assistant to Griffin, reported that he had Griffin's office files in his possession. Although Mollica still worked at the agency, keeping custody of records was not a part of his job, a GSA official told the *Washington Star*.

Griffin told the *Star* that his office records were intact. "Nothing has left GSA. Nothing has been destroyed. Nothing has been laundered."

The impression of a White House effort to impede Solomon's investigations was heightened even more when Griffin, now a member of Carter's staff, wrote to Solomon demanding that the GSA turn over his records, including notes, diaries, telephone logs and other materials. He threatened to sue if the material was turned over to Alto's investigation.

"I hereby demand that all of my private property above described be delivered forthwith to my attorney, William P. Daisley, at the firm of King & Nordlinger . . . and that you refrain from examining my private papers without receipt of the [subpoena] process," Griffin wrote Solomon.

William S. Lynch, who headed the Justice Department's GSA task force, insisted that GSA should keep custody of Griffin's papers, including diaries and telephone logs, because they would be needed in the continuing probe of GSA. However, he did work out an arrangement whereby Griffin could examine the material with the agreement that he could remove only what was purely personal and unrelated to his actions as an official at GSA.

White House sources told this reporter and others that President Carter did not want to curb the investigations but had concluded that Jay Solomon was just not up to the task of getting the "bigger fish" and feared that his easy availability to the press would result in serious legal blunders. It was also reported by others that White House aides Hamilton Jordan and Jody Powell believed Jay Solomon was "hogging the headlines" and the credit, which should have been going to President Carter in order to bolster his image as a corruption fighter.

In late October President Carter made a trip to Nashville, Tennessee, for a Democratic state rally. The purpose of the trip was to bolster the election prospects for Democratic candidates for state and federal offices in Tennessee, and GSA Administrator Jay Solomon went along as a local boy who was doing great things in Washington.

President Carter praised him as "a great businessman from Chattanooga" who "took over as administrator of GSA . . . and he's done as much to let us know about waste and corruption in Government as anyone.

"He's fighting the battles for you to make the Federal Government be better, cleaner, more decent, more honest," President Carter said. "I want to thank Tennessee for giving me Jay Solomon."

Those were among the last public words of praise that Jay Solomon heard about the GSA cleanup until he submitted his resignation the next March after Presidential Assistant Jordan rudely started seeking a successor even before Solomon indicated he was resigning.

In November an unhappy Vincent Alto resigned. Alto had said that he would remain in office for six months. It was reported that he felt the White House and Justice Department were throwing barriers in the way of a complete investigation, so he did not want to continue serving beyond the six months. Solomon then moved independently of the White House and Justice Department in suggesting as Alto's replacement and for the post of inspector general of the GSA Irwin M. Borowski, an aggressive and independent lawyer-investigator from the Securities and Exchange Commission.

Solomon's recommendation for nomination of Borowski was held up in the White House without explanation. This was frustrating for Solomon, who wanted to get a permanent inspector general of his own choice installed before bowing out of the GSA sometime in 1979.

Nothing had moved on the Borowski recommendation in January, and Solomon learned from a *Washington Post* reporter that the White House was searching for Solomon's successor.

"Actually, I sort of assumed this was coming," Solomon told the *Washington Post* reporter. "I mean, I've had a feeling for a while—it was my instinct— . . . Maybe, I've been going too fast, too hard. Maybe I've been getting too close to the truth—what that truth is I don't know."

Solomon told the reporter that he had felt "a lack of support" from the White House in recent weeks in his efforts to pursue the investigation.

In December and January, Solomon complained that he was having difficulty in getting telephone calls returned by White

House officials, including those to Hamilton Jordan. Although White House officials admitted some lack of diligence in returning Solomon's telephone calls, they explained that it would be a full-time job to respond. White House officials insisted there was no lack of desire to continue the investigations of GSA, but there was a lack of interest "in playing it up big all the time." "We're going to make it Jimmy Carter's issue and not Jay Solomon's."

The Carter White House was aware that getting rid of Jay Solomon was a touchy issue, because Jay had become a symbol of the aggressive drive against GSA corruption that had dominated the headlines for nearly a year. If it appeared that he was fired, the public would ask why.

Ham Jordan said there was "no truth" to the reports that Solomon was in the process of being fired. "Jay has reminded me on several occasions that he didn't come up here to stay forever," Jordan told the *Post*. "I've labored under the assumption that he'll be going at some point. But that's his decision. It's really true."

Solomon said he had indeed told Jordan that he did not plan to stay the whole term, but he told reporters that he had not given the White House any indication that he wanted to leave in the immediate future.

Solomon said that he was mainly interested in seeing Borowski installed as inspector general in GSA to ensure the completion of the investigations that were under way and the future independence and integrity of the huge government service and supply agency.

Carter disregarded Solomon's recommendations for Borowski and on January 30 nominated Kurt W. Muellenberg, chief of the Justice Department's organized crime section, to be inspector general of the GSA. By selecting Muellenberg, a man with a reputation as an able, tough prosecutor, the Carter White House managed to avoid the charges of a cover-up while taking a last slap at Solomon.

As he said he would do earlier, in reponse to a *Washington Post* reporter's question, Jay Solomon resigned in mid-March and willingly made it appear that the timing of his leaving had been left up to him. His brief letter to President Carter on March 14, 1979, said, "In accordance with understandings reached in previous conversations, I hereby tender my resignation as Administrator of the General Services Administration effective March 31, 1979. It has been a high privilege and honor to serve my country in the Carter administration, and I am deeply grateful to you for having made that possible."

President Carter's acceptance, dated March 21, said it was "with regret and with gratitude for the services you have rendered.

"Because of your leadership and integrity, decades of waste and corruption at the GSA are now being exposed, and those who have betrayed the public trust are being identified and punished," the President wrote. "That process will be continued and expanded."

But to much of the public it was obvious that Jay Solomon was pushed out as Administrator of GSA, and there was a lingering suspicion that the Carter White House had betrayed the public trust for political expediency. Regardless how well Kurt Muellenberg and Solomon's successor, Rear Admiral Rowland G. Freeman, did with straightening out the GSA, there would be doubts about the motivation in the forced ouster of Jay Solomon.

One point was absolutely clear. The Carter White House had taken the sure-fire political plus of Solomon's crusade against GSA corruption and had turned it into a political headache.

CHAPTER FOURTEEN

Jimmy Carter and the Whistleblowers

Although President Carter abandoned some of the rhetoric of his campaign promises, he engaged in a continuing political dialogue on the need for "reform" of the Civil Service Commission, so that honest government employees would be protected when they spoke the truth about their crooked bosses.

It was true that the Carter White House had done little or nothing to restore A. Ernest Fitzgerald to full effectiveness as a cost-cutting analyst in the Air Force, but Greg Schneiders continued to assert that President Carter's heart was in the right place and that Fitzgerald and others would find satisfaction when Carter's civil service reform was unveiled.

Among Jay Solomon's great accomplishments in connection with the GSA scandals was his forthright and direct action to restore to duty the honest GSA employees who had been fired or demoted for complaining about payoffs, rigged contracts and other corruption at the General Services Administration. In September 1978, when President Carter was publicly praising Solomon's action against corruption at GSA, he as usual accompanied his praise with words to boost "our new civil service reform legislation" that was pending in Congress.

"Our new civil service reform . . . will help us again to have not only better use of worthy and dedicated and honest employees, but a way to correct deficiencies," President Carter said. "And in that we'll have a special counsel, independent [of the agency head] to investigate and to make sure that we don't have a further corruption of your government."

"We inherited a mess," President Carter told a Town Meeting at Aliquippa, Pennsylvania, "but we're getting it under control."

A few weeks later, on October 26, 1978, he boasted to a Nashville audience that "we've passed . . . a very fine civil service reform law to put our good civil servants to work a little harder for you.

"It just happens that [Senator] Jim Sasser [a Tennessee Democrat] is chairman of the Civil Service Reform Committee, and I want to thank Tennessee for giving me this strong ally and friend and supporter in Washington."

While President Carter still spoke of his so-called civil service reform as the centerpiece of his government reorganization to "protect . . . those who are legitimate whistleblowers," many of the most prominent whistleblowers said that Carter's program would not have protected them but would have made them more vulnerable to arbitrary firing.

Air Force cost analyst A. Ernest Fitzgerald, who had blown the whistle on the $2 billion cost overruns on the C-5A jet transport, explained that under the Carter reform his Air Force superiors could have fired him without stating a reason, and he would have had no legal recourse as a tenured career employee or under veterans' preference.

"Under Carter's so-called reform law, Harold Brown [Secretary of the Air Force who was displeased with Fitzgerald's truthful testimony] could have fired me from my [GS-17] job, and all I could have done about it was appeal to an Air Force board that would have been stacked against me.

"Under the old civil service law I was at least able to get a civil service hearing and get into federal court where I established I was wrongfully discharged," Fitzgerald said.

"Carter's reform will politicize the whole top level—GS-16 and above—in the way that Richard Nixon was trying to politicize it," Fitzgerald continued. "I'm probably the only person in the Pentagon above GS-16 rank who has not joined the new executive service, because that would make me even more vulnerable to being fired than sitting tight in my present post."

Fitzgerald stated that he was at a loss to know whether President Carter was intentionally misleading the public or whether he was simply misguided and devoid of any real understanding of the problem.

"I thought he knew about my case when he mentioned it specifically in the 1976 campaign," Fitzgerald said. "But I've listened to him speak and read his speeches during his campaign to get his civil service reform bill through Congress, and he is simply out of touch with the facts."

The Air Force cost analyst related that Carter had made a number of speeches in 1977 and 1978 in which he specifically referred to "the Fitzgerald case" and stated that his "reform" legislation would protect an Ernie Fitzgerald from retaliation. "Representative John Moss tried to straighten him out on it, and my lawyers and I tried to get the message through to him in the White House on a number of occasions," Fitzgerald said.

Fitzgerald recalled one occasion when President Carter had spoken before an audience in Alexandria, Virginia, where those in attendance were largely government employees who were concerned about Carter's legislation. That legislation was admittedly designed to make it easier to fire employees who were incompetent or lazy, and many government employees feared it would open the way for wholesale firing of hard-working dissidents who simply did not agree with their bosses. To assure the government employees that "honest whistleblowers" would not be fired, President Carter made the self-serving statement that "Ernie Fitzgerald" would have been "protected" under his reform bill.

Fitzgerald said later that his first inclination had been to get up and dispute President Carter's misrepresentation of the way his "reform" legislation would have affected a Fitzgerald case. However, he concluded, that would have been pointless since Senator Proxmire, Representative John Moss and Senator Patrick J. Leahy, a Vermont Democrat, had not been able to convince the Carter White House on their objections to his "reform" legislation.

Almost from the time President Carter unveiled his reform program on March 2, 1978, in a speech before the National Press Club, there had been complaints that it did precisely the opposite of what it was supposed to do.

The rhetoric of President Carter's sales pitch was certainly appealing, because he billed it as legislation designed to make government workers perform with spirit and integrity.

"We want a government that can be trusted, not feared; that will be efficient, not mired in its own red tape; a government that will respond to the needs of American citizens and not be preoccupied with needs of its own," President Carter told the National Press Club audience in general terms. "We all want a government worthy of confidence and respect.

"The single most important step we can take is a thoroughgoing reform of the Civil Service system," President Carter said, summing up what Fitzgerald and others had been saying for years. "The two complaints most often heard against the present system are that Federal employees have too little protection against political abuse—and too much protection against legitimate assessment of performance and skills. These charges sound contradictory, but both of them happen to be true. And the system that perpetuates them needs to be changed."

Ernie Fitzgerald and the dozens of others who had been the victims of retaliations for expressing truthful and accurate dissent agreed that something should be done about the dishonesty and political abuse of the civil service system, but they did not believe that Carter's moves to legalize Richard Nixon's political manipulations were the answer.

They cringed when President Carter talked about making it easier for government managers "to reward the best and most talented people—and to fire those few who are unwilling to work." Managers at the Air Force had been opposed to Fitzgerald's truthful testimony on the cost overruns, and they rewarded with promotions those civilians and military officers who falsified records and framed charges to "smear" the honest cost analyst, according to the well-documented civil service hearings and the records of congressional hearings.

Representative Moss, long involved in investigations of retaliation against whistleblowers, examined the Carter civil service legislation and declared in March 1978 that it was "change which will not contribute to meaningful reform." Moss, who conducted a four-year investigation of corrupt patronage practices in the Civil Service Commission as well as the agencies, said he did not believe President Carter's plan to establish a career executive service would create efficiency but could result in "massive political favoritism."

In a speech before the American Federation of Government Employees (AFGE) in the week after the Carter "reform" was unveiled, Moss declared that it would weaken job protection. He said it all looked "distressingly familiar" to him. Carter's proposals "were all, in one form or another, offered by the Nixon–Ford political operatives as specific changes in the merit system to make it work better to their advantage."

He declared that any administration could, by actually establishing a valid case, get rid of government workers who were incompetent, lazy or dishonest and that over the years a great many government employees had been fired or forced out. "You should not, however, be able to fire workers arbitrarily and capriciously," Moss said. He further stated that instead of making it easier for government managers to fire employees, the rights of honest dissenters to hold their government jobs should be affirmed and some effective action taken to restore honest whistleblowers to positions of responsibility.

Lashing out at the first year of President Carter's administration and its "ineffective investigations of the misuse of the Civil Service in the Nixon years," Representative Moss told *Federal Times* reporter Inderjit Badhwar that it was a source of "keen disappointment" to him that "no substantive reform had been effected in that agency."

The California Congressman was referring to the fact that the Carter White House had permitted "a political cover-up" of the role of high Civil Service Commission employees in the Nixon personnel scandals. The Carter administration had approved or condoned the deliberate destruction of important Civil Service Commission records that were evidence of perjury and other personnel frauds.

White House Assistant Hamilton Jordan and Civil Service Commission Chairman Alan K. Campbell had the destruction of records continued in spite of warnings from Representative Moss, consumer advocate Ralph Nader, and Robert Vaughn, a lawyer and author of an exposé of past Civil Service Commission crimes.

The Carter administration's actions were interpreted by congressional critics and others as either gross stupidity or conspiracy to obstruct justice. The cover-up of crimes had been accomplished in 1977 by the following devices:

1. Months of unconscionable delays in asking for an FBI investigation of evidence of corruption of the Civil Service Commission's merit system, which was documented in congressional hearings and in an internal Civil Service Commission report.
2. Justice Department assignment of too few agents to the FBI investigation of the evidence of complicated Civil Service Commission crimes, and resistance to requests for assignment of more FBI agents to the job.
3. Justice Department orders sharply limiting the FBI investigation into the destruction of Civil Service Commission records, and rejection of FBI recommendations that the inquiry be broadened to include other crimes.
4. Permitting Civil Service Commission personnel, including

some of those with potential criminal responsibility, to arrange an in-house investigation that effectively barred the FBI from the broad investigation that was demanded by Moss and others.

5. Pushing for the so-called reform measures at the Civil Service Commission that would legalize some of the most criticized illegal actions of the Nixon administration's steps to politicize the merit system.

Lawyer-author Robert Vaughn presented, in 1974, a well-documented study of Civil Service Commission frauds entitled *The Spoiled System*. That book described the manner in which the commission engaged in arbitrary actions and permitted perjury and the rigging of records to fire Ernie Fitzgerald and others.

Vaughn's book included other examples of the Civil Service Commission policies approving and condoning perjury, record rigging, and malicious harassment of honest employees at the Department of Agriculture, the Department of Health, Education and Welfare, the Department of Labor, the Department of the Interior, the Department of State and the various agencies under those departments.

The Watergate investigations had exposed the Nixon White House politicization of the Civil Service Commission through an infamous manual produced by White House personnel director Fred Malek. Malek explained that the ideas were not original and he had simply pulled together and codified the various ways that earlier administrations had been able to subvert the merit system.

The report of a Civil Service Commission task force under Milton I. Sharon, a retired regional director of the Civil Service Commission, commented on the "widespread and systematic abuses of the Civil Service appointment system." Even though it scored the frauds, perjury and destruction of records that were a part of the abuses, it diplomatically avoided any effort to zero in on the Civil Service commissioners and employees responsible for these crimes. They were among those who selected Sharon to head the study.

That was what Representative Moss wanted investigated thoroughly when he demanded in 1976 that a federal grand jury be impaneled to probe evidence of fraud and cover-up at the top level of the Civil Service Commission. Representative Moss believed that candidate Jimmy Carter's campaign speeches indicated he would move aggressively against the crimes of the past. In the early weeks of the Carter administration, Ralph Nader and Vaughn met with Hamilton Jordan to emphasize the importance of action against the civil service crimes that were undermining the integrity of the entire civil service system.

Despite encouraging rhetoric from the Carter White House, the Justice Department sat on the case through the spring and summer and did not authorize an FBI probe of Civil Service corruption until November 1977—only a few weeks before the statute of limitations was to run out on some of the crimes.

Even then the restrictions frustrated the FBI agents, and there was such a lack of cooperation by the Carter White House, the Justice Department and the Civil Service Commission that critics compared it to the stonewalling conspiracy of silence the FBI faced in its 1972 probe of Watergate.

Instead of broadening the civil service probe, assigning more and independent agents, and giving it the high priority it deserved, the Carter administration continued to permit potential defendants to have a role in control of the investigations.

Civil Service Commission Chairman Campbell, either on his own initiative or with the help of persons responsible for past crimes, drew up the Carter "reform" that would legalize political favoritism in the management of the 2,800,000 civilian government employees.

And it wasn't as if the Carter White House was unaware of the seriousness of the problem. The Carter transition team had followed up the charges of scandalous political favoritism in the Nixon and Ford administrations by soliciting a reliable report on the crimes and political manipulations at Civil Service. That highly critical, single-spaced, twelve-page report laid out details of wholesale disregard of the laws and regulations. It identified Civil Service Commission members and high-level executives of the commission staff as being implicated in perjury, falsification of records, and willful political manipulations.

While Representative Moss and Ralph Nader prodded the White House for action, Civil Service Commission executives, accused of a variety of laxities, crimes and cover-ups, continued to hold important positions where they could actually block further congressional inquiries and establish a commission-controlled investigation that sharply limited congressional and FBI access to civil service records.

Representative Moss was infuriated at the Civil Service Commission's refusal to produce records for congressional committees.

This was not the open government or the cleanup that Jimmy Carter had promised. Even if the President did not have personal knowledge of what was taking place, he was responsible for it, Moss declared. Permitting a commission-named lawyer to take custody of records and to control access to those records was precisely the opposite of the open government and accountability that Carter had promised.

Chairman Campbell defended his lack of follow-through on past civil service crimes and emphasized pushing reform legislation. As for the "reform" measures he was drawing up, Campbell said he thought the major problem was not stopping the Carter administration from using Civil Service jobs as a federal spoils system, but making the system more productive.

Instead of making the U.S. Civil Service Commission independent of political influence, Campbell wanted to move the civil service functions of recruiting, examination and equal opportunity policies to an office of personnel management directly under the President.

"The President . . . must have more discretion in personnel management if he is to run an efficient government," Campbell explained. It was essentially the same logic that Nixon's White House Chief of Staff, H. R. (Bob) Haldeman had used in setting the stage to move Nixon loyalists into more top positions.

Senator William Proxmire and Representative Moss contended that simple, aggressive enforcement of the laws on perjury and destruction or falsification of government records would go a long way toward reforming a civil service system that Moss characterized as "demonstrably rotten to the core."

Senator Proxmire's solution would have included legislation to permit any citizen to initiate action against government officials for crimes of perjury and false testimony, or for retaliating against a government employee who gives honest testimony. The Wisconsin Senator's experience in pursuing the Fitzgerald case had convinced him that the Justice Department's reluctance to prosecute high officials of any administration meant these officials were virtually above the law.

Proxmire's proposal would have provided that any citizen could ask for an investigation or for a written report from the Attorney General as to why he had not pursued the requested investigation. If the Attorney General's reply was not satisfactory, the citizen could then petition a federal court for a special prosecutor to conduct a grand jury investigation.

That was the background of the Carter administration's experiences with Democrats who wanted a real housecleaning and "reform" at the Civil Service Commission at the time that President Carter unveiled his "reform" package in March 1978.

Despite criticism from Senate and House Democrats as well as Republicans, President Carter's program split the Civil Service Commission into two bodies—an Office of Personnel Management to stimulate the productivity and performance of federal employees, and a Merit Protection Board to guard against merit abuses and resolve the appeals brought by employees.

"I will also propose an Office of Special Counsel to investigate merit violations and protect the 'whistleblowers' who expose gross management errors and abuses," the President said.

"Our proposals will mean less job security for incompetent federal employees, but conscientious civil servants will benefit from a change that recognizes and rewards good performance," President Carter concluded in sweeping terms of assurance.

Although the broad assurances satisfied most listeners, there were a few members of the press who paid attention to what the administration had failed to do for Fitzgerald, and to its actual prosecution of Frank Snepp, a former CIA agent who had written a book exposing incompetence and treachery at the Central Intelligence Agency.

Mary McGrory, a perceptive columnist for the *Washington Star,* wanted to know specifically "what sort of protection will the Office of Special Counsel provide for whistleblowers?" She had followed Fitzgerald's ordeal in seeking justice in the Nixon, Ford and Carter administrations and had seen his frustration as the liars and record falsifiers were promoted year after year while Fitzgerald, an expert cost analyst, was barred from the cost-cutting work he did best.

"The Special Counsel will be there [at the Merit Protection Board] independent from me to protect through the courts, if necessary, those who are legitimate whistleblowers and who do point out violations of ethics, or those who through serious error hurt our country," President Carter said. The President ignored the fact that he had promoted Air Force military officers and civilians who had given false and misleading testimony against Fitzgerald. He ignored the fact that by a directive to Defense Secretary Brown he could have personally made certain that Fitzgerald was restored to work on major weapons systems where millions and perhaps billions of dollars could be saved.

It was difficult to believe that the President did not want to do what was right, but those who followed the cases closely had to ask why there was such a gap between Jimmy Carter's words and the actions of his administration.

Mark Goodin of the *Houston Post* asked why "Frank Snepp, one of the most famous whistleblowers" on CIA "incompetence and treachery," was being prosecuted by Mr. Carter's Justice Department. Goodin's question noted that Snepp wrote the book on the CIA deficiencies only after his reports to the CIA inspector general's office failed to get results. It was not contended by the Justice Department that Snepp's book had revealed any secret national security information.

"How does this encourage whistleblowing?" Goodin asked.

"I don't look on Frank Snepp as one of the greatest whistleblowers of all times," President Carter responded. His attitude appeared to be that good and bad whistleblowing is often a matter of personal or political viewpoint.

"He signed voluntarily a contract [of employment with the CIA], later confirmed this agreement with the Director of the CIA that before his book was published . . . it would be examined to assure there were no revelations of secret material."

Although President Carter said he had not read the book and had no knowledge of any national security secrets that Snepp had revealed, "the Attorney General has decided that when a contract is signed that it ought to be honored.

"If everyone who came into the CIA or other highly secret organizations in government felt free to resign because of a dispute . . . and then write a book revealing our Nation's utmost secrets, it would be very devastating to our Nation's ability to protect ourselves in peace or war and to negotiate on a confidential and successful basis with other government leaders," President Carter explained.

Although he did not assert that Snepp had violated national security classifications, Mr. Carter, like so many presidents before him, tried to defend the use of arbitrary executive branch secrecy when the only thing exposed was corruption and mismanagement.

The *Federal Times* editorialized that Congress and the public should not be taken in by the "reform" label that President Carter and Civil Service Commission Chairman Campbell had put on the reorganization, which was a return to the spoils system.

"But what this reorganization package is all about is—as we

keep saying—not reform but political control,'' the *Federal Times* said bluntly. ''And at the very heart of this move for political control is the proposed senior executive service. This officer corps of supergraders [GS-16, GS-17 and GS-18] would enable Mr. Carter, and the Presidents who follow him, to control the bureaucracy in a spoils-system way that has been impossible, legally, since the Civil Service Act became law in 1883.''

The *Federal Times* pointed to an analysis by its columnist Bob Huddleston, which concluded that Carter's so-called reform legislation would virtually assure that the top personnel post in most departments and agencies would be filled eventually on a noncareer basis. ''That is, appointment would be made without regard to the competitive rules of the civil service.''

The harping of the *Federal Times* on that point, on the tremendous power of the Director of Personnel Management, and on the lack of adequate protection for whistleblowers was helpful in getting some amendments to the Carter bill. However, most of the newsmen—particularly those who specialized in general political reporting—failed to grasp the fact that Carter's ''reform'' legalized the very political control that Richard Nixon's administration had been seeking—a destruction of the merit system.

Because President Carter called it ''reform'' and because many Democrats in Congress—critics of Nixon for similar political power grabs—repeated the ''reform'' slogan, the strong opposition was finally worn down to a courageous few. Only a few Democrats or Republicans in Congress would run the risk of voting against a ''reform'' measure a few weeks before the 1978 election.

Many outspoken defenders of whistleblowers were won over to support the Carter legislation through the Democratic leadership's acceptance of amendments. Those amendments seemed to provide additional safeguards for the whistleblower—those conscientious government employees who wanted to be aggressively honest but wanted to avoid the types of retaliation that were visited upon Ernie Fitzgerald.

Many Congressmen and Senators grumbled privately that they were still not satisfied with the legislation but felt compelled to support it to avoid criticism for voting against reform. A few set out their reservations on the House floor, and then voted for the legislation.

Representative Gene Taylor, a Republican from Missouri, said he had ''mixed emotions about some of the 'reforms' we are about to enact." "I support the Civil Service conference report because I have reached the conclusion that Congress ought to give our current President some new tools with which to better manage the Federal Government's vast bureaucracy," Representative Taylor said. "Whether President Carter's administration uses these new tools properly or injects partisan politics into the top levels of Government and endangers the impartial administration of our laws, remains to be seen."

He expressed fear that the provisions of the bill dealing with "merit pay" for Civil Service executives might be used to provide extra pay for political favorites. "It will be up to future Congresses to maintain vigilant oversight over the new office of Personnel Management, and over the new Merit Systems Protection Board," he warned.

Representative Herbert Harris, a Democrat with many career government employees in his Northern Virginia district, declared that the "reform" legislation was "a failure" and that he would not vote for it. He said that many in Congress would go back to the voters and report that they had voted for historic legislation that would "improve and streamline government operations and efficiency while retaining an independent and professional corps of government workers.

"It may be a period of months, or even years, before my colleagues understand the impact of the bill which will open up our Government to increased politicization of the Civil Service," Harris said. He declared that "the average Federal employee will understand the bill's essential failure."

The Virginia Democrat compared the Civil Service "reform" to the Nixon administration's Post Office "reform," which a majority of the members in Congress now recognized as a disaster. Harris recalled that the Post Office reform was pushed through by Nixon's administration for the purpose of "making it run like a business."

"It sounded good at the time, but I do not know too many of my colleagues who voted on that measure . . . who do not today regret their hastiness in 'reforming' the Post Office.

"I want the record to reflect that this House was reminded that it was the career Civil Service [that] kept this Government operating when it was paralyzed in the aftermath of our most recent attempt to politicize the bureaucracy—in the Nixon administration," Harris declared. "The action of the Congress in enacting an open door to political manipulation will require a much greater commitment on the part of Congress to exercise its oversight and investigatory responsibilities."

While Harris said President Carter's new Senior Executive Service would be "meritorious in many ways" in giving flexibility to management, Harris warned that "gaping loopholes left intact . . . will enable the President to name too many of Government's senior executives from the ranks of his political devotees." Harris declared that the law set no standards of qualifications for the filling of top civil service jobs but had opened them up for political manipulation.

The Democratic leadership wanted to give Mr. Carter "a victory" on one of his so-called reform programs, and most of the Republicans did not want to spend the whole campaign explaining why they opposed a "reform" measure. Mr. Carter's "reform" passed the House by a vote of 365 to 8. Representative Moss was among the 59 members "not voting." He explained:

"I am not going to vote to give Jimmy Carter the powers to manipulate and destroy the Civil Service that I would not give to a Richard Nixon. I know that the same people in our Democratic leadership who were up there pushing this so-called 'reform' would have been denouncing it as a political power grab if either Richard Nixon or Gerald Ford had been behind it."

Moss said that "President Carter might try to administer the legislation in an even-handed manner, but even if he does keep politics out I fear what it can be in the hands of another Nixon or Johnson."

The California Democrat declared that "the Carter administration record up to this point [October 1978] leaves serious questions as to the purity of White House motivations or the competency to follow through on a worthy objective.

"President Carter may mean what he says about wanting an open, honest and nonpartisan government, but the abuse and misuse of executive privilege has been worse than in the Nixon administration," Moss said. "It may not be President Carter, but someone at the White House is as ruthless a political operator as either Bob Haldeman or Chuck Colson." It was already apparent that Hamilton Jordan and Gerald Rafshoon were the real forces behind ruthless moves that gave a top priority to political maneuvering aimed at 1980 election politics. Producing effective government programs was secondary to getting Jimmy Carter re-elected.

CHAPTER FIFTEEN

Personnel Problems —Policy with Political Expediency

The firing of Bella Abzug as chairperson for President Carter's National Advisory Committee for Women came as a "totally shocking" affair to the outspoken former New York Congresswoman. The firing by White House Assistant Hamilton Jordan was "totally unjustified," Bella told an astounded press.

What was startling to the White House press corps was the fact that Jordan notified her of her discharge a few minutes after she had met with President Carter and had read a statement that was favorable to the Carter administration.

President Carter, in an hour-long meeting with Abzug's committee on January 11, 1979, had not told her that she was to be fired. He left that chore to Presidential Assistant Ham Jordan, who with Press Assistant Jody Powell and Communications Director Gerald Rafshoon made the initial decision that Bella had to go.

While Bella was totally independent in her pushing for the rights of women, she had been tolerated for months. The final criticism that infuriated Jordan, Powell and Rafshoon was a press release from Abzug's committee that sharply criticized President Carter for failing to place sufficient emphasis on Women's Committee issues.

According to Martin Shramm, political writer for the *Washing-*

ton Post, Jordan, Rafshoon and Powell huddled and then gleefully and unanimously agreed that Bella had gone too far this time and that she should be fired. It was reasoned that firing Bella would send out a message about the limitations on dissent with the White House; it was also assumed that the outspoken and cantankerous former New York Congresswoman was not really popular in feminist ranks.

What the triumphant trio did not know at that time—which they could have found out from Presidential Assistant Sarah Weddington—was that Bella Abzug had actually opposed the circulation of the four-page press release that had enraged Jordan, Powell and Rafshoon.

Less than two hours after the firing of Abzug, Carmen Delgado Votaw, who shared the leadership on the National Advisory Committee, submitted her resignation as a show of solidarity. Within a few days at least twenty of the forty women on the committee quit in protest. Those resigning included Nancy Neuman, Vice President of the League of Women Voters, who said the Carter White House action was comparable to "when you have a few problems on your job and go home and kick your dog."

Even among columnists, reporters and politicians not sympathetic to Bella Abzug's policies of negotiation by confrontation, there were expressions of "shock" at the deceptiveness of President Carter in not advising Bella that she was going to be fired.

The meat-axe method of firing was left to Jordan, and this resulted in derogatory editorial comments and cartoons portraying the President as a man who spoke in terms of being forthright and courageous while leaving the dirty chores to Jordan and others. Even the President's long-time friend, Attorney General Griffin Bell, joked publicly about the courageous "steely-eyed President" who had turned the firing of Abzug over to Jordan.

It was May before the President named Lynda Bird Johnson Robb as the new chairperson for the National Advisory Committee for Women.

By itself the firing of Bella Abzug would have created little furor, for she had piloted her committee on women through a series of incidents that might have justified a direct public firing. The committee had used a State Department mailing permit to send out newsletters that compared the Mormon Church policies on race to the Ku Klux Klan's. Bella refused to apologize for that one. In December 1978 she had canceled a scheduled fifteen-minute meeting with President Carter, because she said she believed her women's committee was entitled to more time.

Bella's firing did not stand alone as a rebuff to outspoken feminists, for it followed, by only a few weeks, the forced resignation of Margaret (Midge) Costanza, who had been Special Assistant to the President for liaison with special interests.

Midge Costanza, a political activist from Rochester, New York, was one of President Carter's earliest supporters and had been the woman selected to share honors with Congressman Andrew Young of Georgia and Peter Rodino of New Jersey in making the seconding speeches for Jimmy Carter's nomination at the 1976 Democratic convention.

President-elect Carter had called her on Christmas Day in 1976 to ask her to come to Washington and join his staff as one of his top six policy advisers. While she was regarded by many as "the token woman" in White House hierarchy, she had a small but high-status office next to the Oval Office from which she directed a staff of ten in the larger offices in the Executive Office Building.

Midge Costanza had been an unsuccessful Democratic candidate for Congress in Rochester in 1974, when she first came to Mr. Carter's attention. He was impressed that she seemed well informed on a wide range of issues, as well as with her political contacts in New York. He selected her to serve with William Vanden Heuvel as co-chairman of Carter's New York campaign.

As a contact with special interest organizations, Midge Costanza was billed as "the President's window to the nation." The self-styled "loud-mouthed, pushy little broad" vowed to speak her own mind on controversial issues that included gay rights, abortion and the decriminalization of marijuana without regard to the Carter White House's official posture on those issues.

Through the first months it worked out reasonably well for President Carter and for Midge Costanza. President Carter was credited with being such a strong and forceful leader that he could tolerate dissent on his White House staff. For Midge Costanza, it gave her the wide exposure that she thrived on. White House Counsel Robert Lipshutz gave his approval for her to have a fund-raising party to pay off a $17,615 deficit from her unsuccessful 1974 campaign for Congress.

As was later reported officially, all but $570 of the $17,615 deficit had been advanced by Costanza personally to the campaign.

Costanza's fund-raiser was a great success, bringing in

$21,035. A large amount of it came from such groups as the Brooklyn Longshoremen, the Communications Workers of America and the United Auto Workers. Many contributions came from individuals who did not know Midge Costanza personally, and only a small amount came from sources in the Rochester area.

While this type of fund raising was legal, some critics raised questions as to whether it was within Carter's ethical guidelines for a White House staff member to use the celebrity of a top White House position to raise funds to take care of a bad financial experience in politics. The Carter White House stuck with Midge Costanza even though she failed to meet the legal reporting requirements of the Federal Election Commission on the fund-raiser.

There was the troublesome problem of how the Costanza fund-raising committee would dispose of the $3,400 surplus that remained after Midge had repaid herself approximately $17,000.

While there was no public or private word of criticism of Midge Costanza on the knotty problems of propriety surrounding the fund-raiser, there was a not-so-quiet rage when Midge decided Bert Lance should resign as Director of the Office of Management and Budget and said so publicly. Jordan and Powell were infuriated, in fact, that Midge would dissent from the President's firm support of Bert Lance on the $400,000 in questionable (later termed illegal) overdrafts on the Calhoun National Bank.

From the fall of 1977, Midge Costanza was in disfavor. She had said and repeated that Lance—one of the Georgians—should resign. A few months later Jordan made the first move to evict her from her prestigious office near the Oval Office to another office in the West Wing of the White House. By the time the internal feuding over offices surfaced in late May 1978, Costanza was resisting a Jordan order to move her out of the White House and across the street into the Executive Office Building.

Although Costanza retained her title—Assistant to the President for Public Liaison—and the $56,000-a-year salary, she said the move would give the impression that she was losing power and influence. Even though she would actually lose no influence with President Carter, she stated publicly, the administration might be hurt politically because of the public perception that the Carter White House did not feel her areas—human rights and women's issues—were very important.

In April Jordan had moved Anne Wexler, a former Deputy

Under Secretary of Commerce, into the White House to take over some of Costanza's duties. Wexler had been brought in at the same Special Assistant level as Costanza. The memorandum from Jordan informed Costanza firmly that Tim Kraft, Carter's Appointments Secretary, was to be moved into Costanza's office.

On May 22, 1978, two days after Edward Walsh of the *Washington Post* reported on Jordan's effort to move Midge Costanza, Costanza was quoted by a United Press International reporter in Northampton, Massachusetts, as saying President Carter had personally assured her she would remain in the White House office next to his Oval Office.

She told a radio station reporter from WSPR in Springfield, Massachusetts, that she had gone directly to President Carter with the office problem. She said she had told Carter, "We live in a very symbolic nation. We have a very symbolic administration. To move me now when I have assumed responsibility of women's issues and domestic human rights issues would tend to give the nation the impression those issues were being moved out of the White House."

But, before her address at Smith College commencement ceremonies in nearby Northampton, she commented that she personally didn't "give two hoots about where I work. The issues are more important to me."

In mid-July Gerald Rafshoon intervened to cancel the appearance of Midge Costanza on a network television show on the energy program. It was explained by the White House that Costanza was canceled to give Stuart Eizenstat, the chief domestic policy adviser, more time to explain the Carter administration policies. It was another sharp rebuff to the feisty Special Assistant, who had been moved to a basement room in the White House and had been forced to give up her more prestigious office to Tim Kraft.

On August 1 Costanza resigned her White House post. White House Press Secretary Rex Granum told the press that Costanza's resignation was "not asked for." But neither did anyone ask that she remain. It was apparent that there were sharp limits on public dissent by White House personnel despite President Carter's statements to the contrary.

Even before Midge Costanza's final exit in late 1978, President Carter had been forced to evict two Georgians from their White House offices despite long and deep personal friendships. They were Dr. Peter G. Bourne, the President's chief adviser on health and drug abuse, and William (Bill) Milliken, a part-time White House consultant on inner-city problems.

Dr. Bourne, a British-born psychiatrist and personal friend of the President, resigned in July 1978, after it was revealed that he had given a White House aide a prescription made out to a fictitious person for a tightly controlled drug—Quaalude. The incident resulted in a criminal investigation, but no charges were lodged against Dr. Bourne or the assistant to whom he gave the prescription. However, in December 1978 Dr. Bourne was publicly reprimanded by the state medical board in Georgia where he held his license to practice.

The action by the Georgia State Medical Board contradicted the three-page statement the White House press office issued in defense of Dr. Bourne after the *Washington Post* revealed Bourne's misconduct.

While Dr. Bourne was unavailable for questioning, the White House statement quoted him as saying the use of the fictitious name was "what I believed to be legitimate precaution . . . to protect the confidentiality of the individual involved."

It was noted in editorial and news stories at the time that use of a fictitious name was a violation of most state laws, and also was a violation of the Federal Controlled Substance Act, which requires the correct name and address of the patient.

There were published reports in Jack Anderson's column that Dr. Bourne had taken hard drugs at a Washington party. Gary Cohn, of Anderson's staff, said he possessed written statements from three witnesses who said they saw Bourne use drugs at the party. Although the White House issued a statement denying it and indicated on July 19 that Bourne intended to stick it out, a letter of resignation was released on July 20.

In the letter to President Carter, Dr. Bourne pictured his use of a fictitious name as "a mistake of the heart and not of the mind." He characterized it as "a prescription written in good faith to a troubled person.

"Last evening following your granting of my requested leave of absence . . . I watched and read the press and television reports of my problem," he wrote. "In the last 18 hours, I have seen law enforcement officers release to the world the name of my patient [and] other articles containing the grossest innuendos and obviously emanating from law enforcement sources. . . .

"Now the attacks move from my medical conduct to my personal conduct," Dr. Bourne wrote. "Underlying all of these developments are constant and unrelenting attacks upon me by those who seek to hurt you through my disparagement."

He said his decision to resign, rather than go on a leave of absence, resulted from his fear of hurting President Carter and the White House staff.

"Due to the use of me to injure you, I am sorry that I no longer feel that I can be a productive part of your administration." He signed, "Your friend, Peter G. Bourne."

The *Washington Post* declared that "the White House and Dr. Bourne have done the right thing in arranging his departure, and they have done so with appropriate dispatch."

"What Dr. Bourne did represents a serious, unaccountable lapse of judgment—at best," the *Post* commented editorially on July 21. "Our sympathy for the unhappy end of his government career is tempered, however, by the overwrought and overbearing quality of his letter of resignation to the President. Whatever may be involved in this matter, it can in no way be seen as Dr. Bourne portrayed it in his letter to Mr. Carter—as an attempt by law-enforcement or media figures 'to hurt you through my disparagement.'

"If anyone has hurt the President in this matter, it is quite simply and exclusively Dr. Bourne," the *Washington Post* editorial concluded.

Less than a year after his resignation from the White House staff, and only a few months after his reprimand by the Georgia Medical Board, Dr. Bourne was hired by the United Nations to help in the organizaton and preparation of a major U.N. program for development and conservation of water resources. At the time of the announcement by the U.N. Development Fund and the World Health Organization, Dr. Bourne's salary was still under negotiation. U.N. officials reported to the *Washington Post* that no special pressures were brought by the Carter administration to obtain the U.N. post for Dr. Bourne.

Nearly as sad for President Carter and Mrs. Rosalyn Carter was the need to sever the White House ties of Bill Milliken, an Atlanta man who specialized in working on the problems of minorities in the inner cities. Although Bill Milliken was only a part-time White House consultant on inner-city problems, he was a long-time friend of the Carters. He frequently spent the night at the White House.

Milliken's effort to intercede with federal housing officials on behalf of George Zamias, a wealthy Johnstown, Pennsylvania, developer was admitted to be "a stupid mistake" that caused great embarrassment to President Carter. It left the impression that Milliken was using his well-publicized White House connections to seek special consideration for Zamias on an application for a $15.5 million federal grant.

White House Counsel Robert Lipshutz investigated Milliken's intervention for Zamias and indicated that he and President Carter agreed with Milliken's assessment that he was involved in "mistakes of judgment."

White House Press Secretary Jody Powell said that it has been concluded that Milliken's actions were "done innocently" and that no submission to the Justice Department was contemplated, nor was there to be any change in Milliken's relationship with the White House.

There was no quarrel about the questionable acts that Milliken had "done innocently," and neither Powell nor Milliken challenged these basic facts.

Zamias, who had been turned down by the Department of Housing and Urban Development on his first application for the $15,500,000 federal development grant at Johnstown, was a longtime friend of Bill Milliken's brother, Ken Milliken, who was based in Pittsburgh. He mentioned his problem to Ken Milliken, and Ken told him, "My brother is in the Carter administration."

In April 1978 they were in Atlanta for a convention of the International Council of Shopping Centers, and Ken Milliken brought Bill Milliken to Zamias's suite.

Zamias later told a *Washington Post* reporter, Fred Barbash, that he explained his project to Bill Milliken and said he was interested in talking to someone at HUD. Milliken then volunteered that he and Richard Fleming, Deputy Assistant Secretary of HUD, were "very close friends," and he would see what he could do about getting Zamias an audience at HUD.

Later, at the convention, Bill Milliken asked Zamias if he would give $10,000 to two of Milliken's inner-city projects—Exodus, Inc., and Institutional Development Corporation. Zamias said he would agree to give Milliken $5,000 at that time "and $5,000 down the road." Both insisted that there was no linking of the request that Milliken was to ask of HUD and Zamias' agreement to give $10,000 to Milliken's nonprofit corporations.

There was no question that Zamias did send Milliken two checks for $5,000 each, one shortly after the Atlanta convention and the other in late August or early September.

Milliken said he did call his friend at HUD, Dick Fleming, who arranged meetings between Zamias and HUD officials. That point was corroborated for the *Washington Post* by Zamias and Fleming, and was not denied by the White House. Zamias was also quoted by the *Post* as saying Milliken had been helpful in getting access to the HUD officials.

"The toughest thing is getting an appointment," Zamias was quoted as saying. "That's what it's all about."

Jody Powell said that the President accepted Bill Milliken's statement that there was no connection between his interceding for Zamias at HUD and the $10,000 contribution Zamias had made to Milliken's nonprofit corporations. Powell related that, after a three-day investigation, White House counsel Robert Lipshutz reported he could find nothing that cast any doubt on Milliken's story. That ended the Milliken affair. The White House didn't even ask Milliken to return the $10,000 to Zamias.

Milliken occupied an unusual position with the Carters. Their acquaintanceship went back to Atlanta, where Milliken had established two programs—one to provide supplemental services for students in poverty area schools, and the other for street academies for dropouts and youths with personal problems. Milliken served as an "adviser" to Mrs. Rosalyn Carter, and the First Lady was so impressed with his programs that she became his patron. She set up appointments with Cabinet officials for Milliken, who arranged for $1.2 million in federal grants for his projects.

Milliken also became a close friend to James Earl (Chip) Carter, Jr., one of the Carters' sons. For a short time, Chip Carter was employed by Milliken in Washington. That paid employment ended after a critical article appeared in the *Washington Monthly* suggesting that Chip Carter's job was a form of reciprocation for the federal funds that Milliken's projects had received. Chip then became an unpaid volunteer, Milliken told reporters.

In addition to a $26,000-a-year salary and expenses from his nonprofit corporations, Milliken had received $13,000 over a period of a few months for serving as a consultant to Mr. Carter's Office of Management and Budget.

Although Powell said that Bill Milliken still had the trust and confidence of President Carter and the First Lady, he no longer had an office in the Executive Office Building.

Milliken's admitted "mistake of judgment" was not unlike the calls that Sherman Adams, Chief of Staff for President Eisenhower, made to two regulatory agencies to set up appointments for his multimillionaire friend, Bernard Goldfine. President Eisenhower characterized the intervention by Adams as "indiscreet" but added, "I need him." A few months later criticism from Democrats and a few Republicans in Congress caused President Eisenhower to ask for Adams's resignation. The difference with regard to the Milliken case seemed to be that Carter knew Milliken as a deeply religious man who "innocently" intervened for his brother's multimillionaire friend because he did not understand the problem of influence-peddling and any related gifts or money.

The brief furor over Midge Costanza, Dr. Peter Bourne and Bill Milliken was overshadowed by the turmoil caused by Jack Anderson's column which charged that fugitive financier Robert Vesco was trying to manipulate a "fix" at the highest levels in the Carter White House. Representatives of Vesco were reported to have made contact with Atlanta attorney Charles Kirbo as well as one of Hamilton Jordan's top assistants.

The Vesco saga demonstrated that Bill Milliken was not the only "innocence abroad" in the White House whose admitted actions raised questions about the propriety of even listening to the sordid propositions or questionable suggestions of men with problems at government agencies.

CHAPTER SIXTEEN

Vesco Fix— An Aborted Deal

The name of Robert Lee Vesco, a fugitive financier from New Jersey, was one of the most publicized in the Watergate era. The free-wheeling financier had been accused by the Securities and Exchange Commission of looting $224 million from the funds of Investors Overseas Services (IOS, Ltd.) a mutual fund corporation.

It was alleged that Robert Vesco, then living as a fugitive in Costa Rica, had made an effort to fix his problems with the SEC and the Nixon administration's Justice Department by making a $250,000 cash campaign contribution in the 1972 election. One of the most highly publicized trials of the Watergate period involved charges that former Attorney General John Mitchell and former Commerce Secretary Maurice Stans had accepted the Vesco cash in exchange for a promise to help Vesco stop the SEC and Justice Department investigations.

Although the General Accounting Office (GAO) traced the cash contributions of $200,000 and $50,000 to the treasury of Nixon's Committee to Re-elect the President (CREP), Mitchell and Stans denied that the contributions were related in any manner to their actions. They specifically denied any knowledge of arrangements Vesco was reported to have had with lower-level Republican fund raisers. Both Mitchell and Stans were acquitted, and Vesco refused to return to the United States to face criminal charges.

Robert Vesco remained a fugitive, living in luxury in Costa Rica and successfully defying the efforts of the United States government to extradite him to face trial during the Ford administration.

By the time Jimmy Carter was elected President in November 1976, it was obvious to those experienced in Washington politics that direct or indirect contact with Robert Vesco was dangerous. Any effort Vesco made—except through open legal representation in open court—must be reported immediately to the Justice Department in an open and forthright manner that left no doubt as to the motivation of the person contacting the Justice Department. It was to be expected that the wealthy, free-wheeling fugitive would try to use his money to obstruct the wheels of justice by buying political connections. Vesco's political asylum in Costa Rica was a political issue, and the indications were that a new President might force him to leave his luxurious exile and might even cooperate with the U.S. Justice Department.

Shortly after Carter was elected, the shrewd Robert Vesco made an assessment of his problem, saw that Georgians were taking over Washington and concluded that the best way to Washington was through a well-connected Georgian. By early January Vesco was in contact with Robert L. Herring, an Albany, Georgia, businessman. Herring, from Hamilton Jordan's hometown, had a lawyer, Spencer Lee IV, who claimed to be a long-time friend of Hamilton Jordan.

Vesco and Herring entered into an agreement. Herring would propose that Spencer Lee contact his friend Hamilton Jordan, who was to be Jimmy Carter's White House Chief of Staff, to see if he could help get the Justice Department off Vesco's back. Initially, Lee was to be paid $10,000 to take the first step—to make contact with Jordan to discuss Vesco's problem.

On January 15, 1977—five days before Jimmy Carter's inauguration—Herring and Lee flew to Costa Rica on a private jet for talks with Vesco. They returned on January 16 with a plan for Lee to go to Nassau to establish a Bahamian corporation to be called Southern Ventures Ltd. The major asset of Southern Ventures Ltd. was to be $12 million in stock from the Vesco corporation known as Property Resources Ltd (PRL).

PRL stock was to be channeled to Southern Ventures Ltd. as the vehicle for making millions of dollars available to Herring and any other Georgians he found it necessary to deal with in taking care of Vesco's problems.

On January 27, 1977, Lee flew to the Bahamas to oversee personally the details of establishing Southern Ventures Ltd.

With the Vesco contacts behind him and with Southern Ventures established, Lee, accompanied by Herring, flew to Washington on February 7 or February 8, 1977, for the purpose of making contact with Hamilton Jordan to arrange for someone in authority in the administration to talk with Vesco. They stayed at the Washington Hilton Hotel.

Herring went to the State Department to deliver some Vesco papers, and Spencer Lee went to the White House for the purpose of seeing Hamilton Jordan. According to Lee, he did not see Jordan but saw Richard Harden, a mutual friend who worked as an assistant to Jordan on the White House staff.

Lee and Harden agree that Harden spelled out the essence of Vesco's proposition, including the fact that "Spencer said he would get a large sum of money if the thing got worked out." It is contended by Lee and Harden that Harden talked Lee out of making any contact with Jordan, and that Harden said he would relate the Vesco incident to President Carter directly at the first opportunity.

As Harden and Lee explained months later, Lee said in that February 8 conversation that he was backing out of the whole Vesco deal and would make no other efforts to contact Jordan. Lee states that he told Harden to inform President Carter that he was backing out of the Vesco deal rather than embarrass the Carter administration.

On February 15, 1977, Richard Harden went to the Oval Office and told President Carter of Vesco's contact with Spencer Lee and of the offer of "a lot of money" for Lee. He also asserts that he told President Carter of Lee's decision to back out of the Vesco deal.

In Harden's presence, President Carter penned a personal note to Attorney General Griffin Bell: "Please see Spencer Lee of Albany when he requests an appointment." The handwritten note, dated February 15, 1977, and found later in the Justice Department files, was initialed "J.C."

As far as the White House was concerned, that ended the Vesco matter. Attorney General Bell says he never received the personal note from President Carter and never had any contact with any of his subordinates in the Justice Department relative to efforts to extradite Robert Vesco from Costa Rica to stand trial on criminal charges.

Attorney General Bell stated months later that there was no known relationship between the Vesco effort and a switch in tactics by the Justice Department; namely, to drop the effort to press formal extradition against Vesco, and instead to seek immediate expulsion of Vesco from his plush and heavily guarded estate in Costa Rica.

Attorney General Bell states that he was totally unaware of any effort Vesco or his representatives had made to obstruct justice through a political fix at the White House until Jack Anderson made inquiries of the Justice Department in the summer of 1978—more than eighteen months after President Carter had penned him the personal note to see Spencer Lee. The Justice Department states that Lee did not call on Attorney General Bell, and Lee asserts that he made no other efforts to talk with Georgians in Washington on the case.

In the summer of 1978 Jack Anderson received a call from Robert Vesco with the hint of a big story if Anderson would meet him in Nassau. Even with Vesco's assurance that it was a story of substance, Anderson was not overly enthusiastic about the fugitive financial manipulator as a source. Anderson had met Vesco on one occasion when he had gone to Costa Rica to film a television interview, and he had found Vesco to be an amiable sort of fellow, as most con men are.

But even as he was making arrangements to go to Nassau, he knew that every aspect of the Vesco story would have to be checked and rechecked, and he knew that often the most crucial aspect of the story would not be subject to verification from other, more reliable sources.

Also, Anderson was prepared for the trip to be just one more of those expensive trips that wasted money as well as time in a schedule that was always too full to give him time with his wife and family. In this case he decided to kill two birds with one stone and take his wife, Olivia, along for a few days' vacation.

The Andersons left Baltimore airport on August 3, 1978, for the flight to Nassau, where Jack Anderson contacted Vesco for the first meeting of what turned into a three-day visit. At first Vesco talked only about a story of alleged persecution by the United States District Attorney's office in Southern New York. It was a complicated story, and even if Vesco's version was precisely accurate, Anderson was not certain of the public's interest in some speculations about rough stuff and highly technical violations of the rights of a man accused of looting IOS investors of $250 million.

In the course of the conversation, Vesco mentioned what he

considered the broken promises of some high officials of the Carter administration with regard to his troubles with the Justice Department. Jack Anderson did not let his enthusiasm show while questioning the story that Vesco believed he had bought peace with the Carter administration in transactions he had made with a group of Georgians. These Georgians included Robert L. Herring of Albany and Spencer Lee IV, a long-time close friend of Hamilton Jordan. Vesco explained to Anderson how the money was to be paid through Southern Ventures.

Sensing Anderson's interest in the Southern Ventures project, Vesco suggested that he would cooperate with Anderson on the Southern Ventures story if Anderson would relay the message to the Securities and Exchange Commission that he was ready to cooperate on the investigations of "some of the bigger boys" in exchange for immunity. Vesco, the mastermind in IOS manipulations, regarded the political figures he bought off or tried to buy off as being "the bigger boys."

Anderson said he would relay his message to Stanley Sporkin, chief of enforcement at the SEC and a major nemesis of Vesco. Immediately, Vesco became more cooperative and open about the Southern Ventures arrangement with the Georgians. Vesco spoke in general terms of his conversations with Herring and Spencer Lee, and of their reports to him on their contacts with the Carter White House. According to reports from Herring and Lee, Vesco said he understood that contact had been made with Hamilton Jordan and with Charles Kirbo in January or early February.

Upon learning from the United States Embassy in Costa Rica that the Justice Department had dropped the intense pressure to extradite him, the fugitive financier said he took this as "a signal" that the Southern Ventures deal was in progress. Vesco said that upon receiving this "signal" he transferred $12 million of Property Resources Ltd. (PRL) stock to the Southern Ventures Ltd. corporation, which Spencer Lee had set up in the Bahamas in late January. Vesco said he had continuing contacts with Herring and Lee through which he was assured that matters were progressing slowly and cautiously but in a generally satisfactory manner.

Jack Anderson, still unconvinced by the vagueness of the account, pressed for details and documents to support the case. Vesco said he would not give Anderson the documents but would save them to deliver to the SEC investigators or other government investigators when he had made his deal for immunity.

At Anderson's insistence that he at least show him some of the documents to demonstrate good faith, Vesco produced some documents dealing with the travels of Herring and Lee. As Anderson pressed him for more specifics on time and precise conversations of Herring's and Lee's contacts with the Carter White House, Vesco took Anderson to his place in Nassau where he could get more details. Some details Anderson wanted could not be supplied unless he consulted other documents that were at his estate in Costa Rica, Vesco insisted.

Anderson's mind was focusing on the kind of record he could get to substantiate the fact that he had even had such conversations with Vesco. Accustomed to dealing with unreliable sources who would back away from a story when it served their purposes, Anderson asked Vesco to write a general chronology of events so he would not be confused on any point as to what Vesco said had transpired in the Southern Ventures plan.

Robert Vesco agreed, and in his own handwriting laid down a chronology of the major points they had covered in three days of conversations on Southern Ventures. On some dates Vesco said he could not be precise, but he assured Anderson that the events had taken place on or about the times listed in the handwritten chronology.

One of the witnesses Jack Anderson knew he wanted to talk to quickly was Robert Herring, the Albany businessman, who was reported to have dealt directly with Spencer Lee—who was purported by Vesco to represent his long-time friend Hamilton Jordan.

While Anderson and his wife were at Vesco's place in Nassau, Herring called Vesco, and Anderson asked that Vesco make arrangements for him to talk with Herring. Herring said he was going to fly to Nassau that night to see Vesco and might be able to squeeze in a short interview with Anderson before returning to Georgia on some pressing business. Anderson said he would wait in Nassau for the opportunity of at least a brief interview with Herring.

Later that evening, Vesco received a telephone call from Herring's lawyer stating that the Albany businessman would not be coming to the Bahamas. He had been arrested at the airport by law officers who believed he was fleeing the country to avoid prosecution on business fraud charges unrelated to his dealings with Vesco.

The lawyer wanted a sworn statement from Anderson stating

that Herring's trip to the Bahamas was not to flee prosecution, but was with the stated intention of returning to Georgia within twenty-four hours. Anderson viewed this as an opportunity to ingratiate himself with Herring—a vital source for checking out the Southern Ventures story—by doing no more than to state the truth about Herring's plans as far as he knew them.

Anderson had his wife, Olivia, change their return reservations for a stopover at Albany, Georgia, so he could interview Herring, Herring's lawyers and others. The quid pro quo was for Anderson to simply make a truthful affidavit to help Herring establish that he did not intend to flee prosecution.

Anderson spent two days in Albany questioning Herring in jail and questioning Herring's lawyers, Herring's wife and Herring's secretary. Mrs. Cindy Herring and the secretary, Gerolyn Hobbs, cooperated fully in answering Anderson's questions and producing desk diaries to establish dates. They also produced letters that were purported to be copies of letters written by Spencer Lee to Hamilton Jordan. Anderson was told by Herring and Ms. Hobbs that Lee wrote the letters and made telephone calls from Herring's office because he did not want his own law associates to know what he was doing.

Still not satisfied with the corroboration on the Southern Ventures plan when he returned to Washington, Anderson sent a reporter to Albany on August 10 in the first of a series of further efforts to establish the dates of the flights and the closeness of the relationships between Spencer Lee, Hamilton Jordan and Richard Harden—the three Albany men reported to be a part of the Southern Ventures scheme.

The pilot of the plane that flew Herring and Lee to Costa Rica was contacted. He verified the flights and corroborated it with the flight logs. Richard Harden was contacted. He admitted the dinner meeting with Spencer Lee and remembered meeting Herring, but declared he had never taken the Southern Ventures scheme up with Hamilton Jordan. Harden said he had urged Spencer Lee not to contact Jordan, and he said he had never discussed Southern Ventures with Jordan.

Anderson asked Attorney General Griffin Bell if the Justice Department had dropped its efforts to extradite Robert Vesco in the spring of 1977. Attorney General Bell said that the extradition of Vesco had been dropped because it was expensive and because it had been long and futile. Anderson had two conversations with the Attorney General to verify that point and to be sure there was no mistake that the Justice Department had indeed dropped the Vesco extradition effort. He asked no more questions, because he did not want to tip his hand.

At the White House, Anderson talked with Hamilton Jordan while Jody Powell was present. He took along reporter Gary Cohen as a witness and to share in the questioning and judgment of Jordan's responses. Jordan denied having received any letters from Spencer Lee and denied ever having discussed Southern Ventures or anything like Southern Ventures with Lee, with Harden or anyone else.

Then Jordan went a step further and denied he had ever heard of the Southern Ventures–Vesco proposal until he was questioned about it by Anderson. Anderson believed that his skepticism of Jordan's denials was justified when he learned later that agents from the Federal Bureau of Investigation had questioned Jordan on the same subject several weeks earlier. If Jordan was misrepresenting on one point, there was reason for viewing all of his denials with some skepticism in the light of the assurance from Herring's secretary, Ms. Gerolyn Hobbs, that she had typed and mailed letters for Spencer Lee that were addressed to Hamilton Jordan.

Anderson's office made several attempts to contact Charles Kirbo, but the Atlanta lawyer was reported to be unavailable and did not return the calls. Satisfied in his own mind that Kirbo was dodging him, Anderson decided to write his first column and scheduled it for publication on Monday, September 11, 1978.

When the column on the allegations of Vesco and Herring was circulated to nearly 1,000 newspapers, it stated these sound facts:

1. Fugitive financier Robert Vesco was trying to buy peace with the Carter administration by dealing through a group of Georgians, including Spencer Lee, long-time friend of Hamilton Jordan.

2. Spencer Lee had accepted a $10,000 down payment on the scheme and had gone to Nassau to set up a Bahamian corporation known as Southern Ventures, Ltd.

3. Spencer Lee and Herring had gone to Washington for the purpose of talking with Hamilton Jordan. They had talked to Richard Harden and spelled out the Southern Ventures scheme, even though there were loud denials from Jordan that he knew anything about Southern Ventures.

4. The Justice Department had suddenly dropped its long-time

pursuit of extradition to force Robert Vesco to return to the United States to stand trial on five different fraud indictments.

5. Vesco, believing the Justice Department's decision to drop extradition was "a signal," proceeded to transfer $12 million in PRL stock to Southern Ventures, Ltd., in a major action to transfer a large amount of money to the Georgians who, he had been told, were working with Herring and Lee.

Attorney General Bell contacted Anderson and said the dropping of the formal extradition action against Vesco was not a sellout to Vesco, but was simply a change of tactics because of the futility of years of efforts to extradite the fugitive financier. He said the new tactic was to seek immediate expulsion of Vesco from his heavily guarded refuge in Costa Rica as a first step in what was hoped would be a more successful effort to seize him for prosecution.

Attorney General Bell said this change in tactics was unrelated to Vesco's attempted manipulation of the White House through the Southern Ventures scheme. Bell could not explain how the new tactic was to work.

Jack Anderson knew he did not have all of the facts on Vesco's effort to make a deal with the Carter administration, but he believed he had about as many admissions from Harden, a top White House aide to Jordan, as he needed to break the Southern Ventures story. From past experience he knew that publishing those facts would force the Carter White House and the Justice Department to make public explanations and, perhaps, to initiate the full federal grand jury investigation that the case warranted.

At the time he wrote the first column, Anderson did not know that Harden had told President Carter of the details of Vesco's Southern Ventures scheme. Nor did he know that on February 15, 1977, President Carter, in the presence of Harden, had scribbled the handwritten note to Attorney General Bell, "Please see Spencer Lee of Albany when he requests an appointment. J.C."

That handwritten note from President Carter to Bell was found later in a Justice Department file—the only documentation to support Harden's later admission that such a note was written after he had told President Carter that Vesco had offered Spencer Lee "a lot of money."

President Carter said he had no memory of discussing the Vesco case with Harden or of writing a note to Attorney General Bell. Attorney General Bell said he had no memory of any discussion with President Carter of the Vesco matter or Spencer Lee, and he denied that he had ever seen the handwritten note from President Carter that was found in the Justice Department files.

What was the purpose of President Carter's note to Griffin Bell? Since President Carter had no memory of the incident, it was possible for critics to speculate as to whether it was a suggestion for Attorney General Bell to make some accommodation for Spencer Lee. If it was President Carter's intention to have Attorney General Bell make a thorough investigation of evidence of a conspiracy to obstruct justice by Vesco and the Georgians, it was certainly a strange and subtle way to express concern over evidence that Vesco was trying to corrupt his White House.

Since it had to be assumed that President Carter had no tape of his Oval Office conversation with Harden, the public knowledge of the precise conversation was to be dependent upon the credibility of Richard Harden—a Georgian, a personal friend of Jordan and a White House official who owed his job to President Carter and Jordan.

In the aftermath of Anderson's series of columns it was established that the copy of a letter from Spencer Lee to Hamilton Jordan was not a true copy. Kirbo and Jordan claimed it was a total fabrication of false evidence to implicate them in Southern Ventures.

Herring, who gave the letter to Anderson, admitted it was not a true copy of a letter from Lee to Jordan but insisted he had put the letter together with the help of his secretary for the purpose of providing Anderson with documentation to support a direct contact between Spencer Lee and Jordan. Herring and his secretary insisted that it was "a reconstruction" of the contents of a letter that was actually mailed to Jordan from Spencer Lee.

The White House and Atlanta attorney Charles Kirbo referred to it as a "fabricated letter" and contended that it undermined the soundness of Anderson's thesis that Vesco had been successful in penetrating the Carter White House with his Southern Ventures scheme. It was suggested by the White House Press Secretary that Anderson was irresponsible in relying upon "a phony letter" to show a link with Jordan.

While Herring's admission of the fabrication of the letter did undercut the proof that Herring's efforts had made direct contact with Jordan, it did not undercut the admissions by Harden that he had been told of the Southern Ventures "fix" effort and had relayed those facts to President Carter.

Nor did the admissions that the letters were not true copies change other relevant facts that were emerging in Jack Anderson's probe. Anderson and his staff learned that Spencer Lee had continued to have telephone communications with Robert Vesco and Robert Herring for months after the February date when he claimed Harden had talked him out of going forward with the Southern Ventures scheme.

It was even more disturbing for Anderson and his staff to learn that Spencer Lee was named to one of President Carter's legal committees to screen judicial appointments. The appointment of Spencer Lee to the Carter judicial screening committee took place three months after President Carter had been told by Harden of Lee's role in the Vesco payoff scheme. Either too little attention was being paid to the people named to these important committees, or President Carter or Attorney General Bell had gone ahead with the appointment of Jordan's friend to the committee in brazen disregard for evidence linking him to Vesco's payoff effort.

Attorney General Bell said that he stayed out of the ensuing Justice Department investigation, which was under the direction of Assistant Attorney General Philip Heymann, head of the Criminal Division.

Heymann, also a Carter administration appointee, contended that he could be objective in an investigation involving the Carter White House. Critics found it difficult to distinguish between Heymann's assurances of objectivity and comparable assurances given by former Attorney General Richard Kleindienst, a Nixon appointee, who contended he could be objective and thorough in exploring the extent of the Nixon White House involvement in the Watergate burglary and cover-up.

Although Attorney General Bell kept out of the Justice Department investigation, he was in almost daily contact with his former law partner, Charles Kirbo, who was engaged in a personal and nonofficial investigation of Jack Anderson. It was apparent that Kirbo's investigation had the blessing and the aid of the White House. He arranged to talk with Cindy Herring, wife of Robert Herring, by going through Tina Harden, sister-in-law of Richard Harden. Harden was still a member of the White House staff and a key figure in the question of whether President Carter, when he was informed of the Vesco plot, had performed his constitutional duty to see "that the laws are faithfully executed."

In the eighteen months after he was given information of Vesco's plot to corrupt his White House, Carter had made no effort to follow through on his note to Attorney General Bell. Perhaps President Carter was so lacking in experience with the federal government that he did not recognize that Richard Nixon's failure to take immediate action to investigate the Watergate cover-up was Nixon's most vulnerable position in Watergate. It was argued by many critics that Nixon's failure to initiate an immediate investigation involved him in obstruction of justice or misprision of a felony.

It was possible that in his ignorance of the criminal law Mr. Carter failed to grasp the criminal nature of Vesco's fix effort and was simply negligent in failing to follow through on his note to Attorney General Bell. Or perhaps Mr. Carter did not want to create the embarrassing spectacle of initiating an investigation that involved his White House staff. Mr. Nixon said that was his initial motivation in the Watergate affair, and that those initial misjudgments led him into deeper and deeper trouble in trying to protect White House Assistants H. R. (Bob) Haldeman and John D. Ehrlichman.

There were also legal hazards and questions of propriety in the White House cooperation with Kirbo on an unofficial probe of Jack Anderson. Even though Kirbo was regarded as a wise political strategist and a wily legal operator, his contacts with Cindy Herring provided Anderson with ammunition that represented an embarrassment to the White House and tended to nullify their gains in establishing that the letters Herring gave to Anderson were not true copies.

Cindy Herring had helped in the letter reconstruction process because her husband was hoping he could get immunity in exchange for testimony on Vesco's allegations. She later explained that the only way her husband could possibly get the whole story aired was to convince Jack Anderson that the letter was authentic documentation.

It was after Anderson's first columns appeared that Cindy Herring, on September 22, informed Anderson that the key letter was not authentic. She did it through a private investigator named Richard Bast, a long-time Anderson friend, who was retained by her husband's lawyer.

Jack Anderson was "extremely distressed" when he was told that some important aspects of his columns had been based on what Cindy Herring said were "reconstructions" of the original letter. While it raised a question of credibility, it did not reflect upon the truth of the account if it was indeed an accurate reconstruction of the original letter sent by Lee to Jordan.

When Kirbo made contact with Cindy Herring, she retained her husband's lawyer, Benjamin Brown of Rockville, Maryland, and was playing her own cautious game. Brown, in turn, hired Richard Bast. Bast had Cindy Herring put a tape recorder in her purse when she visited Kirbo "to preserve the integrity"' of the conversations.

Those recordings were used by Jack Anderson as the basis for a column in which he contended that Kirbo tried to persuade Cindy Herring to state that the letters and records were not "reconstructions" but had been "fabricated" by her husband. Kirbo also urged her not to be "too open" with the FBI, and not to place too much trust in Jack Anderson.

In the column accusing Kirbo of being in league with the White House in an effort to "destroy our reputation," Anderson said that Kirbo and Harden "tried to persuade one of our news sources to change her story." Anderson also noted Kirbo's comment that Mrs. Herring should not be "too open" with the FBI.

Initially, Kirbo issued a flat denial that he had told Mrs. Herring not to be "too open" with the FBI. He withdrew that denial when he discovered that a recording existed but said that, taken in the context of the whole conversation, he did not feel he had said "anything wrong."

Kirbo, interested in evidence to protect himself and the White House, advised Mrs. Herring that she was much too "inclined to trust everybody."

"That's a mistake," Kirbo said. "You need to really have a lawyer talk with you and help you analyze it. . . . I think it would be a mistake for you to put too much trust in me, 'cause I'm trying to protect my reputation. I think you've got some misplaced trust in Jack Anderson. And it's a mistake to be too open with the FBI, because they've got another thing they are working on."

It was understandable that Kirbo would urge Cindy Herring against having too much trust in Anderson because of his own personal interest in undermining the thesis of Anderson's columns. His recorded conversation with Mrs. Herring had certainly reflected unfavorably upon him and on the Carter White House. But why did he advise caution in dealing with FBI agents who were simply trying to get all of the relevant facts on federal crimes? In the absence of evidence that the FBI agents were prejudiced against the Carter administration, anyone wanting the whole truth told should have been urging full cooperation.

Although Attorney General Bell had disqualified himself from the Vesco investigation, he offered the opinion to reporters that "the White House is under attack by con artists." Assistant Attorney General Heymann defended the Kirbo investigation and the one-way flow of information from Kirbo to the Justice Department. Heymann said he would be "worried about" any indication that there was "a two-way flow" of information where Bell also was feeding information back to his friend and former law partner, Charles Kirbo. "We don't have that," Heymann said with finality.

Under public pressure, the Justice Department launched a federal grand jury investigation with the officials cognizant of the same troubles in which various Nixon administration lawyers found themselves when they failed to take immediate steps to initiate investigations of evidence of White House crimes. The twenty-four-member federal grand jury in the District of Columbia operated quietly under Foreman Ralph E. Ulmer, whose aggressive questioning and voluminous note-taking did not permit the more familiar prosecutor dominance of the investigation.

Foreman Ulmer was not satisfied with the manner in which the Justice Department lawyers were proceeding, and in July 1979 he made his first effort to resign in a letter sent to United States District Judge William Bryant, charging that the Justice Department was actually obstructing the efforts of the grand jury to get all of the facts.

In late August Ulmer wrote a second letter to Judge Bryant resigning as foreman and charging, "The cover-up activities are being orchestrated within the Department of Justice under the concept that the administration must be protected at all costs."

The grand jury foreman said his resignation was in protest "against the President's reluctance to take the steps called for by the involvement of his own aides." Ulmer told the *Washington Post* that the grand jury secrecy rules barred him from being more detailed in his criticism of the Justice Department for withholding information from the grand jury, delays in the calling of witnesses and efforts to restrict the questioning of witnesses by the grand jurors.

The Justice Department in releasing Ulmer's letter also released an affidavit from Herring taken last April in which the former Georgia businessman said he had talked with Foreman Ulmer on several occasions. Justice Department officials said that, while there is no rule against a grand juror having contact with a witness, such as Herring, outside of the grand jury room, it is "quite unusual."

The Justice Department defended its conduct. Michael E. Shaheen, Jr., head of the Justice Department's internal investigation unit, said his office had investigated Ulmer's charges and found them "to be without merit." Assistant Attorney General Heymann said the Vesco investigation had been troubled by changes in attorneys and some administrative irregularities. He characterized the Justice effort as "absolutely rigorous and quite exceptionally probing."

On August 31, 1979, the *New York Times* reported that Heymann had been before the grand jury a month earlier and had told the panel that Harden, still a member of Carter's White House staff, had committed perjury. In response to the *New York Times* story, Heymann issued a statement declaring that "at no time in that meeting [with the grand jury] did I suggest or state a belief that Richard Harden had committed perjury."

There appeared to be some doubt as to whether Harden had testified accurately on some of his conversations. The Justice Department issued its clarification of Heymann's statement because of "the unfairness" that would exist if the *New York Times* story went unchallenged.

President Carter told reporters in Plains, Georgia, that there was nothing to the charges of a Justice Department cover-up for the White House.

"There is too much at stake for the Attorney General or the President of the United States to try to subvert the legal system," Mr. Carter said. "It would be politically suicidal . . . it's inconceivable."

However, Mr. Carter acknowledged that he did give a statement to federal law enforcement officials concerning the "hazy" recollection he had that Harden told him something about Robert Vesco.

A full year after the Anderson columns on the Vesco fix effort, the Justice Department was still trying to decide whether conditions existed that required the appointment of a special prosecutor under the new ethics law.

The direct point at issue was the credibility of Richard Harden, who claimed that he talked Spencer Lee out of contacting

Hamilton Jordan and convinced him that he should back out of the Vesco fix scheme. Spencer Lee's continued contact with Vesco and Herring after the February 8, 1977, meeting with Harden was one indication that Spencer Lee did not make an immediate break with the Southern Ventures schemers.

It was possible that Harden believed that Spencer Lee had indeed given up the dishonest project and mended his ways, but Richard Harden and President Jimmy Carter had some other obligations when they became aware of the evidence of Vesco's efforts to corrupt the Carter White House. By hindsight, they were at least guilty of negligence and naiveté. They had failed to learn some of the important Watergate lessons.

CHAPTER SEVENTEEN

Peanut Loans— The Tie That Binds

When Bert Lance resigned as Director of the Office of Management and Budget, President Carter said he still believed that his banker friend had done nothing wrong, that Lance was "a good man" and that the records produced by the Senate Government Affairs Committee had "only confirmed" his belief.

Frequently Presidents have made such comments about departing friends who have become a political embarrassment, but they have then proceeded systematically to cut the ties with the resigned official, making it apparent that their comments were intended to help a former associate save face and re-establish himself outside of government.

Regarding his relations with Bert Lance, President Carter was indeed different from other Presidents. He continued to associate with Lance in private and in public. Lance was permitted to keep his White House pass. Ham Jordan and Jody Powell arranged for the State Department to permit Lance to continue to carry a diplomatic passport (number 000045). Bert and LaBelle Lance continued to travel abroad as personal representatives of President Carter in the private peace crusade known as Friendship Force International, an Atlanta-based people-to-people program.

It was, indeed, strange that in the image-conscious Carter administration there would continue to be such overt displays of affection for Lance, who, at least in the eyes of some Democratic critics, had been the source of great political embarrassment. But President Jimmy Carter fondly embraced his old friend at a Democratic fund-raising affair in Atlanta, spoke of him warmly in press conferences and permitted Hamilton Jordan and Jody Powell to speak of his continued good will and friendship for Bert. Even Gerald Rafshoon, who was concentrating his efforts on image-building for the 1980 election, found no fault in a continued personal and political association with the resigned OMB Director.

The continuing criticism of William Safire, the *New York Times* columnist, finally forced the Carter White House to ask Bert Lance to turn in his diplomatic passport. Safire's barbed criticism was aimed at the special privilege of not having to be searched when Bert and LaBelle Lance traveled in and out of foreign countries as diplomats. Safire also called attention to Bert Lance's wide international travels to deal with wealthy oil-rich Arab leaders in the Middle East and to the difficulty of distinguishing between Lance's personal financial ventures and his travels as a representative of President Carter. These same questions had been raised when former Treasury Secretary John Connally was assigned to international travel duties by President Nixon at a time when he and his law firm were representing a number of oil companies.

Senate Republicans had forced Benjamin Civiletti, head of the Justice Department's Criminal Division, to admit his concern over President Carter's continued association with and public praise of Bert Lance at the same time as a criminal investigation of Lance was being conducted before a federal grand jury in Atlanta. Although Civiletti reluctantly admitted that prosecutors had complained of President Carter's association with Lance, he said he had never communicated his feelings to President Carter.

Senator Malcolm Wallop, Republican of Wyoming, accused Civiletti of being "insensitive" to the complaints of three attorneys working on the Lance case because Civiletti contended he had no legal duty to advise President Carter of "the chilling effect his [President Carter's] actions might have on the administration of justice."

It seemed that President Carter did avoid public displays of affection for Lance in the period in 1978 after Wallop's specific criticism that he might be obstructing the even-handed administration of justice.

Following the sharp criticism of Civiletti in connection with his controversial nomination as Deputy Attorney General, the Justice Department did intensify its investigation of the alleged banking frauds of Bert Lance. The prosecution team, headed by Edwin Tomko, was eager to proceed aggressively, and there was no inclination on the part of Deputy Attorney General Civiletti or Assistant Attorney General Philip Heymann to take any step that might be interpreted as interference with a full investigation and prosecution.

In mid-1978—months after the Justice Department had promised a full investigation of all the allegations against Lance—Justice Department lawyers contacted Billy Lee Campbell, who had been convicted of embezzling more than $300,000 from the Calhoun First National Bank in the period from 1971 through mid-1975. In September 1977 Billy Lee Campbell told Senate Government Affairs Committee investigators that Bert Lance was his silent business partner in Campbell Farms, which had been the recipient of the so-called embezzled funds.

Campbell also told the investigators that Bert Lance had encouraged his borrowing from the Calhoun First National "to make Campbell Farms a showplace," which they would eventually sell and split the profits.

Campbell explained to the investigators that his deal with Lance started to come apart when a federal bank examiner discovered lax banking practices, which included the lack of sufficient collateral to cover the Campbell Farms loans. Campbell told government investigators that initially Lance told him "don't panic," and then in a few weeks Lance informed him he would have to turn him in to the Federal Bureau of Investigation.

Campbell told the Senate investigators he had no documents to support his claim that Lance was involved in Campbell Farms with him as a secret partner, but he said a close examination of the financial records of the Calhoun bank might produce needed supporting evidence.

Apparently, the resignation of Lance as Director of the OMB ended the interest of the Senate Government Affairs Committee, as well as its investigation, and there was no serious effort to obtain corroboration until Justice Department lawyers questioned and then requestioned Billy Lee Campbell in the latter half of 1978. It was then that the Justice Department lawyers obtained additional records from the Calhoun bank and from the National Bank of Georgia in Atlanta. After grilling Campbell over and over, eventually they concluded that he was "a credible witness" who could be used in a criminal trial in which Lance might be one of the defendants.

While the FBI and Justice Department lawyers quietly went about the business of subpoenaing records from the Calhoun First National Bank and the National Bank of Georgia to corroborate more fully the testimony of Billy Lee Campbell, Bert Lance operated with a lower profile in his connection with President Carter and the Carter White House.

Bert Lance's personal financial crisis was avoided when he was able to dispose of his stock in the National Bank of Georgia —his major asset—at a premium price to Ghaith R. Pharaon, an oil-rich Saudi Arabian financier. Neither Lance nor Pharaon paid any significant attention to the charges implying that this transaction was linked to Pharaon's and Saudi Arabian oil lobbyists' wish to curry favor with President Carter's administration.

By November 1978 it was apparent to most observers that the Justice Department team was searching for all financial records they believed relevant to the Lance inquiry. This included records of loans the National Bank of Georgia made to the Carter Warehouse in 1975 and 1976, when Lance was president of that bank.

Full exploration of those transactions for bank law violations or for possible election law violations required that subpoenas be issued for Billy Carter and the financial records of the Carter Warehouse.

Examination of those records demonstrated a need to question Billy Carter in the federal grand jury in Atlanta to determine the circumstances surrounding several million dollars in loans that appeared to have been given preferential treatment at Lance's National Bank of Georgia. In 1975 Jimmy Carter turned over the Carter Warehouse operations to Brother Billy and contended he had no part in the details of the financing arrangements, because he wished to give all his time and energy to campaigning for the Democratic presidential nomination.

In November Billy Carter interrupted his international travels to Libya and the entertainment of his radical Libyan friends long enough to go before the federal grand jury in Atlanta. On November 25, 1978, Billy Carter emerged from the federal grand jury and informed reporters that he had invoked the Fifth Amendment "a few times" by refusing to swear to some details of some of the loans from Lance's bank. Those questions dealt with a $1 million loan to the Carter Warehouse and the personal loans he received from Lance's bank.

Billy Carter said he just could not remember the dates and details of the transactions but was certain that the grand jurors found nothing wrong with his borrowing from Lance-controlled banks.

In an emotional outburst after his three hours of testimony,

Billy Carter lashed out at the "Republican and Yankee press," who, he said, were in a plot to hurt President Carter through interminable investigations of Bert Lance. He said the investigation of Lance was "a fishing expedition."

Little of the details of the investigation had been made public, but reporters had been able to make some investigation of the public records of taxes paid in Sumter County, Georgia, and certain tax credits that President Carter had taken on his federal tax returns for 1975 and 1976. The President had made his federal tax returns public, and they disclosed that he had claimed a tax credit of $695,000 in 1975 for a peanut sheller that was appraised at $300,000 in Sumter County records. The President claimed an investment credit of $367,000 in 1976 for a truck bin and elevator that was valued by the county at $50,000 for local tax purposes.

Billy Carter, a member of the Sumter county tax assessment board, said there was no impropriety in using different values for federal and local tax purposes. He explained that the Sumter County assessments were lower than actual value to keep them in line with the assessment on equipment owned by "eight or nine" other peanut growers in that county.

Inquiry by Jeff Gerth, a *New York Times* reporter, unearthed evidence that an equipment and improvement loan of about $1 million from Lance's National Bank of Georgia was not fully collateralized for more than a year in 1975 and 1976. Gerth's story reported that local officials characterized this lack of collateral as "improper but not illegal."

This was the first public report to show that the federal grand jury in Atlanta was investigating the question of whether Bert Lance's loans to the Carter Warehouse from the National Bank of Georgia amounted to a favoritism that might constitute an unsound banking practice.

Billy Carter later told syndicated columnist Jack Anderson's staff that it was questions relative to these loans that he would not answer for the federal grand jury, because he did not have access to the records at the time he was testifying.

Billy Carter and the White House press office denied that any of the millions of dollars borrowed by the Carter Warehouse from Bert Lance's bank went into the Carter primary or general election campaigns in 1975 or 1976. However, this did not keep *New York Times* columnist William Safire and others from suggesting that the Carter Warehouse might have been "a money laundry" for making bank money available to the Carter campaign in an evasion of federal election laws.

Safire, Jack Anderson and other critics contended that only a thorough and complete investigation of all details of the Lance loans to the Carter Warehouse and the warehouse's financial dealings with all Carter family members could determine if the federal election laws were violated.

Even as public attention was focusing on the loans to the Carter Warehouse, more documented information became available through reports made to the Securities and Exchange Commission and the Comptroller of the Currency by a "special committee" established by the Board of Directors of the National Bank of Georgia.

The SEC and the Comptroller filed a complaint against Bert Lance, the Calhoun First National Bank, and the National Bank of Georgia on April 26, 1978, alleging "unsafe and unsound banking practices and financial irregularities." As part of the civil settlement of those problems, the National Bank of Georgia agreed to name two independent outside directors and a Special Counsel and Special Auditor to review all complaints and to recommend remedial action. At the suggestion of the SEC staff, that special committee expanded its investigation to include two loans not mentioned in the original complaints of the SEC and the Comptroller of the Currency.

That report by Lance's former colleagues at the National Bank of Georgia was devastating in its implications. These were the former friends and business associates of Bert Lance trying to be as understanding as they could be in their interpretation of what had been called "unsound and unsafe banking practices," while retaining a credibility with the federal regulatory agencies.

The auditing committee conducted sixty-nine interviews—sixty-one in person and eight by telephone. "No interviews were conducted under oath or recorded stenographically," they stated. Officials and directors of the bank would be less likely to agree to interviews if they were put under oath, where they might be subject to prosecution for perjury or other crimes.

Because of the extensive investigation by the SEC, the National Bank of Georgia's "special committee" did not initially intend to interview Lance, but in early January 1979 some new matters arose that made them seek an interview with Lance.

Unable to get Lance to agree to an interview on his loan activities, the "special committee" agreed to a suggestion by Lance's lawyer that written questions be submitted. "We submitted a list of written questions to Lance, through his lawyer, concerning these matters," the special committee reported. "We did not receive a response to these questions."

That 130-page report of the auditing committee of the National Bank of Georgia established these hard facts:

1. Bert Lance's National Bank of Georgia bolstered the business and personal financial stability of Jimmy and Billy Carter during 1975 and 1976, when Carter was campaigning for the Democratic nomination.

2. Those loans and lines of credit (which reached a peak of more than $3,650,000 on election day in 1976) were arranged, directed or influenced by Bert Lance. The reasons for lowering the interest rate on the Carter Warehouse loans from a favorable prime plus 2½ percent in 1975 to a prime plus 2 percent were "undocumented moves" and made at the direction of Bert Lance, president and chief executive officer of the bank.

3. The line of credit of $3,000,000 to the Carter Warehouse to finance peanut crop purchases was approved by the National Bank of Georgia loan committee on July 18, 1975, as Carter was embarking upon his drive for the Democratic nomination. In August 1976, just after Carter received the Democratic nomination, the interest was dropped from 2½ percent to 2 percent above prime rate.

4. On September 23, 1976—in the midst of the presidential campaign—the National Bank of Georgia increased the line of credit for the Carter Warehouse to $9 million.

While the special committee of the National Bank of Georgia found much to criticize in the false and misleading financial reports that were accepted by the bank during Lance's tenure as president and chief executive officer, it found that the loans made to Gerald Rafshoon and the Gerald Rafshoon Advertising, Inc., firm "were sound loans made to a good customer at prevailing interest rates." That committee made no effort to determine if these loans to Rafshoon were, in fact, financing expenditures in Jimmy Carter's campaign for the Democratic presidential nomination. The loans to Rafshoon "began on April 30, 1975, when Lance instructed a loan officer to make Rafshoon an unsecured loan of $15,000," the report said.

"The proceeds of this loan were used to repay a $10,000 loan at The Mercantile National Bank and for a down payment on some property purchased by Rafshoon."

That loan to Rafshoon by the National Bank of Georgia, during the period when Rafshoon was extending credit to the Carter campaign, went up to $155,000 in the spring of 1976. At the time of the report in December 1978, Rafshoon still owed the National Bank of Georgia $48,021. It was secured by a pledge of accounts receivable and Rafshoon's personal guarantee. In addition to explaining that the loans were "at prevailing interest rates" and to a "good customer," the auditing committee said the largest loan to Rafshoon, and "the one most susceptible to diversion of funds," was disbursed in connection with problems with a bankrupt agency client.

The publication of the National Bank of Georgia's audit report on January 17, 1979, provided further documentation on the Carter Warehouse loans, stirred more press interest, and raised more questions about whether Attorney General Griffin Bell should appoint a special prosecutor.

A few days later, on January 20, 1979, the *Los Angeles Times* investigative reporting team of Ronald J. Ostrow and Robert L. Jackson reported that Billy Carter took out large personal bank loans in 1977 during the same period that the Carter Warehouse was having problems paying its debts. According to the Ostrow–Jackson account, those personal loans totaled $300,000 in addition to the $148,908 that Billy had borrowed from the Carter Farms Inc., another family business.

This heavy borrowing by Billy Carter took place in the same period of time that the Carter Warehouse, which Billy was managing, incurred nearly $500,000 in overdrafts at the National Bank of Georgia.

During the last week in January 1979 a federal grand jury in Atlanta issued subpoenas for still more records of the Carter Warehouse, and it was reported that the investigation now included serious questioning of whether some of the Carter Warehouse funds might have found their way into the Carter campaign in 1975 or 1976.

By late January Brother Billy's antics and his careless comments had ceased to be entertaining to the press or to the Georgians in the White House. Billy Carter, comic relief for many months because of his colorful redneck jargon, had stirred an international storm with his ethnic quips, his rude anti-Semitic comments and his open association with officials of the government of Colonel Muammer Qaddafi, President of Libya. Colonel Qaddafi had financed and harbored Arab terrorists and was one of the most outspoken advocates of wiping Israel off the map.

While waiting for the arrival of his Libyan friends at an Atlanta airport, Billy Carter casually urinated against a wall. He then offered the political observation that he was launching a new era of American–Libyan friendship and shrewdly noted: "There's a hell of a lot more Arabians than there are Jews." He added a bit later that "the Jewish media tears up the Arab countries full time, as you well know."

The President, who had defended Brother Billy frequently in the past, found himself in a position where he had to authorize White House Press Secretary Powell to disassociate the White House from Billy's crude actions and comments.

Critics of President Carter were beginning to raise the question of whether Mr. Carter was free to express himself critically on either Bert Lance or Billy Carter. Seldom had the nation seen a more long-suffering President than Jimmy Carter, who permitted himself and his administration to be embarrassed month after month by Lance and Brother Billy.

As more details on the National Bank of Georgia loans to the Carter Warehouse emerged, the question was raised as to whether Lance or Billy Carter might have some information that might bring President Carter more directly into the loan controversy.

Republican members of the Senate and House became more and more vocal in demanding that Attorney General Griffin Bell appoint a special prosecutor to investigate Lance and carry on a broader and deeper investigation of the Carter Warehouse loans. As it was announced by Atlanta lawyer Charles Kirbo that the Carter Warehouse was for sale, the Republicans put more pressure on Attorney General Bell for a special prosecutor.

On March 12, 1979, Minority Leader Howard Baker stepped up to lead the Republican chorus of complaint when Attorney General Bell indicated he had "confidence" that the lawyers in his department could conduct an objective investigation of the Carter Warehouse loans. A week later, the Justice Department acknowledged that a search for a special prosecutor for the Carter Warehouse investigation was in progress.

On March 21, 1979—more than four months after the Carter Warehouse loans had emerged as an issue—Attorney General Bell named Paul J. Curran, a forty-six-year-old New York City attorney, as special counsel. Curran, a Republican, had served as United States Attorney in the Southern District of New York as an appointee of President Nixon. During his term he had seen the return of indictments against two former Nixon Cabinet officers—Attorney General John Mitchell and Commerce Secretary Maurice Stans—in connection with an illegal campaign contribution of $200,000 from fugitive financier Robert Vesco. Mitchell and Stans were acquitted, and Vesco remained a fugitive.

While there were some Republican complaints that Attorney General Bell had not appointed the special prosecutor under a new law guaranteeing independence of the Justice Department, Bell clarified Curran's role and his independence until it was apparent that Curran could make investigations and prosecution decisions without consulting the Justice Department.

Deputy Attorney General Civiletti had been promising some grand jury action in the Lance investigation since February, and it seemed to drag on and on with no end. On March 27, 1979, the so-called Lance grand jury returned its first criminal charges. A four-count indictment was returned against Larry Beasley, a former president of the Newton County Bank. Beasley was charged with misapplication of bank funds in connection with a loan of $37,000 to Richard Carr.

Carr was a business associate and personal friend of Bert Lance. Thus it was apparent that the criminal indictment returned against Beasley was to provide a lever to force him to testify freely on information deemed important in the Lance investigation.

On May 14, 1979, Beasley changed his plea from not guilty on all four counts to nolo contendere (no contest) on one count and part of another. It was a clear plea bargain with the aim of obtaining cooperation in the Lance investigation.

A week later, on May 23, 1979, the federal grand jury in Atlanta returned a seventy-one-count indictment against Lance and three business associates charging conspiracy, fraud and misapplication of loan funds. The others indicted with Lance were Thomas M. Mitchell, who served as trustee for Lance's financial affairs while Lance was in Washington; Richard T. Carr, a one-time banking associate; and H. Jackson Mullins, a Calhoun, Georgia, druggist. Mullins was alleged to have let Lance use his name in a variety of financial manipulations.

The indictment disclosed charges of a conspiracy to obtain

hundreds of illegal loans totaling more than $20 million for themselves and for their families from forty-one banks. Although most of the banks were in Georgia, other banks from which loans were obtained included banks in New York, Chicago, Luxembourg and Hong Kong. The indictment spanned the period from the unsound loans that the Calhoun First National Bank was making to Billy Lee Campbell in the 1971 to 1975 period, through the loans Lance was negotiating with New York banks and Chicago banks in 1976 and 1977 in connection with his purchase of stock in the National Bank of Georgia.

Lance and his codefendants entered pleas of not guilty to the federal criminal charges and immediately prepared lengthy challenges to the indictment, charging that it was the work of biased prosecutors. Lance was particularly vociferous in his attacks upon Billy Lee Campbell, the former successful Georgia farmer whom he had brought into the Calhoun First National Bank as an employee and later as a director.

Campbell, who pleaded guilty to embezzlement charges, entered federal prison in December 1976. After waiting for months for help from Lance, he started cooperating with Edward Tomco's Justice Department prosecution team and was scheduled to be a key witness against Bert Lance in efforts to establish that Lance had been aware of Campbell's heavy borrowing from Calhoun First National Bank and of the false statements on his financial reports.

In his pleadings and his private conversations, Lance tried to brand his former friend and business associate as "a malicious liar" who repaid Lance's friendship by embezzling more than $300,000. Lance declared that Campbell was bitter because it was Lance who turned him in to the FBI in July of 1975. Lance contended that Campbell manufactured the story of his business arrangements with him and also fabricated the account of an agreement with him to keep quiet and serve his prison term.

Campbell had told prosecutors that Lance was to profit from Campbell Farms and that Lance knew of the lack of collateral for loans and even encouraged him to spend beyond his means on the farm. When the bank examiner moved in on the Calhoun National Bank in 1975, Lance told Campbell "don't panic," then turned him in and promised to help him get off without a prison term.

Lance's attack on Campbell centered on the fact that Lance had told the FBI about Campbell's embezzlement. He also said

Campbell had not accused him all through the months of the investigation and prosecution. Lance said specifically that Campbell never at any time told his own lawyer or the prosecutors that Lance had any role in the embezzlement. Lance pointed out that Campbell told the sentencing judge that the embezzled funds went into Campbell Farms for improvements and into livestock operation and was lost.

Lance said that federal prosecutors had demonstrated their bias by failing to call Billy Lee Campbell's lawyer, Bobby Joe Cook, to testify that Campbell had never at any time stated that Lance had any interest in Campbell Farms. Lance, in his pleadings, named several other witnesses who he said would testify that Campbell had told them that Lance had no responsibility in connection with the embezzlement upon which he was convicted.

As the battle of court pleadings continued in preparation for the trial of the Lance indictment, Special Prosecutor Curran continued his investigations of the peanut warehouse loans. The Curran investigation into the Carter Warehouse loans had the potential for embroiling Bert Lance and Billy Carter in still more trouble at some future time.

Special Prosecutor Curran's investigation also carried the potential for more direct damage to President Jimmy Carter than he had suffered up to then. Jimmy Carter had already been identified as having some conversations with Bert Lance with regard to the warehouse loan arrangements. While President Carter admitted some brief conversations in July 1976, after he had won the Democratic Presidential nomination, Mr. Carter denied that he had any role in the actual "negotiations" on the loans involved in the $500,000 deficiency in collateral.

Although Jimmy Carter owned 63 percent of the peanut warehouse business, he said he had turned over all of the operations and decisions to Brother Billy during the time he was campaigning for President in 1975 and 1976. After he was elected President, Carter established a "blind trust" under the direction of his friend and counselor, Charles Kirbo.

On October 16, 1979 Special Counsel Paul J. Curran issued a 180 page report that concluded, "none of the proceeds of the peanut loans (from Bert Lance's National Bank of Georgia) were used in Jimmy Carter's primary or general election campaign for the presidency."

"My conclusion, necessarily expressed summarily in this public report, is that based on the evidence and the law no criminal charges can or should be brought," Curran stated. An additional secret report to Attorney General Ben Civiletti discussed "in detail all of the evidence developed and applies that evidence to the relevant criminal statutes and the case law."

That secret report to the Attorney General contained the details of President Carter's explanation of his role in the borrowing from Bert Lance's National Bank of Georgia by the Carter Warehouse in 1975 and 1976 when he was running for President. The public report by Curran had a disclaimer that it was "based solely on our analysis of documents, and is, therefore, incomplete."

Curran stated that if Congress decides that the total report made to Attorney General Civiletti should be made public he would release it, but in the meantime "I may not lawfully release the report I have made to Attorney General Civiletti and I will not do so."

"Thus I stress right here at the beginning, this public document can not and does not purport to set forth the totality of the investigation and, in fairness to the parties involved and to the government it must be examined with that understanding," Curran said in making a significant caution that could justify later revelations that might prove politically embarrassing.

Significantly, while the report cleared President Carter of law violations, it clearly documented the chaotic financial condition of the Carter warehouse business during the period when Jimmy Carter was running for President and promising to straighten out the multi-billion dollar finances of the nation. And while President Carter asserted that he himself had virtually nothing to do with the operation and management of the family peanut business during the time he was running for President, he selected brother Billy to conduct the affairs of the peanut business despite his long time knowledge of Billy Carter's casual attitude toward financial affairs. The result was that the Carter warehouse went deeper and deeper into debt to Bert Lance's bank during Carter's campaign for the Presidency. Because of Billy's relaxed management practices the Carter warehouse was constantly in arrears on payments on its bank loan. Meanwhile Billy and Jimmy Carter withdrew a total of more than $200,000 from the business. According to the Curran report, Jimmy and Billy Carter withdrew $114,000 from the Carter warehouse in 1975 and $112,000 in 1976. Of this $226,000 the allocations to "salaries" for Jimmy and Billy Carter totaled $90,000 in the two year period. This left $136,000 for general business and living expenses that might or might not be related to the heavy campaign expenditures in the same time frame.

Curran's report also examined in detail the financial relationship between the NBG-financed Gerald Rafshoon Advertising Agency, Inc. (GRAA) and the Jimmy Carter Presidential Campaign (JCPC). Curran revealed that JCPC's payments to Rafshoon's firm reached a peak of $671,243.52 in May 1976—the time of the crucial Pennsylvania primary. The key question here was whether the Rafshoon Agency had used money it borrowed from Lance's bank to finance Carter's media purchases. Curran's investigation stated that Rafshoon's firm collected a total of $3,062,057.39 of Jimmy Carter's campaign funds during the period from December 1974 through October 1976, and made a gross profit of $456,062.72 on the Carter candidacy.

Curran noted that the Rafshoon Agency had earned sufficient money on the Carter campaign account by May 1976 to defray the $240,125.07 Curran said had actually been expended for Carter's campaign by that time. Curran noted that Rafshoon had sufficient funds available to advance credit to the Carter campaign without relying on the borrowing from Lance's bank.

Although Rafshoon's unpaid invoices for Carter's campaign totalled $671,243.52, Curran stated that this sum actually had not been expended because it included "media reservations" of $236,152.74 and "productions payables" of $194,965.71. Curran accepted the Carter-Rafshoon explanation that this $431,118.45 total would not be normally payable until the media showings.

As the Special Prosecutor figured it, this left only a $243,125.07 in Rafshoon Agency funds that were actually expended on Carter's behalf.

"In effect, by May 31, 1976 GRAA (the Rafshoon Agency) had expended most of its earned commissions on behalf of JCPC (the Carter Campaign)," the report said. "We express no opinion as to whether the activities described in this section constitute a violation of the federal election laws," Curran stated. The Carter-appointed Federal Election Commission stated that the Rafshoon Agency's financial expenditures for the Carter Campaign did not constitute a law violation.

The Curran report, while admittedly not complete, contained sufficient facts and conclusions for the Carter White House to treat it as complete absolution for the Carter Campaign financing in 1975 and 1976. But the still secret report on the details of Curran's conclusions in relating the law to facts justifiably left critics in a skeptical mood. Critics—made cynical by clever whitewash reports on Watergate and other matters—grumbled privately of another "whitewash" and "coverup." It was doubtful, however, whether any committee of the Democratic Congress would create the kind of sustained criticism necessary to jar loose from the Justice Department the full Curran report without which many questions are left in the air.

CHAPTER EIGHTEEN

MEOW—Energy Policy

On April 18, 1977, President Carter gave his first major speech on energy policy in a televised address to the nation. "I want to have an unpleasant talk with you about a problem unprecedented in our history," Mr. Carter said in that speech. "The energy crisis has not yet overwhelmed us, but it will if we do not act quickly."

The public knew he was right in stating the seriousness of the problem, which had been growing by leaps and bounds because of neglect in the Nixon and Ford administrations. When Jimmy Carter said that this difficult effort of the nation would be the "moral equivalent of war," there were public expressions of approval and a willingness to follow his lead when his program was unveiled, which was to take place before a joint session of Congress on April 20.

The Carter plan was drafted by nonpolitical technicians under the tightest secrecy. This alienated special interest groups, congressional leaders and even members of the Carter administration who felt they had expertise that was not used. This situation created an automatic opposition to even the most carefully devised energy program.

However, there was an additional problem. The new administration rushed through its drafting, which caused technical flaws that undermined confidence in the entire program.

Those technical flaws were used by special interest lobbying groups—particularly the oil and gas industry—to ridicule the Carter energy program and to raise questions about the competency of those who were advising the White House. Despite those problems and the fact that the Carter White House did a poor selling job in Congress, the Carter program was passed by the House on August 5, 1977, with only minor modifications. The House action was largely a result of President Carter's continued high standing in the polls and the work of House Speaker Thomas (Tip) O'Neill.

In the Senate it was a different story. Lobbyists were more effective in the Senate and took advantage of the sharply declining popularity of the President resulting from his ill-advised public support of his resigned Budget Director T. Bertram Lance.

The troubles of Bert Lance emerged in late July and early August, just as President Carter was signing the legislation creating a new Energy Department to consolidate the functions of the Federal Energy Administration (FEA), the Energy Research and Development Administration, the Federal Power Commission (FPC) and parts of other agencies with energy-related functions. This job of establishing the new Cabinet Department coincided with rising problems in the Senate. President Carter named his chief energy adviser, James R. Schlesinger, as Secretary of Energy.

If Schlesinger had been totally free to handle the energy problems on his own terms there would have been problems of such proportions that it might have overwhelmed him. Secretary Schlesinger, however, was not given a free hand in the selection of personnel or in the determination of policy. Omi Walden, a young Georgia woman, was pushed off on him as an Assistant Secretary. He inherited Douglas Robinson, who had the strong backing of White House Special Assistant Stuart Eizenstat. John O'Leary, the Deputy Secretary, was inherited from the FEA, where he had been the administrator. O'Leary, also former administrator of the New Mexico Energy Resources Board, came with an entourage that included William S. Heffelfinger, who became director of administration in the new agency.

All were the source of continuous controversy with influential Senators and Congressmen, who raised questions as to whether these were "the best" government officials that President Carter and Secretary Schlesinger could find for important policy and administrative positions in the new Department of Energy. Secretary Schlesinger gamely defended them against congressional critics, even though it occasionally made him look venal or foolish. Privately, he said he believed he had no alternative if he was to stay on President Carter's team.

Perhaps the best qualified of the top-level personnel in the

Energy Department was Dale D. Myers, the Under Secretary of Energy. Myers worked for Rockwell International from 1943 to 1970, starting as an aeronautical engineer and working his way up to vice president and program manager for the Space Shuttle program in 1969 and 1970. He served as associate administrator for the manned space flight at the National Aeronautics and Space Administration (NASA) from 1970 to 1974. Then he returned to Rockwell International as a corporate vice president and as president of North American Aircraft Operations.

However, Under Secretary of Energy Myers held the number three post in the Department of Energy. He was outmaneuvered by O'Leary, a clever career bureaucrat who had served as Chief of the Bureau of Natural Gas at the FPC and director of the Bureau of Mines in the Interior Department. O'Leary shrewdly built a constituency among officials of the department he regulated. He was expert at stonewalling congressional committees and at hiring management experts to help him grab areas of responsibility initially assigned to Myers. Myers finally resigned in frustration.

O'Leary was not Secretary Schlesinger's choice for the number two post in the Energy Department, but he accepted him at the insistence of the Carter White House. John Francis O'Leary, as noted, brought with him William S. Heffelfinger, whose background as Assistant Secretary of Transportation in the Nixon administration had created major controversy with important Democratic congressional committee chairmen. The investigations of Heffelfinger's activities and his misrepresentation of his background covered more than two years, resulted in the transmittal of the investigation file to the Justice Department for possible criminal prosecution and launched a full-scale examination of the policies and personnel performance in the thoroughly ineffective Department of Energy. This investigation had not been resolved completely when Charles P. Duncan, Jr., replaced Schlesinger in August 1979.

By the time President Carter moved Duncan from his position as Deputy Secretary of Defense to the Energy Secretary position, the President's "moral equivalent of war" on energy problems was being referred to generally and disparagingly by the acronym "MEOW." Although Mr. Carter defended Schlesinger against congressional attacks until the end, it was recognized that the aloof former Harvard professor was thoroughly disliked by key members of the congressional committees that dealt with energy legislation.

Even if Schlesinger had the ability to devise and implement the comprehensive energy plan the nation needed, the Carter White House never gave him the full opportunity to prove it. His programs were compromised by the political demands of Hamilton Jordan and the public relations demands of Gerald Rafshoon. He was saddled with Omi Walden as an Assistant Secretary of Energy, because she was from Georgia and because she had some limited experience in the disastrous operations of the Georgia State Energy Office.

It was at White House insistence that Schlesinger accepted O'Leary as Deputy Secretary, Douglas Robinson as a top lawyer in the enforcement division and William Heffelfinger as the director of administration. Robinson's controversial actions on the Ven-Fuel Company violations in the Ford administration were indicative of a general policy of softness with the oil industry and seemed at odds with President Carter's talk of getting tough with the oil industry.

Robinson was defended by O'Leary and other top officials of the Energy Department, who by doing so alienated important House and Senate members, who contended that while Mr. Carter talked tough against the oil industry lobbyists, the enforcement actions of his Energy Department said "Meow."

Heffelfinger, who served as a Deputy Assistant Secretary of Transportation and Assistant Secretary of Transportation in the Nixon administration, had been accused of questionable and illegal political manipulation for the Nixon White House. Heffelfinger and his supporters defended his questionable personnel actions by explaining that he was carrying out orders from superiors and the Nixon White House.

On March 14, 1978, Heffelfinger was grilled for more than an hour by Representative John D. Dingell (D.—Mich.), chairman of the House energy and power subcommittee. Most of that grilling centered on a staff report containing "evidence indicating that Heffelfinger falsified his government resumés, threatened federal officials and contractors, tried to rig a Coast Guard procurement, abused the merit system, ordered the destruction of government property and offered to provide a female companion to a management consultant who was studying Heffelfinger's agency." The *Federal Times* reported this summary of the complaints of Chairman Dingell and Representative Richard L. Ottinger, a New York Democrat.

Dingell's and Ottinger's questioning of Heffelfinger and O'Leary in the House subcommittee coincided with a similar attack by Senator Henry M. Jackson, Chairman of the Senate Energy and Natural Resources Committee. Chairman Jackson wrote a personal letter to Secretary Schlesinger asking that he review Heffelfinger's record and consider removing him from his position as director of administration.

Heffelfinger denied the direct evidence against him, and O'Leary contended that he was unfamiliar with the charges against Heffelfinger, although committees of the Senate and House had been raising questions about Heffelfinger's actions for several weeks. O'Leary and Frederick P. Hitz, director of congressional relations for the Energy Department, said that, as far as they were concerned, the charges against Heffelfinger were "unsubstantiated allegations," and they would conduct their own investigation within the agency.

Secretary of Energy Schlesinger was reported to have taken the position that he would not let congressional committees tell him whom he should fire or hire, and he had reportedly turned the problem over to O'Leary. Congressional staffers noted that O'Leary was Heffelfinger's mentor in the agency.

Grenville Garside, staff director of the Senate Energy and Natural Resources Committee, told the *Federal Times* that the Dingell subcommittee hearings had "confirmed" charges that were sufficient cause to dismiss Heffelfinger, even if all the allegations were not established with firm evidence.

"There's enough on the public record already so one doesn't wonder about what's left [unconfirmed]," Garside said.

Prior to the House hearing, staff investigators had informed Hitz of the questions that O'Leary should be prepared to face on the allegations against Heffelfinger. However, when O'Leary appeared, he said he was not aware of many of the charges leveled against Heffelfinger or of the evidence supporting those charges.

It was obvious that O'Leary did not want to know the charges or the supporting evidence, because he kept Heffelfinger in the job as director of administration throughout an internal investigation that resulted in the Heffelfinger files being sent to the Justice Department for consideration for criminal prosecution.

The first report of Inspector General J. Kenneth Mansfield spelled out the woeful lack of enforcement activity in the Department of Energy, as well as the efforts of O'Leary to cripple the new independent Inspector General's office and to keep major auditing and enforcement functions under his personal control. Mansfield, an independent-minded and experienced government investigator, had been named to the newly created Inspector General post on the urging of Senator Jackson.

By the time Mansfield's first report was issued in March 1979, the new Department of Energy had been in operation nearly eighteen months. It had been nearly two years since President Carter had promised the program that would be the "moral equivalent of war" on the nation's energy problems. There had been no effective leadership from the Carter administration, and the programs had floundered in Congress. President Carter and Secretary Schlesinger had become the whipping boys for the public and Congress, and there were demands for Secretary Schlesinger's ouster.

Periodically, President Carter and White House Press Secretary Jody Powell berated the oil lobbyists and promised to get tough with the oil industry, but the Department of Energy launched no prosecutions against the oil companies or oil company executives. Regardless of the good intentions of President Carter or Secretary Schlesinger, it seemed to be a policy of talking tough while playing soft with Big Oil.

Cartoonists, editorial writers and columnists found Carter's "moral equivalent of war" to be a joke and derisively took up the acronym "MEOW."

John Iannone, an analyst for the American Petroleum Institute (API), was called before Congress to explain his access to internal documents of the Energy Department, which included advanced drafts of proposed Energy Department regulations.

Iannone identified Gerald P. Emmer, director of petroleum allocation regulations, as one of his chief sources of material from within the Energy Department. One document included in the leaked material was a copy of a letter from Senator Edward M. Kennedy to David J. Bardin, chief of the Department's Economic Regulatory Administration.

Although Emmer denied leaking the Kennedy letter to Iannone, he admitted to being the source of advance proposals for department rules and regulations. He explained that these proposed rules could be obtained by anyone walking into the reception area of his office. He also explained that these documents containing information worth millions of dollars to the oil industry were "standing around in piles" in his office.

"We don't have any security procedures" for anything except classified documents, Emmer told a Senate Energy Subcommittee headed by Senator Howard Metzenbaum of Ohio.

Chairman Metzenbaum called another Department of Energy witness, who testified that the draft of a department rule intended for "limited circulation" to "15 people" was in fact made available to about three hundred people attending the Gas Processors Association convention in Dallas. Bardin promised to tighten the agency's security but said he did not want to isolate the agency from the industry.

Senator Metzenbaum lashed out at the seeming "insensitivity" of officials of the Energy Department in its dealing with oil lobbyists:

"We're talking about an agency's credibility. We're talking about an agency's integrity. We're talking about an agency's reputation." Metzenbaum was particularly critical of Energy Secretary Schlesinger for declining an invitation to be present at the hearings in order to explain the leaks of information to Iannone and other oil industry representatives. He criticized Schlesinger's "insensitivity to the concerns of Congress."

The March 1979 inspector general's report gave support from within the agency to the views of such critics as Senators Metzenbaum, Jackson and Proxmire, and Congressmen John Dingell and John Moss. Although Mansfield and his new team of investigators had been on the job only a few months, they were appalled at the lack of any enforcement action by the Energy Department. The Inspector General before Mansfield had operated under the direction of Deputy Secretary O'Leary, but Mansfield, operating under a new law guaranteeing independence of operation, had no need to be soft on O'Leary or anyone else in the agency.

Under the new inspector general law, Mansfield was not subject to removal by anyone but the President, and there had to be "good cause" for the removal. His report was not cleared with Schlesinger's office and became available, without censorship by the Energy Department, to the oversight committees in Congress.

Pointing out the great potential for fraud, waste and abuse in the Department of Energy, Mansfield charged that his superiors were using their authority to control the size of his staff, hoping to undermine the effectiveness of the Office of Inspector General. He did not accuse either Schlesinger or O'Leary by name or position, but the accusation was aimed at O'Leary, who was the major operational official responsible for the lack of any prosecution in the past.

In the fifty-six-page report, Mansfield called attention to the fact that the Energy Department was trying to keep his staff at one hundred—far below the 150-slot level that O'Leary had promised Congress. At the same time O'Leary was cutting Mansfield's staff level for "economy" purposes, he was expanding by more than 11 percent the number of internal auditors who would be reporting directly to O'Leary's office.

"Programs totaling billions of dollars are being audited only glancingly," Mansfield stated. "We think it is almost certain that the amount of fraud and abuse in DOE [Department of Energy] programs now being undetected, unprevented and unpunished because of our present inability to adopt a forward investigative strategy, is large."

Mansfield reported that there were four general areas where there had been essentially no investigation in the past and where the programs were "unusually susceptible to waste and . . . fraud." He cited the following:

"(1). Areas where large amounts of money are being spent in accordance with timetables and schedules requiring rapid commitments of funds. The Strategic Petroleum Reserve Program is an example.

"(2). Areas where the monetary gains resulting from successful evasion of laws and regulations can be very large. Regulations concerning permissible oil prices provide an example.

"(3). Areas of high technological risk-taking. These would include a wide array of energy projects including coal gasification and liquefaction, and certain solar projects.

"(4). Areas presenting unusually difficult monitoring and control problems. These would include the programs for providing weatherization assistance to low-income families."

While Mansfield was praised widely in Congress for his forthright criticism of the Energy Department's enforcement efforts, Deputy Secretary O'Leary took issue with him. In a prepared statement, O'Leary said that Mansfield's comments on frauds were "potentially misleading and could be unfair."

O'Leary argued that his efforts to limit the investigators available to Mansfield's office was in line with President Carter's interest in keeping government payroll costs down and was not intended to curb Mansfield's investigations of fraud and mismanagement.

Mansfield came back with specifics on the types of mismanagement that had wasted millions of dollars. He called attention to the Strategic Petroleum Reserve Programs for storing emergency reserves of oil in salt domes in Louisiana and Texas.

"We found that DOE had paid over $1 million for standby time while four expensive well drilling rigs were going idle and unused," Mansfield told Congress. "Our expression of concern contributed to actions taken by DOE to make management changes in the drilling contractor operations and to develop procedures for minimizing standby time.

"We issued an investigative report in which we concluded that the Department had been maintaining a double standard of access to information that favored the American Petroleum Institute over members of the public who relied on DOE's formal procedures," Mansfield said. "The information in question included drafts of proposed rulemakings that would directly affect the financial interests of API's member oil companies. Corrective action has been taken or is in prospect."

Mansfield reported that "the H-Coal project" was behind schedule on a coal liquefaction pilot plant project and "is experiencing a more than $100 million overrun." "Our review focused attention on management weaknesses which resulted in the waste of millions of dollars," Mansfield said. "The Department informs us that 'massive' corrective action is under way."

Mansfield reported that the inspector general's office was ready to turn over to prosecution authorities any action "that bears upon possible criminal wrongdoing in the Strategic Petroleum Reserve Program."

"The suspected criminality relates to such matters as bribes and large-scale thefts of costly DOE-financed capital equipment items," Mansfield reported. Mansfield told a Senate Government Affairs subcommittee that his staff had only scratched the surface on the corruption and mismanagement that had been festering for months in the Department of Energy and its predecessors.

In the summer of 1979 evidence from the investigations of Inspector General Mansfield and his staff was emerging in the form of prosecutions and documentation of past DOE actions that served the interests of the oil industry rather than the consumer.

It was against this background that the gasoline shortages developed. President Jimmy Carter prepared to make a major energy speech in early July and retired to Camp David with the stated purpose of putting the last touches on this important address.

At Camp David on July 4, President Carter read over the original draft of the energy speech that his aides had written for him. His first impression was that it was a good speech, but after discussions with Rosalyn, Hamilton Jordan and White House pollster Patrick Caddell, he changed his mind. Without explanation to the press, the public, or anyone else except his most intimate advisers, he canceled the speech and started a week of soul-searching about his personal political problems, the nation's economic problems and the general public impression that he was not a good leader.

Public opinion polls were uniformly consistent in rating him at about the same low levels that Richard Nixon reached that period in the summer of 1974 just before his resignation. Those same polls were consistent in indicating that Senator Edward M. Kennedy was much more popular with the Democratic Party and would probably be a shoo-in for the Democratic nomination if he would so much as indicate his availability in 1980.

The press and public reaction to the suddcn unexplained cancellation of a major Presidential speech was one of bewilderment and shock. Had President Carter lost his senses under the pressure of the job? What was ahead for a floundering nation if Jimmy Carter became a recluse at Camp David?

Just as suddenly, President Carter and his top aides started contacting politicians and "religious and ethical leaders," who were flown in and out of Camp David for a feverish week of activity. Carter, Jordan, White House Press Secretary Jody Powell and chief image-builder Gerald Rafshoon were setting the stage for the President to emerge with a new leadership image. They also had the job of providing some reasonable and sane explanation for the sudden cancellation of the energy speech scheduled for the first week in July. It was an almost impossible task for any White House staff, and the Carter White House staff had not demonstrated a reputation for high competency in solving difficult problems.

The new speech that emerged from those twelve days of political, economic and spiritual soul-searching was a disappointment even as it achieved one of its main goals—getting the nation's attention on the new Jimmy Carter and his energy program initiatives. Even though that speech on Sunday night, July 15, was given with more forceful gestures and was spoken in a louder voice, it seemed contrived and wooden. Democrats and Republicans tried to find laudatory comments that would apply to either the President's presentation of the substance of the vague "new initiatives,'' which he had stated for the third or fourth time. Over and over, in the July speech and in follow-up speeches in Detroit and Kansas City, he spoke of his ''leadership'' and of the forceful direction he intended to give the new programs from a reorganized government and a reorganized White House.

On July 17 President Carter started the massive shake-up of the Cabinet to demonstrate the forceful ''new Carter'' leadership; he promised drastic changes in the White House staff, which was generally regarded as the heart of the problem. When President Carter fired Secretary of Health, Education and Welfare Joseph Califano, Secretary of the Treasury Michael Blumenthal, Secretary of Transportation Brock Adams and Secretary of Energy James Schlesinger, he left an impression that survival was linked with obedience to White House dictates and the ability to get along with Hamilton Jordan and the other Georgians.

The impression of chaos in the purge planning was heightened by the fact that the announcements on the first firings included the resignation of his old Georgia friend, Attorney General Griffin Bell. Bell's desire to resign was well known. He had already hand-picked his successor—Deputy Attorney General Benjamin Civiletti. Attorney General Bell commented publicly on the ''poor timing'' involved in the acceptance of his resignation during the same time period as the firings.

It was generally believed that the massive purge was handled in such a brutal manner that it destroyed any sympathy Mr. Carter had won with his new attacks on the admittedly overwhelming problems of inflation and high fuel costs.

While it was debatable whether it would be helpful to the nation to shift Secretary of HUD Patricia Harris to replace Joseph Califano at the Department of Health, Education and Welfare, or whether G. William Miller, chairman of the Federal Reserve Board, would bring some important new quality to the post of Secretary of the Treasury, there seemed little doubt that replacement of Secretary of Energy James Schlesinger was essential. Secretary Schlesinger had become a target for the barbs of Senators, Congressmen and others who were displeased with the energy mess and did not wish to place the blame on President Carter. Secretary Schlesinger had certainly been ineffective in keeping the White House tamperers out of important personnel and policy decisions.

Deputy Defense Secretary Charles W. Duncan, Jr., seemed to be a good choice as Schlesinger's replacement because of his sharp contrast in style. While Schlesinger was regarded as a brilliant man, he either did not know how to manage or was unable to manage effectively because of White House interference. Duncan, as the number two man in Defense, had a reputation as a good manager, was independently wealthy and was able to make it clear he would not tolerate White House meddling in the housecleaning he proposed at the Energy Department. Meanwhile, John O'Leary and a number of others who were considered by Congress to be "bad influences" in the administration of the Energy Department announced their intentions to resign.

In wielding the new broom at the Department of Energy, Secretary Charles Duncan made at least one significant compromise to please the Georgians in the White House: Duncan asked Omi Walden to leave her $52,750-a-year job as Assistant Secretary of Energy for Conservation and Solar Application, but at the same time, he created a new $50,112-a-year position for the Georgia Peach as his Special Advisor for Conservation and Solar Energy. Despite a poor to mediocre record, Omi Walden was still clearly a "must" in the new Duncan-directed Department of Energy. Duncan, who was an executive with Coca-Cola in Georgia when Carter was governor, was another of the earlier "connections."

Duncan, a quiet fifty-two-year-old Houston businessman, had a long-time personal relationship with President Carter that had started when he was serving as president of Coca-Cola in Atlanta and Carter was Governor of Georgia. At the Defense Department he had been regarded as an effective and essential manager for Defense Secretary Harold Brown over a period of more than two years.

If Duncan was the right man to handle the mammoth Energy Department, why had not President Carter replaced personnel in the Energy Department earlier, when he had declared the "moral equivalent of war" on the nation's energy problems? Duncan's job included fending off White House political tampering if he was expected to change the weak "MEOW" image to the true "moral equivalent of war." However, there was little change in the White House staff, only the solidification of Hamilton Jordan's power as the White House Chief of Staff. This was the final step to centralize the power in a White House Chief of Staff that President Carter had said he would never take when he criticized the structure of the Nixon White House under H. R. (Bob) Haldeman.

CHAPTER NINETEEN

Seeking the Leader Image

President Carter, with his top advisers, succeeded in getting the nation's attention in order to deliver his major energy speech for 1979, again seeking to rally the Congress for quick action on his energy program in September. Mr. Carter, Rosalyn, Ham Jordan, Gerald Rafshoon and Pat Caddell, while not conceding publicly that there was any lack of leadership qualities in the President, did recognize that there was a public perception that Jimmy Carter was not a leader. That perception was interfering with the Carter game plan for the 1980 re-election of the President.

President Carter and his Georgians were forced to acknowledge that the public perception of Jimmy Carter as an ineffective President had something to do with his failure to persuade the Congress to respond to his programs for dealing with the twin horrors—inflation and the energy crunch. In addition to the continued presence of these nagging insoluble problems, there was the ever present Senator Edward M. Kennedy, smiling and confident, repeating his carefully thought-out one-line response to questions concerning his political intentions in 1980.

There was no comfort for the White House in Senator Kennedy's repeated assertions that he assumed that President Carter would be the Democratic Presidential candidate in 1980 and that if Carter was the nominee, he would support him. The repetition of that position by Ted Kennedy had reached the point of high political comedy, even though the Massachusetts Senator managed to suppress the smile on most occasions.

It was unsettling for the Carter White House when friends and supporters of Senator Kennedy went about the country establishing political organizations for 1980 even as Senator Kennedy said they had no encouragement from him or his political staff. The Georgians believed that Senator Kennedy could have stopped all of the activity of Kennedy for President movements in California, Iowa, Florida and New Hampshire by passing along a private word that he was not interested in the Presidency. They believed that Senator Kennedy was influential enough with his supporters to have stopped them from the politically brutal attacks on President Carter, which pictured him as a "weak" and "ineffective" President and a well-intentioned religious zealot who was incapable of carrying out his presidential responsibilities.

If such campaign tactics were used by Republicans, that might be written off as partisan political judgments. But when Democrats attacked other Democrats, that represented a political hazard for the future. Privately, the White House Georgians and others with a stake in Carter's re-election fumed and blamed Kennedy for their problems. They argued that the Massachusetts Senator should come out in the open and engage in "a fair fight."

T. Bertram Lance, under federal indictment for alleged bank frauds, was still a low-profile Carter supporter who asserted with confidence that Carter would win the Democratic nomination and would go on to win re-election in 1980. The way Bert Lance viewed it in August 1979, Senator Kennedy could not win the Democratic nomination unless he openly declared himself as a candidate for President some months before the primaries.

"You can't beat somebody with nobody," Lance declared in his wooded retreat near Calhoun, Georgia, where he was planning for his defense against the indictments. "The minute that Kennedy declares his candidacy, he becomes fair game on Chappaquidick and on his programs," Lance said. "Even those who lack confidence in Jimmy Carter's leadership have great admiration and respect for his Christian principles. It is a respect they won't have for Kennedy when the Chappaquidick issue gets worked over in the primary campaigns."

Lance declared that Senator Kennedy "may have charisma, but when his programs are analyzed beside Jimmy Carter's more moderate approach, I am certain the majority will be with Carter." Lance gave as an example the national health program, on which Carter was in a better position "on the issues" than Kennedy, whose "program is so irresponsible it would bankrupt the nation."

While Lance declined to discuss his continuing contacts with

President Carter and others in the Carter White House, he said he did not consider President Carter or Attorney General Bell responsible in any manner for the multicount bank fraud indictment that was returned against him and three others in May 1979.

Lance said that he was certain that President Carter still viewed him as innocent of criminal wrongdoing and as the victim of Carter's political enemies and the press, who "are trying to hurt Carter through prosecution of me." Nor did Lance, a political realist, blame Attorney General Bell for not stepping in and blocking the indictments. Lance blamed "the press" and "some ambitious prosecutors" for stirring up resentment against him and creating a situation in which "neither President Carter nor the Attorney General could have done more than they did."

The former Calhoun banker spoke confidently of winning his case "in the end." He hopes to have the indictments tossed out by a United States District Judge in Georgia, and he is also confident that a Georgia jury will not be moved by the evidence amassed by "ambitious prosecutors." "They will recognize that what I did was what takes place in almost every small town bank in our part of the country where the banker is trying to help his friends and the community," Lance said.

If all of his hopes for an understanding federal judge and a sympathetic jury are swept away in a conviction, Lance said, "I won't panic, and am prepared to take whatever is ahead," in the criminal trial which at that time was scheduled tentatively for early 1980.

In an interview at his wooded country office, Lance told this reporter he did not fear indictment for helping to arrange the multimillion-dollar series of loans from the National Bank of Georgia to the Carter Warehouse in 1975 and 1976. "They were simply business loans, and only unusual in that they were a new field of agribusiness," Lance said. "I was president of the bank and left the day-to-day handling of the mechanics to subordinates. It was no conspiracy to get [illegal] money into the Carter campaign [for President]. If Billy Carter put some of that money into Jimmy's campaign, I didn't know anything about it, and I still don't know anything about it.

"As far as I am concerned, these were good loans to the Carter Warehouse, and they have been repaid in full," Lance said. "The same thing is true as far as Rafshoon's loans were concerned." Lance declined to answer any specific questions about the details of the loan arrangements to the Carter Warehouse or to Rafshoon, "because I don't know anything about the day-to-day work on these loans. I was president of the bank."

Lance said he did not believe that Carter would be hurt politically by his trial, scheduled for early 1980. "I expect to be acquitted, and that will be vindication for me and for Jimmy Carter for supporting me," Lance said. Although confident of acquittal, Lance said that a conviction might do some small political damage to Carter.

At the height of the controversy over Carter's Cabinet purge, it was suggested facetiously by an Atlanta newspaper columnist that President Carter should take a leaf from President Ford's book and "pardon Bert Lance before he is convicted" and bring him back to Washington to provide some knowledgeable leadership in the White House.

Critics of the continuing close relationship between President Carter and Lance comment that the Calhoun banker might have good reason for total confidence that he will never go to prison in connection with the bank fraud indictments. It was so reasoned since President Carter often stated his belief that Lance is "a good man" and that he was not involved in illegal actions. It would take no radical change in that rationalization to justify a pardon for Lance after the 1980 election.

Jimmy Carter, whether re-elected or defeated in 1980, will be in a position to use his absolute power to grant an unconditional pardon to relieve his friend of any convictions, pending indictments or potential future indictments. After the 1980 election, Carter would not have to be concerned about the political impact of a pardon for Lance. Is it likely? Jimmy Carter has already demonstrated the greatest of loyalty and appreciation for Lance's friendship in public comments when it meant political risk. Would it be likely that he would demonstrate less loyalty when the political risks are behind him?

Either as a lame duck President or as a victorious presidential candidate, barred by law from seeking a third term, Jimmy Carter would have less reason to be concerned with public opinion that President Gerald Ford had when he granted Richard Nixon a full and unconditional pardon for any crimes he might have committed while President.

However, in the fall of 1979, the positive-thinking Bert Lance said he was not thinking in terms of being convicted of federal crimes or of Jimmy Carter's losing the Presidency. Granting that Hamilton Jordan was short on the qualities required to administer the White House, Lance still viewed the thirty-four-year-old Albany, Georgia, man "as a kind of a political strategy genius," and he viewed Jimmy Carter as "the most determined man I have ever known.

"When Jimmy wants something, he will do absolutely anything to win," Lance said. Lance recalled that it was Jordan who put together the famous planning paper that Carter used in 1974, 1975 and 1976 to win the Democratic nomination and the Presidency.

Lance disavowed any role in the Carter–Jordan planning for 1980 but declared that President Carter can defeat Senator Kennedy for the nomination "because Kennedy's programs will not stand scrutiny because they are too expensive and because they cannot be administered.

"Jimmy Carter's more moderate programs will have more appeal because they are in tune with the moderation that is the majority sentiment in the country," Lance said.

Bert Lance scoffed at the idea that Jimmy Carter's July massacre would have any lasting impact on his political future either inside or outside of the Democratic party. "The average voter out there doesn't know much about Joe Califano or Schlesinger, and doesn't care much about what happens to them," Lance said. "They probably don't even recognize the names of Mike Blumenthal or Brock Adams, and figure that any change must be for the better."

Those with any knowledge of Joe Califano will be those who hated him for his crusade against smoking, so it will be a plus for Carter in the tobacco growing states, Lance explained. "Those who know Schlesinger's name will identify him with the energy program and the congressional demands that he be fired," Lance said. "They will probably figure that the President was right to have fired him."

As far as the overall impact of the Cabinet purge was concerned, Lance said he expected "it would put the fear of God" into others at the top level in government "who have been leaking out stories that have hurt Jimmy Carter."

Lance said he did not view with alarm the naming of Hamilton Jordan as White House Chief of Staff. "Jimmy needs Hamilton and he can trust him to do what is best for the Carter administration,'' Lance said. While he was mildly critical of Jordan for ''a careless life style'' in his first months in the White House, Lance said he believed Jordan had ''learned from some mistakes, and will work to do a good job.''

Lance said that he believed the White House would be strengthened by moving Robert Lipshutz out of the White House Counsel post and appointing to fill his post an experienced lawyer who knew the Washington scene. Lance said that Bob Lipshutz, an Atlanta lawyer, had done an excellent job as treasurer for the Carter presidential campaign in 1975 and 1976 but had ''been out of his element in the White House.'' Lance said he believed that Lipshutz should be replaced by a well-respected Washington lawyer like Clark Clifford. Clifford had served as counsel for Lance when he appeared before the Senate Government Affairs Committee and had given such a spectacular performance that many casual observers believed he had saved Lance's job as Director of the Office of Management and Budget.

Within a few days after this reporter's interview with Lance, it was announced that Robert Lipshutz was resigning as Counsel to the President and was being replaced by Washington lawyer Lloyd Cutler. Cutler, sixty-two, was a member of one of Washington's largest and most prominent law firms—Wilmer, Cutler and Pickering. Cutler, a long-time Democrat, was one of the first prominent Washington lawyers to be identified with the antiwar movement. Just prior to his appointment, he was involved in advising President Carter on the plan for getting Salt II approved.

Although Cutler was a classic liberal in his opposition to the Vietnam War, his corporate clients and his reputation as a lawyer-lobbyist won him the disfavor of some consumer advocates such as Ralph Nader and a few like-minded members of the Senate and House. Cutler, as a representative of various corporate interests, had supported the idea of giving the President a veto power over most government regulatory agency decisions. In the week before his appointment he had spoken in support of those views at a meeting of the American Bar Association in Dallas. This caused some grumbling from liberals, who saw broadening of the presidential veto power over regulatory agency decisions as an overconcentration of power in the hands of the President.

However, the Cutler appointment as White House Counsel did not require Senate confirmation, and there was no organized forum where critics could voice their displeasure over Lloyd Cutler. It was doubtful that President Carter would have paid any attention if they had been able to find a forum, for he was convinced that his entire reorganization was "in the best interest of the nation."

To demonstrate his new leadership, he rejected the minor objections to his nomination of former New Orleans Mayor Moon Landrieu to be Secretary of Housing and Urban Development. Questions of "conflicts of interest" were raised in connection with the Landrieu nomination because of his involvement with various real estate ventures in Louisiana and Florida.

One of the alleged "conflicts of interest" involved the fact that Mr. Landrieu was hired by a New Orleans real estate developer named Joseph C. Canizaro shortly after leaving office as Mayor of New Orleans in May 1978. While he was Mayor of New Orleans, Landrieu had taken part in arranging a land swap through which Canizaro's real estate firm had been given 3.7 acres of city land that was important to the firm's multimillion-dollar development on the riverfront known as Canal Place. Landrieu was made a partner in Canizaro's firm without putting up any capital only a few months after leaving city office. He explained that it was not an improper relationship because his 10 percent share was to be paid out of future profits, so could not be a reward for past favors.

President Carter and the White House staff were unaware of Landrieu's dealing with Canizaro at the time Mr. Carter announced Landrieu as his choice for Secretary of HUD to replace Patricia Harris, who was named Secretary of Health, Education and Welfare. Nor was Mr. Carter aware of Landrieu's interest in Pier House, a Key West land deal involving the purchase and plans for redevelopment with grants and loans from HUD.

However, Landrieu quickly announced that he would insulate himself from any HUD decisions dealing with the Canal Street Project or Pier House if he were confirmed and would also divest himself of his interest in those properties. President Carter accepted Landrieu's solution to the conflict problem, and sent the nomination to the Senate for scrutiny by the Senate Banking Committee. Moon Landrieu had the warm endorsement and backing of Senators Russell B. Long and J. Bennett Johnston, both Democrats of Louisiana and key figures in the handling of energy legislation.

While the newspapers examined in as much detail as possible the circumstances under which Landrieu had acquired his controversial holdings in several properties at virtually no cost, neither the Republicans nor the Democrats were disposed to challenge the nomination, which could have resulted in an early confrontation on the leadership qualities of the "new Jimmy Carter." It was to the benefit of the whole nation if President Carter was not discouraged immediately in his new leadership initiatives.

William Proxmire, Chairman of the Senate Banking Committee, led the extensive questioning of Landrieu in exploring details of the explanations of how Landrieu obtained the properties, his plans for disposal of those properties, his pledges to insulate himself from HUD decisions on those properties and his promise that he would not return to work for Canizaro after his term as Secretary of HUD ended.

Landrieu told the Banking Committee that he would lose millions by his decision to sell his interests in the Canal Street Project in New Orleans. He characterized that prospect as "painful" but said he was willing to make the sacrifice because of his interest in public service in political office.

The former New Orleans mayor put his net worth at about $280,000 in papers filed with the committee and explained that selling the 10 percent interest in the Canal Street Project could cost him $5 million in anticipated profits over the next five years and as much as $30 million over the next thirty years. He told the Banking Committee that Canizaro conceived the idea of the Canal Street Project river development when Landrieu was Mayor of New Orleans. The $350 million riverfront development was contingent upon Canizaro's being able to persuade the city to trade him 3.7 acres of land near Canal Street for 1.5 acres of more valuable downtown land that Canizaro owned, Landrieu said, admitting a role in getting that swap approved.

Landrieu related that later, when he left his job as mayor, he received job offers from Canizaro and others to work as a land development expert. Canizaro's first offer was $75,000 a year plus a 5 percent interest in the Canal Street Project, Landrieu said. He accepted when Canizaro boosted the offer to $100,000 and a 10 percent interest. Landrieu estimated that the 10 percent interest might be worth as much as $500,000 today.

At the time Landrieu was confirmed, there was an application pending at HUD for a $5 million grant to New Orleans that would be beneficial to the Canal Street Project, and Landrieu pledged to insulate himself from that decision and from pending decisions on a HUD grant being sought by the Pier House project in Florida.

Landrieu testified that he bought a 5 percent interest in the Pier House project for $5,000 and estimated that it might be worth $200,000. The unliquidated estimated profits from Pier House and the Canal Street Project were not included in his estimated $280,000 net worth.

He said he went into the Pier House project with Leon Irwin, a close friend and former political campaign leader. He explained a third profitable real estate project with another friend and campaign manager, Blake Arata.

Landrieu related that he put $300 into the Port Madison Project, which was organized by Arata in 1971, and he wound up in 1978 with a $58,000 profit when the partnership was dissolved. He said that this transaction took place while he was Mayor of New Orleans but explained that the property was outside of New Orleans. The big profit was achieved because the purchase was made almost entirely on loans and doubled in value in the period that he and Arata held it.

When the Landrieu hearing was concluded, Chairman Proxmire said that he believed he had done his job in exploring in detail the controversial transactions and in getting Landrieu to state that he would insulate himself from HUD actions. He said he was certain that Landrieu would be confirmed promptly by the Senate. And he was—on a voice vote.

Senate sympathy for a floundering Jimmy Carter seemed to have helped the Landrieu nomination in the Senate, where there were often major political confrontations on nominations with less evidence of conflict of interest. A floundering Jimmy Carter had declared that Moon Landrieu was one of the members of the new team that he needed to make the government more effective. No one in the Senate wanted to give the Carter White House the excuse that the Senate had stood in the way of his getting the people he said he needed to run an effective government, least of all Senator Proxmire, who feared he was acquiring the image of "the abominable no man" for his opposition to Carter's policies and people.

While Moon Landrieu might turn out to be the strong and effective leader that HUD needed, the nomination of a man with so many potential conflicts of interest was a far cry from the higher standards that President Carter had said he would impose upon the government in the 1976 campaign and in his first months as President.

Mr. Carter's problem of demonstrating leadership was further compounded in September 1979, when his newly designated White House Chief of Staff was accused by the owners of New York's Studio 54 disco of having sniffed cocaine. It was an allegation by men who were at that time under income tax fraud investigation, yet it created a condition in which the Federal Bureau of Investigation was required to investigate under the provisions of a new federal ethics law.

There were loud denials by Jordan and by two other Carter administration officials who had accompanied him to Studio 54 in 1978, but the new law requires a federal investigation of all charges of law violations against high-level government officials. While there was considerable press sympathy for Jordan and a willingness to believe that his denials were true, it had to be conceded that he had visited Studio 54, where the use of illegal narcotics was commonplace and was even encouraged.

Before that allegation had been investigated and disposed of, Ham Jordan was hit with still another charge that he had sniffed cocaine at a political party in Beverly Hills in October 1977. Again the FBI had to be brought into the investigation of a matter that would have normally been handled by local law enforcement officers, and another cloud of suspicion was cast over the White House Chief of Staff while he was trying to give some centralized direction to the Carter White House.

Such charges, whether true or false, made both Jordan and President Carter vulnerable to critics who resented the tougher political line required to discipline the government. A tougher line was being taken to curtail the political adventures of those who supported Senator Edward M. Kennedy for the Democratic presidential nomination in 1980.

It was difficult to say that the accusations against Jordan were important in sending Mr. Carter's stock to new lows in mid-1979. A poll sponsored by the National Broadcasting Company and the Associated Press showed that only 19 percent of those polled believed that Mr. Carter was doing either a "good" or "excellent" job of running the government. It was a lower rating than either President Truman or President Nixon had in their darkest political hours.

While the relaxed living style of Hamilton Jordan might have contributed to Mr. Carter's problems, the eccentric diplomatic activity of Ambassador Andrew Young shared in the responsibility for the doubts about President Carter's leadership qualities.

CHAPTER TWENTY

Andy Young—Ambassador Extraordinary

When Andrew Young, a Democratic Congressman from Georgia, was sworn in as Ambassador to the United Nations, President Carter outdid himself in praise of the black Georgian who had been his contant shield against critics accusing him of any type of racism.

"Of all the people I have ever known in public service, Andy Young is the best," President Carter said at the swearing-in ceremony in the large East Room of the White House. In that one sentence he outdid former Presidents Lyndon Johnson and Richard Nixon, who usually lavished unrestrained praise on those they were appointing to high office. In praising their appointees, they, of course, were praising themselves for being able to attract men of such quality to serve in high office.

President Nixon spoke of "the special dimension" of each of his Cabinet officers, but at no time did he designate any one of them as "the best" of the Cabinet or as "the best" he had ever known in his whole public life.

President Carter, after reviewing the various traits of brilliance, courage, sensitivity and independence that Young possessed, told the assembled group of Young's friends and admirers that Young "did not want or ask for this job." "I wanted Andy to be the Ambassador of our country to the United Nations for a long time," Carter said. "And it was only with the greatest reluctance on his part that he finally agreed to do it for me and for our country."

President Carter told the group that he, Andrew Young, Secretary of State Cyrus Vance and National Security Adviser Zbigniew Brzezinski had spent a full two hours discussing "the most difficult and challenging international questions that our country faces.

"It was a reassuring thing to have Andrew Young there," Mr. Carter said. "I hope to measure up as President to the standards that he sets as Ambassador to the United Nations. His status will be equal to that of Secretary of State or the Secretary of the Treasury or anyone else. And his closeness to me personally will ensure that there is never a division of sense of purpose . . . as he deals with almost 150 other nations' leaders in New York and around the world."

Even before he took his seat as Ambassador to the United Nations, the outspoken Andy Young made the first of a long series of controversial comments that were periodically to result in embarrassment to President Carter and Secretary of State Vance. In a television interview on CBS, Young declared that the Cuban troops then fighting in Africa "bring a certain stability and order to Angola." He pictured Premier Fidel Castro's troops and tanks as "basically doing technical assistance" and philosophized, "I don't believe that Cuba is in Africa because it was ordered there by the Russians. I believe that Cuba is in Africa because it really has shared in a sense of colonial oppression and domination."

It was a position that was at odds with U.S. policy in Africa, and later he scrambled to explain his views in terms that did not make him appear as an apologist for Cuba's adventurism.

Young's comments at various points on a trip through Africa caused further controversy, but there was little or no reaction from President Carter or Secretary of State Vance, who viewed Andy Young as the point man on evolving changes of policy with regard to South Africa and Rhodesia, and their relationships with various Black African nations.

On April 11 Young held a news conference at the State Department to explain his statements in the context of U.S. policy. He declared that former U.S. policy in Africa had been based upon seeing that continent as an extension of the "cold war" between the United States and the Soviet Union.

"The only thing I'm thinking is, don't get paranoid about a few Communists," Young said. He noted that Egypt, Nigeria,

Zambia and Tanzania had some military or economic missions from the Soviet Union or Mainland China, and that had not meant Communist domination. He criticized the "knee-jerk reaction" in U.S. policy that viewed every Communist mission as a Communist takeover effort.

From the outset, it was apparent that Andrew Young was to be the point man for Jimmy Carter's effort to woo the Third World nations of Africa, Asia, South America and the Middle East. That was all in keeping with President Carter's campaign for human rights, which, at least in theory, was to be pushed with single-minded courage and without regard for whose feelings were irritated. Certainly it would be commendable that, when Jimmy Carter became President, he affirm and reaffirm from time to time the interests of the United States in pushing human rights for all persons in all parts of the world without regard for race, color or religion.

But it was perceived by many liberal as well as conservative columnists that President Carter and Ambassador Andrew Young were harping on that subject on many occasions when it was ill-advised to raise the subject. Occasionally, it was done by President Carter under circumstances that gave the appearance of being a gratuitous slap at the Soviet Union and had no particular relevance to the arms control talks or other international topics upon which we were seeking accommodations. Frequently President Carter, Andrew Young and others in the administration raised questions of "human rights" in a way that created problems for authoritarian rulers in Iran, Nicaragua and other nations who were generally aligned with the United States. There was a constant barrage of charges of "human rights" violations in South Africa and in Rhodesia, where governments—generally aligned with the Western world—were fighting for survival against Marxist-led guerrilla groups financed and supported by the Soviet Union or Cuba.

It took months for President Carter to drop the "human rights" evangelism from his speeches. He finally learned to use that action only if there was a direct issue that had to be confronted. However, Ambassador Young continued to use his forum at the United Nations and his celebrity as a traveling representative of the United States to sympathize with revolutionary groups, such as the Palestine Liberation Organization (PLO) terrorists, and to dramatize the fact that he was one American official who could be objective and even sympathetic to the positions of the Soviet Union and Premier Fidel Castro in Cuba.

Because President Carter refused to rebuke Andy Young publicly, it was difficult or impossible to tell whether Andy Young was carrying out his own foreign policy or speaking with President Carter's private encouragement and approval. The unspoken anguish of Secretary of State Cyrus Vance made it obvious that, on at least a few occasions, he was not fully in accord with Ambassador Young's comments or his timing.

The unusual freedom with which the handsome and articulate Ambassador spoke was unique in American history. It was hard to imagine any other President in the last fifty years who would have had the high tolerance level that Mr. Carter exhibited where Andy Young's comments were the issue. Certainly, Midge Costanza, Bella Abzug, Joseph Califano, Michael Blumenthal and Brock Adams were fired for demonstrating independence in much less flamboyant ways.

Andy Young went his own free-wheeling way with the confidence that his personal relationship with Carter would save him from any public rebuke. However, in July 1978 Andy Young told a Paris-based Socialist newspaper, *Le Matin,* that there were "hundreds, perhaps even thousands, of political prisoners in the U.S."

That interview was published on July 12, only a few hours before Secretary of State Vance was to meet in Geneva with Soviet Foreign Minister Andrei Gromyko for the purpose of delivering a personal message from President Carter deploring the Soviet treatment of dissidents Anatoly Shcharansky and Alexander Ginzburg.

It appeared that the Soviets were going ahead with the trial of Shcharansky and Ginzburg on the eve of the scheduled SALT negotiations in defiance of the expressed U.S. criticism. The message Vance carried to Gromyko from Carter was again to emphasize the strong U.S. opposition to the mistreatment of these dissidents. With the knowledge of the scheduled SALT negotiations, and with the knowledge that President Carter was pushing the "human rights" issue for dissidents Shcharansky and Ginzburg, Andy Young had felt free to comment in an area that was sensitive to Soviet–American relations.

Secretary Vance had criticized the Shcharansky and Ginzburg trials and declared that those trials would "inevitably affect the climate of our relations and impose obstacles to the building of confidence and cooperation between our countries." There was sharp criticism of the Soviet Union in Congress, and there were suggestions that the SALT talks, as well as two pending major business transactions, should be canceled.

In that climate, Young said he did not believe that the Soviet trials of the two dissidents should call for suspension of the SALT negotiations. In trying to put the Soviet Union's trial of dissidents in perspective, Young compared the Soviet Union favorably with the United States and also made reference to his own incarceration in Atlanta for his role in a civil rights protest movement.

"After all, in our prisons as well, there are hundreds, perhaps thousands of people whom I would call political prisoners," Young said. "I myself was sentenced ten years ago in Atlanta for having organized a protest movement. And three years later I was a Representative for Georgia. It is true that things don't change that quickly in the Soviet Union, but they do change there also."

Tass, the Soviet news agency, grabbed the quotation from Ambassador Young and characterized it as an admission by a high U.S. official that "political persecution is widespread" in the United States.

Faced with congressional calls for Young's resignation or impeachment, the Carter administration issued its first public criticism of Andy Young. But it was probably the most diplomatic rebuke ever orchestrated by any administration for an Ambassador who had, through carelessness or by design, made public statements so much at odds with what a President and Secretary of State were seeking to get across to the world.

First, White House Press Secretary Jody Powell said that Ambassador Young's statement "does not represent the policies of this administration." Then, Secretary of State Vance met with Young and afterward issued a statement that he was "very displeased" with Young's remarks. Finally, Powell told reporters that President Carter had telephoned Young and "told him he was unhappy" about his choice of words. Powell said that Young had told the President that it was "a mistake" to have made the comments to the reporters for *Le Matin,* and Young had "apologized for the troubles he had caused."

With that cautious reprimand, it was no surprise to the Washington press corps or to the Congress that Ambassador Andy Young continued on his free-wheeling way, seeming to pay little or no attention to the words of caution given to him in his private talks with President Carter and Secretary Vance. His was a special portfolio with special responsibilities to be supportive of the Marxist-led blacks who were not satisfied with the new moderate black government that had been installed by a free election in Rhodesia.

Ambassador Young gave the revolution against the Shah of Iran a big boost when he pronounced that the Ayatollah Khomeini was a misunderstood "saint." Young's comments were made in the period just before the religious leader returned to Iran to embark upon a zealous and bloody purge that was to shock the world for months. With Khomeini's actions mocking the "saint" label nearly every day, Ambassador Young embarked upon still another controversial diplomatic venture with representatives of the terrorist revolutionaries in the PLO.

The secret meetings with the representatives of the PLO were flatly contrary to U.S. policy in the sensitive negotiations to bring about a peaceful settlement in the Middle East. Apparently Ambassador Young, without consultation with President Carter or Secretary of State Vance, launched his own exploratory diplomatic mission at a particularly sensitive time. Israeli Prime Minister Menachem Begin and Egyptian President Anwar Sadat were relying upon the United States to abide by a pledge of "no recognition" and "no diplomatic contact" with representatives of the terrorists who were trying to destroy the agreements President Carter had helped to forge at Camp David.

When the admittedly questionable talks with PLO representatives first surfaced, Young misrepresented the facts to the State Department, with the result that the State Department issued denials that there had been any meeting between Young and representatives of the PLO. Later it was determined that there had been a meeting but that it was a social meeting, and there were no discussions of any matters with diplomatic substance.

Finally, caught up in his own contradictions, Ambassador Young admitted he had met with Terzi, an influential PLO representative, at the New York apartment of Abdullah Yacoub Bishara, Kuwait's U.N. ambassador. Without clearing with Secretary Vance or anyone else in the State Department or with the White House, Young had gone to Bishara's apartment with full knowledge that Terzi was to be there for discussions of Arab bloc support for the postponement of a Security Council debate on Palestinian rights.

What he did was to seek a compromise in the interests of the United States by appealing directly to Terzi as a representative of the PLO. However, his actions were admittedly a violation of U.S.

policy as established when former Secretary of State Henry Kissinger pledged to Israel that the United States would not "recognize or negotiate with" the PLO until the PLO recognized Israel's right to exist.

Although Ambassador Young had frankly told Israel's U.N. Ambassador, Yehuda Blum, about his meeting with Terzi, he had not explained it fully to the representative of the U.S. State Department, Assistant Secretary of State Charles William Maynes. The result was a series of errors by State Department spokesmen in explaining Young's actions to the press.

The State Department was embarrassed to be caught peddling falsehoods, and the State Department, in turn, said it was because Young had lied or misrepresented to Maynes. It was a no-win situation for the Carter administration, and Secretary of State Vance was not prepared to have the State Department shoulder the responsibility for Mr. Carter's free-wheeling, duplicitous ambassador.

Secretary Vance called Young and asked for the straight story. He criticized Young for his lack of veracity in dealing with the State Department and passed on the direction that Young was to make a command appearance at the White House to meet with President Carter. In that ninety-minute meeting with President Carter, Young submitted his resignation, and it was accepted. He said later, "I didn't want in any way to be used to obscure or diffuse some of the things he's [Carter] trying to do."

It was an unrepentant Ambassador Young who spoke before a press conference to explain his resignation. "I really don't feel a bit sorry for what I've done." As he gripped the lectern, Young said he noted "sharks smelling blood in the water," and added, "but I think I come before you not at all bloody, and in a way I come because I'm unbowed."

President Carter's aides sought to portray the resignation of Young as a showing of Jimmy Carter's new leadership to the country and the world. But to many critics as well as political friends it seemed to be only more evidence of a President's inability to control his own appointees.

President Carter's appearance was sad at the departure of his long-time political friend, and his words were almost apologetic as he tried to smooth out the political and foreign policy problems that Young had created by his unorthodox diplomacy and his duplicitous comments.

Young contended that he had not falsified but had only failed to tell the whole truth. The President, who had said he and his administration would never lie, did not comment upon Young's lack of veracity but stressed the "superb performance" of the departing U.N. Ambassador. He told the nation that Andy Young would have a role in the political operations of 1980.

Andrew Young remained at the U.N. until Carter named his successor in mid-September and continued with his undisciplined dialogue throughout a tour of African nations, where he was accorded the treatment usually reserved for a head of state rather than a fired Ambassador. In typical Andrew Young style, he paid little attention to whether or not his off-the-cuff comments were particularly helpful to U.S. policy on such sensitive international matters as Castro's Cuba or the Strategic Arms Limitations Treaty being negotiated with the Soviet Union.

Career diplomats at the State Department as well as many Carter appointees breathed a sigh of relief at Young's departure and what they hoped was the end of his direct and indirect influence on sensitive U.S. policy questions. Many believed that Secretary Vance, by nature a cautious man who disliked confrontations, would have been able to steer a steadier course in helping Carter establish international policies if it had not been for the erratic conduct of Andy Young.

Aware of Andy Young's special personal relationship with President Carter, Secretary Vance did not have the raw courage for a showdown if he had wanted it. In the Kennedy and Johnson administrations, Cy Vance was recognized as a man of few personal convictions or principles that would keep him from trying to do what his superiors wanted. If there were strong, sure policies flowing from the White House, Vance would have been able to provide reasonably efficient administration and articulate projection of those policies. But, President Carter was a man with little experience in foreign affairs and was constantly influenced by the special pleadings of Andy Young with his special affinity for Third World revolutionary causes.

This had been recognized as an impossible situation from the outset, but it was not understood just how it would influence American foreign policy and the U.S. economic picture. A pliable Secretary of State might be an asset in accommodating the shifting winds of domestic and international politics, but it was a mistake to believe that a steady course was possible with an undisciplined free-wheeler toying with the aft steering wheel.

It might be argued that any President and Secretary of State would have had a difficult time wrestling with the complicated international problems that the Carter administration faced, but it was agreed by the overwhelming majority of the nation's newspapers that Andy Young's unorthodox diplomacy had made a bad situation more difficult.

It was also clear to most political observers that President Carter had created some of his own problems by not putting a firm hand on Andy Young or not firing him after observing the tenor of Andy Young's first comments justifying the Cuban troops in Angola. It is difficult to believe that President Carter approved the radical rhetoric of Andy Young.

Even as he was pledging continued political support for President Carter, the resigning U.N. Ambassador made public statements and sat for a series of interviews in which he was highly critical of U.S. defense policies on matters ranging from Cuba through Vietnam and including our nuclear defense. Even as Senator Frank Church, a liberal Democrat from Idaho, was taking a stiffer line with regard to Soviet troops in Cuba, Young was stressing that the United States should end its trade restrictions on Castro's Cuba.

As Israel was hit by more and more of the terrorist raids for which the PLO claimed credit, Andrew Young continued to take a more and more sympathetic line toward this Soviet-financed and -trained international outlaw organization. He equated it in broad terms with the fight of blacks for civil rights in the South.

In the face of repressions in Vietnam that forced the exodus of nearly a million refugees from Southeast Asia, Young urged immediate steps to establish diplomatic relations with that Soviet-aligned and -dominated nation. He blamed U.S. policies for the refugee problem, alleging it was caused by the U.S. destruction of agricultural land in Vietnam.

Young was a leader in opposition to increased defense spending and was sharply critical of President Carter's proposal to build the MX missile system assuring a U.S. counter to the Soviet's emerging power.

Most of Young's critics gave him credit for "good intentions" and blamed his unusual sympathy with Third World revolutionaries on sentiments derived from his personal experiences as one of the top lieutenants of Dr. Martin Luther King, Jr., in the battle for civil rights. But even some of his long-time defenders said he had used "bad judgment," and the *New York Times* accused him of "clumsy, foolish diplomacy that led his government into a lie, violated its policy, and broke its promises."

While some leaders in the congressional Black Caucus hinted broadly that Andy Young had been "done in" by American Jewish supporters of Israel, the hard fact was that Andy Young's usefulness was destroyed by the permissiveness of a weak and ineffective President. It was difficult to find anything in the manner in which the Andy Young affair was handled to demonstrate the leadership qualities that Mr. Carter wished to project.

CHAPTER TWENTY-ONE

SALT II—Questions of Credibility

The political and diplomatic turmoil resulting from Ambassador Andrew Young's lack of credibility had not ended when other questions of credibility arose that created chaos in connection with Senate approval of the pending Strategic Arms Limitation Treaty, known as SALT II.

On August 31, 1979, the administration reluctantly reported that a combat unit of some three thousand Soviet troops was stationed in Cuba. The belated admission came more than a month after Senator Richard Stone, a Florida Democrat, had pushed administration witnesses to comment on reports he had heard that a Russian combat force was in Cuba. In explaining the announcement in a September 5 press conference, Secretary of State Cyrus Vance related that the Soviet force numbered between two thousand and three thousand men with about forty tanks. But, in minimizing the threat, he noted that the force had no airlift or sealift capability that would make possible an attack on any other Latin American country. He said evidence indicated that the force had been in Cuba since the early 1970s.

While the Carter administration argued that the combat unit in Cuba was an issue unrelated to the SALT II treaty scheduled for debate on October 1, Senate Majority Leader Robert C. Byrd recognized it as an issue that could seriously damage the possibility of favorable Senate action on SALT II and indicated he would not call SALT II up until November, December or even later. He wanted time to give the administration maneuvering room on the issue.

While the Carter White House and its spokesmen, placing high political priority on Senate approval of SALT II, argued fiercely that the issue of Soviet combat troops in Cuba was not linked with the issues involved in the limitation of arms for the two superpowers, there were vociferous objections by opponents who claimed that the Soviet combat unit was a violation of past agreements and demonstrated that the Soviet Union was not to be trusted.

Carter administration spokesmen, including Secretary of State Vance, tossed out a statement to imply that the Soviet brigade might be simply a "training" mission for Cuban troops. That effort did not defuse the issue, and even Senator Frank Church said he would oppose Senate ratification of SALT II until the troops were removed. Senator Church, chairman of the Senate Foreign Relations Committee, was a Senator the Carter White House had been able to rely upon to balance the more military-minded leadership in the Senate Armed Services Committee.

The controversy arising over the Soviet troops in Cuba raised questions about the competence or credibility of the Central Intelligence Agency (CIA) under former Admiral Stanfield Turner. It also raised more serious questions about the credibility of Secretary of State Vance, Secretary of Defense Harold Brown and the members and Chairman of the Joint Chiefs of Staff.

It was expected that President Carter, the White House Chief of Staff and White House Press Secretary Jody Powell would shift their judgments because of a perceived political necessity to get Senate ratification of SALT II. Before the forced public admissions that there were Soviet combat troops in Cuba, they had been counting on the approval of SALT II to demonstrate President Carter's leadership in international affairs.

However, it was not expected that Secretary Vance, Secretary Brown and the Joint Chiefs would be so politically pliable on an issue that was critical to the future of the nation's defense posture. Even before the Cuba-based combat troop issue surfaced, members of the Joint Chiefs had compromised on their written memorandum, which expressed serious reservations about SALT II.

That earlier position was outlined most clearly in an October 12, 1978, memorandum to Defense Secretary Harold Brown. General David Jones, who signed that memorandum as Chairman of the Joint Chiefs of Staff, supported SALT II in July, 1979, despite the fact that certain minimum conditions had not been met with "unambiguous resolution." The efforts of defense-oriented Senators to obtain copies of this memorandum of the Joint Chiefs ran into a stone wall of executive branch secrecy from the Carter administration, which feared that the documentation would have been devastating to the credibility of its supporters who up to that time were able to rationalize support of the political goals of the Carter White House.

While President Carter's address to Congress had characterized the SALT II agreement he had negotiated with Soviet President Leonid Brezhnev as "a truly national achievement" and said it would "keep the peace and prevent a war," his critics said it would assure Soviet superiority in arms. Senator Henry M. Jackson, a senior member of the Armed Services Committee, said Carter had given a "foolish" address to Congress and described SALT II as one of the long list of gratuitous concessions made to the Soviet Union by an administration that was too eager to maintain the appearance of "detente."

"In the areas of trade and technology, the right to emigrate, and strategic arms, the signs of appeasement are all too evident," Jackson said. Senator Jake Garn of Utah said President Carter was deceptive in indicating that SALT II would achieve an actual arms reduction.

The admission that there were Soviet combat troops in Cuba gave credence to the views of Senator Jackson and the other opponents, and those Senators who were reported to be undecided on SALT II were interested and concerned because Lieutenant General Edward Rowny, the Pentagon's military representative to SALT II, took early retirement so he could testify against ratification.

Senator Sam Nunn, a Georgia Democrat, and Senator John Stennis, a Mississippi Democrat, had indicated their skepticism about SALT II before the Cuban affair. Senator Nunn said he could not support SALT II unless there was a guarantee of at least a 5 percent boost in the Defense Department budget to assure that the United States was at least trying to maintain basic parity with the Soviet Union.

Senator Nunn, Senator Stennis, Senator Jackson and Senator John Glenn, a Democrat from Ohio, were concerned as to whether U.S. intelligence had the capacity to verify that the Soviet Union would indeed stay within the general framework of the SALT II agreement. The United States had lost important listening posts in Iran when the Shah of Iran was deposed, and the presence of those sophisticated listening posts on the Soviet border had been an important factor in the ratification of SALT I.

Testimony by Admiral Stanfield Turner, Director of the CIA,

demonstrated strong misgivings about the U.S. ability to prove that the Soviets were complying with SALT II. However, the testimony and statements by Defense Secretary Brown and Secretary of State Vance were deceptively vague on the issue of verifications. They used such opinion words as "adequately" to justify acceptance of a less than complete capability to verify. Also, Vance testified there had been no "significant" violations of SALT I by the Soviet Union. He said this to minimize the importance of the known violations that members of the House and Senate considered "very significant" because they were indicative of the Soviet Union's attitude toward agreements. Although the presence of combat troops in Cuba, verified by U.S. intelligence in late August, was not directly related to the SALT II agreements signed by President Carter and Brezhnev only two months earlier, it did raise serious questions of the competence and credibility of President Carter and his top aides. Among those questions:

1. If the United States has the intelligence capability to police SALT II after losing its listening posts in Iran, why was it so tardy in establishing that there were Soviet combat troops in Cuba in violation of agreements made by President John F. Kennedy at the time of the Cuban crisis in 1962?

2. Is the testimony by Defense Secretary Brown and the Joint Chiefs of Staff who are in favor of SALT II the frank opinions of those men, or has their testimony been carefully honed to fit the demands of the Carter White House?

3. Was President Carter paying any attention to his men who had depth experience in military and diplomatic affairs, or was his approach to the problems of the military budget, the PLO and the Mideast, and the Soviet troops in Cuba being influenced largely by advice from political cronies concerned with the 1980 election?

While the criticism of President Carter on these points by Republican presidential candidates could be discounted as politically motivated, it could not be charged that partisan politics motivated such critics as Senator Jackson, Senator Nunn or Senator Ernest F. Hollings, a Democrat from South Carolina.

Nor was it partisan politics that moved Senator Russell Long, a Louisiana Democrat, to announce his unequivocal opposition to SALT II. Long, who had backed the Panama Canal treaties in 1978, declared that the Soviet troops in Cuba represented bad faith on the part of Moscow. He also declared that he was not convinced of the frankness of administration witnesses on the crucial issue of the capability of U.S. intelligence and, in fact, had concluded that the treaty was not verifiable.

The atmosphere was not improved by the negative results that flowed from Secretary of State Vance's meetings with Soviet Ambassador Anatoly Dobrynin, which dragged on for days with no outward evidence that the Soviet Union was backing down from its claim of the right to keep troops in Cuba. *Pravda,* the Soviet Communist Party newspaper, had stated editorially that the Russian troops were in Cuba at the invitation of Fidel Castro and that the United States had no right to object.

Faced with apparent intransigence on the part of the Soviet Union, high administration spokesmen leaked stories to newsmen that the Soviet troops in Cuba might be "simply a training brigade" to help Castro prepare Cuban troops for action in Africa or South America. That move by the Carter administration was met head-on by Senator Jackson and others, who declared that the presence of any combat troops in Cuba was "bad faith" and that it did not make any difference if they carried a "training unit" label or something else.

Marvin Stone, editor of *U.S. News & World Report,* summed up the "real issue in the SALT debate" as unrelated to weighing the effectiveness of complicated weapons systems possessed by the United States and the Soviet Union.

"The issue, to put it simply, is Jimmy Carter," Stone wrote. "Do we, or don't we, have confidence in the President's judgment in dealing with questions of national security and the growing Soviet military threat?"

Stone capsuled the Carter record in one paragraph: "One of the first Carter decisions—to withdraw American ground forces from South Korea—caused consternation in Japan, this country's most important Pacific ally. Slowdown of the MX-missile project, cancellation of the B-1 bomber, shelving of the neutron bomb at the cost of a major crisis in NATO, the administration's equivocal response to the Soviet challenge in Ethiopia, indecision in the Iranian crisis—all further eroded Carter's credibility in the national-security field."

Editor Stone said that after making those impetuous and controversial decisions, President Carter has been "scrambling desperately" to repair the damage by suspending further troop withdrawals from South Korea, giving approval to development of the MX missile, and planning a quick-reaction force to protect

U.S. access to Mideast oil. Stone concluded that opposition by the Senators was a "singular contribution to this country's future security" to force Carter into military spending commitments that would "reverse the slide toward Soviet superiority in the 1980s."

The testimony of Defense Secretary Harold Brown on September 19, 1979, that the Carter administration might be willing to spend more money to meet the nation's security needs was far from a firm position indicating a sincere desire to bolster the U.S. defense posture.

"The door is open in fiscal 1981 and fiscal 1982 to more than 3 percent after inflation [the increase in the defense budget that the administration had been pushed into favoring] if we conclude that it is needed to carry out the major objectives of the five-year defense plan," Secretary Brown told the Senate Foreign Relations Committee.

Secretary Brown's statement was regarded by many critics as "weasel worded" and motivated by a desire to win Senate approval without actually promising to meet any level of spending. It was understandable why defense-minded members of the Senate and House questioned Brown's sincerity. In a vague comment later they said that a Senate vote supportive of a 5 percent increase in the defense budget would be taken into account in revising the defense budget plans.

"This is making the sound of the [Carter] trumpet uncertain," commented Senator Hollings, who led the fight to put the Senate on record as backing a 5 percent increase in military spending. He added that Carter administration spokesmen were "doing the same thing all over again."

Carter's efforts to project a new image of leadership had failed, and as public opinion polls indicated, the American people had less confidence in President Carter than they had in Richard Nixon at his lowest point—just prior to his forced resignation in August 1974.

But White House Press Secretary Jody Powell noted that President Harry Truman had dropped almost as low in the polls as President Carter and had bounced back to win the Democratic nomination and the election in 1948. While admitting that the political future was clouded, Powell said that President Carter was indeed "a leader" and that the public viewed him otherwise because of the unprecedented number of complicated problems he had faced in his first years in the White House.

President Carter proclaimed himself "a fighter" who was not going to retreat or drop out in the face of the emerging threat of a fight for the Democratic nomination from Senator Edward M. Kennedy. "I'll whip his ass," President Carter was quoted as boasting privately to political leaders and reporters at the first hint that Kennedy might be available.

In public President Carter and White House Press Secretary Powell used less colorful language to assert their confidence that, although Senator Kennedy had the mystique of the Kennedy name and a personal charisma, he could be "beaten on the issues."

It was pointed out at the White House that President Carter's domestic programs were modest in comparison to the additional billions that would be spent under Kennedy's suggestions. It was noted also that on the issue of SALT II and military spending Senator Kennedy had voted with the liberal bloc in the Senate—those who had voted against a 5 percent increase in future Pentagon budgets.

CHAPTER TWENTY-TWO

The Politics of Justice

Attorney General Griffin Bell swept the corrupting influence of partisan politics out of the Justice Department and, in the wake of Watergate, had restored "absolute integrity" to an institution contaminated by Richard Nixon's administration.

That was the often-stated view of President Jimmy Carter as Bell was preparing to leave the Justice Department in August 1979. President Carter would not have listened to the critical comments of those who pointed to the firing of David Marston, a United States Attorney, as being "political," for Mr. Carter had never admitted that politics had any part of it.

President Carter did acknowledge that he had taken a call from Democratic Representative Joshua Eilberg in which Eilberg demanded that Marston be fired. But the President said he did not know that Eilberg was the subject of a fraud investigation by Marston at the time he called Bell "to expedite" the Marston firing. In Carter's view, his ignorance of Eilberg's problems with the Marston investigation exempted him from responsibility for trying to obstruct justice and placed him above any proper political criticism.

The Marston matter was not the only controversy that Mr. Carter overlooked in determining that Attorney General Bell had operated with "absolute integrity." There were Democratic and Republican complaints about the failure of the Justice Department to appoint special prosecutors in several investigations.

Because Bell was a stockholder in Bert Lance's National Bank of Georgia, it was necessary for him to bar himself from any role in the Lance investigation, but he permitted it to be handled by his Justice Department subordinates and adamantly refused to establish a special prosecutor. True, federal indictments were returned against Lance and others in May 1979, but only after sharply critical public reports of the SEC and the Comptroller of the Currency's office had forced the issue.

Also, there seemed to be every reason in the world for Bell to initiate the appointment of a special prosecutor in the investigation of Robert Vesco's effort to bribe high officials of the White House and the Justice Department in order to avoid extradition from Costa Rica. The foreman of the federal grand jury in the Vesco case had tried to resign, charging the Justice Department with "cover-up" and "obstruction of justice."

With the record of Bell's admission that the firing of Marston was a political act, and with the Lance prosecution not yet completed, the Vesco investigation in turmoil and the investigation of the Carter Peanut Warehouse loans still unresolved, it was a bit premature for President Carter to draw any definitive conclusions on Griffin Bell's record.

For months it had been apparent that Benjamin Civiletti, Bell's hand-picked successor, would be nominated by President Carter as the new Attorney General. Civiletti, a Democratic lawyer from Baltimore, had been moved up the ladder from Assistant Attorney General in charge of the Criminal Division to Deputy Attorney General. He had been named an Assistant Attorney General at the suggestion of Charles Kirbo, Carter's political confidant from Atlanta.

Within the department, Civiletti had established himself as a reliable administration man. He had been cool under the critical fire of Republicans on the crucial issue of the firing of David Marston when both President Carter and Attorney General Bell were accused of a political fix. Although he was criticized for his slow handling of the Lance investigation, Civiletti managed to place the direct responsibility for questionable actions on others. As Deputy Attorney General, Civiletti managed to have the criticism of the grand jury directed at Philip Heymann, who was Civiletti's successor as head of the Criminal Division.

Civiletti was so skillful fending off questions on the Marston affair and the Lance case that most of the Republicans and all of the Democrats believed it was futile to oppose him when Carter nominated him as Attorney General. Although his positions were frequently preposterous, Civiletti remained firm and unsmiling with confidence in his stonewalling.

"We have to have something new to challenge him on," one cautious Republican said. "I don't think we can stop him with a rehash of the accusations in the Marston firing or the handling of the Lance investigation."

In 1979 only Senator Malcolm Wallop, the aggressive Wyoming Republican, raised any serious questions about the Marston firing or the Lance case. The Wyoming Senator also asked Civiletti how he could be truly nonpolitical in his decisions under a President who demanded total loyalty.

Civiletti answered that he would indeed bar any political tampering from the White House and that this rejection of political pressure would include resistance to President Carter. He promised the then Chairman Edward M. Kennedy and various others on the Senate Judiciary Committee that he would assure the delivery of documents and records that had been improperly withheld by the Justice Department for several months.

Attorney General Bell was lavish in his praise of Civiletti when endorsing him for the nation's highest law enforcement position. "He has never shied from even the toughest issue. He is firm, decisive, a leader and a manager. He is a man of the law, a lawyer's lawyer. He will continue and even enhance the policies of professionalism, openness, and independence that are a Justice Department tradition."

When the nomination came up on the Senate floor on August 1, Senator Kennedy forgot his past disputes with the Department. He spoke of the thoroughness of the staff investigation into the matters of Civiletti's handling of affairs at the Justice Department and of his financial records.

"Mr. Civiletti has passed each test with flying colors," Kennedy told the Senate.

Only Senator Wallop spoke against the nomination, although a number of Republicans said privately that they considered Civiletti "a political operator" at the Justice Department. "The skids are greased for his confirmation. A vote against him won't do any good and it might make him mad," one Republican said in explaining his failure to raise any questions or oppose Civiletti.

The vote was 94 to 1. Senator Wallop was the only man to vote against Civiletti or to speak openly on the floor of his own continued misgivings about Civiletti's independence from White House political pressures.

Wallop called attention to his earlier opposition to Civiletti as Assistant Attorney General and as Deputy Attorney General when many others had been courageous enough to stand beside him. "The issues of the day included the firing of David Marston as United States Attorney in Philadelphia, his responsibility for the investigation of allegations against Bert Lance, his handling of the Korean bribery cases, and the disposition of the Helms case."

The Wyoming Senator said he was not only concerned about Civiletti's handling of the cases, but he was concerned about his capacity as an administrator because of Civiletti's claimed ignorance on crucial details in the manner in which others had handled the cases.

"In light of problems occurring in the recent past involving communications with attorneys in the Department, and in the light of noted failures to supervise attorneys under his charge, I am concerned that, if Mr. Civiletti assumes the No. 1 position in the Department, [the] management problems will be compounded rather than cured," Wallop said. His objections were drowned in the overwhelming vote of approval.

Only a few days after the Senate vote, Civiletti accompanied President Carter on a political tour of Baltimore's Italian sections. Such political posturing was precisely the type of activity that Civiletti had told the Senate Judiciary Committee he would not engage in as Attorney General.

David Broder, the *Washington Post* political writer who traveled to Baltimore with Carter, wrote:

"There was a time, when he was running for President, that Jimmy Carter was so keen on insulating the attorney general from politics that he urged taking the job out of the Cabinet and making it independent.

"But today, Carter carried Attorney General-designate Benjamin R. Civiletti like a good luck charm through Civiletti's home town of Baltimore and told the Sons of Italy convention that they could look to the team of Carter for help on increasing the number of Italian–American judges."

When Charles Caputo of Pittsburgh asked President Carter about the chances of increasing the number of Italian–Americans on the federal bench, Carter replied:

"I will make you an offer. . . . If the Sons of Italy and other distinguished groups around the country make recommendations for federal judgeships and if you cannot get an adequate hearing from Benjamin Civiletti's office, you can come directly to me."

Broder reported that President Carter kept shoving Civiletti into the spotlight, identifying him as his "chief adviser" on judicial appointments.

In a brief interview with Broder, Civiletti acknowledged that he had told the Senate Judiciary Committee, "I am not going to do political events." Then the man the Senate had confirmed as the nation's top law enforcement official added, "But this is not a political event. The President is not a candidate. The campaign has not begun. And besides, this is my home town."

The distinctions Civiletti drew were not sufficient as far as the *Washington Post* editorial page was concerned. An editorial on August 8, 1979, labeled the President as "Boss Carter" and compared him unfavorably to Boss Tweed of New York's infamous and corrupt Tweed Ring.

The *Post* editors led off with a sarcastic comment that they wished to say "something nice about Jimmy Carter." "He is a crummy ethnic politician, heavy handed beyond imagining, an absolute washout as a cynical, wheeler-dealer in last-name politics.

"To what we regard as Mr. Carter's eternal credit, he does it so vulgarly and awkwardly and badly that it almost doesn't matter that he does it at all," the *Post* said. Calling specific attention to Mr. Carter's "demeaning assurances" that if Civiletti wouldn't give them a proper hearing "you can come directly to me," the *Post* added:

"The most notable time anyone came straight to him, of course, concerned a different kind of Justice Department nomination—the David Marston–Congressman Eilberg affair."

The *Post* commented that the ill-advised Marston firing should have raised "the danger signs"—particularly on the part of "a President who has made such a big deal out of unpolitical appointments."

Noting that the Justice Department was just recovering from the low level of the Watergate era, the *Post* expressed the hope that Mr. Carter's desire to please the Italian–Americans in Baltimore was "not a true reflection of his attitude toward the Attorney General's role in helping to select judges."

The *Washington Post* suggested that the American people would rather see pictures of Carter at his desk, with his jacket off and sleeves rolled up doing diligent work than cavorting at ethnic clambakes. "If Jimmy Carter wants to play Boss, it should be as the presidential kind, not the kind that went out of fashion with Boss Tweed."

Senator Wallop declared that the Carter–Civiletti political act in Baltimore demonstrated that Civiletti's promises to the Judiciary Committee "were on the surface the kind of political posturing that he pretended were alien to his nature." Wallop said that after the Baltimore act a number of his Republican colleagues had come to him and said they wished they had opposed the nomination.

However, when Civiletti went to the White House on August 16 to be officially sworn into office as Attorney General, there was nothing in the remarks of President Carter or Civiletti to indicate any awareness that they stood accused of sleazy ward-heeler politics on a par with Richard Nixon's standards.

President Carter paid brief tribute to the departing Griffin Bell for having "brought to this Department, to the position of Attorney General, a sense of absolute integrity, of professionalism and of merit, and of justice in the finest and most all-encompassing meaning of the word.

"Under Ben Civiletti, as the new Attorney General, we will build on the standards of excellence that have been established here in the Justice Department," Carter said. "He will be the highest law enforcement officer in our land, entrusted with complete confidence."

There was no repetition of a belief that Ben Civiletti would be nonpolitical or independent of the White House. Carter said, "He's a courageous man, and this is a job that requires courage."

In his response, Civiletti reminded the President of earlier discussions of independence and integrity in the Justice Department. "The President said that he thought one of the most important legacies of his administration to the American people would be that concept of independence and integrity of the Department of Justice in the handling of prosecutions and cases of investigation," Civiletti said.

Without making reference to what cases he had in mind, Civiletti said that one of the big problems in the Justice Department was interminable investigations with no conclusions.

"We must work faster," he said, as if setting the stage for closing many cases that had been bothering him for some time. "We must have the courage to end cases, to end investigations, whether it be through successful and vigorous prosecutions, or . . . in closing a case that does not merit the exercise of the prosecutorial or the civil power to bring suits."

Civiletti's remarks were comparable to the speeches that President Ford made in taking office in August 1974, when he was setting the stage to justify the pardoning of former President Richard Nixon.

Even as Civiletti was being sworn into office on August 16 in the White House ceremony, the Justice Department was on notice that there were at least a half-dozen politically sensitive investigations pending in the Criminal Divison. A grand jury foreman had charged Assistant Attorney General Philip Heymann with "cover-up" and foot-dragging to protect the White House.

Known to be pending when Civiletti took office were the knotty problems of the Vesco investigation, involving the general question raised as to whether President Carter and Attorney General Bell had acted expeditiously when they first learned of evidence of Robert Vesco's plan to buy government favoritism with a multimillion-dollar stock gift.

Also pending was the still incomplete investigation of the Carter Peanut Warehouse loans, with the general charges that Billy Carter used the warehouse operation as "a money laundry" to get Bert Lance's bank loans into the Jimmy Carter campaign.

There was certainly a motivation for the White House to try to bring any or all of these investigations to a close quickly so they would not impede the 1980 campaign. It was the stated White House position that there were no criminal acts or even improprieties in any of these matters, so there was every reason to believe that some of President Carter's White House aides might suggest to Civiletti that the investigations be killed off prematurely.

An even greater problem was dropped on Civiletti's desk when two defendants in a criminal investigation in New York charged that Hamilton Jordan, newly appointed as Carter's White House Chief of Staff, had sniffed the illegal drug, cocaine, at Studio 54, a New York disco. While the motivations of those making the charge were seriously questioned, still more charges of illegal use of cocaine were made against Hamilton Jordan and other White House aides stemming from a visit to a Berkeley restaurant and a party at the home of a former Carter political fund-raiser.

Under the new ethics law, the Justice Department is required to make a preliminary investigation of all such charges filed against high public officials and to make a decision as to whether a special prosecutor should be appointed to conduct a more thorough investigation and to prosecute. As Attorney General, Civiletti was the man who was required to make that determination with the whole political establishment and the nation's press corps looking over his shoulder.

But, as a preliminary step, Civiletti was required to make a decision as to whether a woman who purported to be a witness to Jordan's indiscretions in California should be granted immunity from prosecution if she would give testimony. The woman's lawyer said his client would not cooperate with the Justice Department unless Civiletti would give her immunity to testify against the White House Chief of Staff.

President and Mrs. Carter defended Jordan and said he was the victim of malicious lies. Rosalyn Carter went so far as to call Jordan "one of the cleanest, nicest young men that I know." The First Lady's impression seemed to be contradicted by Jordan's relaxed life-style and his highly publicized pub-crawling exploits.

With 1980 politics saturating the air, it was obvious that Civiletti had his work cut out for him if he had any intention of keeping any part of his pledge of nonpartisan administration of the Justice Department.

Even as the Ham Jordan affair was escalating, President Carter was laying down a tough patronage policy at the White House with regard to more than 275,000 temporary jobs for the 1980 census. First, President Carter signed an executive order taking the census jobs out from under the merit provisions of his much-heralded Civil Service Reform law. Then, with census jobs free for distribution in a totally partisan political style, Carter invited the Democratic members of Congress to a White House dinner, where he complained bitterly about lack of political support and threatened retribution.

One Democratic member quoted President Carter as commenting, "I'll be damned if I'll send my wife into your district for a fund-raiser." The *Washington Post* reporters quoted the congressman as saying that Carter was particularly upset because the House had just rejected legislation to implement the Panama Canal treaties. White House aides indicated that Mr. Carter did not intend to handle any of the census jobs—particularly the top supervisory jobs in the Census Bureau's 409 district offices—through the offices of Senators and Congressmen who consistently opposed the Carter administration programs.

Several days before the White House dinner, Mikel Miller, a former official of the pro-Carter Communication Workers of America, sent letters to the Capitol in his capacity as director of recruiting for the 1980 census. Miller was quoted in the *Washington Post* as explaining the White House game plan on the census jobs in this way:

"Christmas is coming and this year the role of Santa Claus will be played by the President. I and my staff are Santa's elves who work in Santa's workshop. We open the mail addressed to Santa. We check to see who has been naughty and nice, and then we load the sleigh."

Miller was reported to have said that the Congressmen understood his message immediately.

There were screams of outrage by Democrats who considered that the White House was playing juvenile political games and was being as bitterly vindictive as were Haldeman, Ehrlichman and other top Nixon aides in the Watergate era. But President Carter, seeking to project a new tough-leader image, paid no attention to the screams from outraged Democrats, the barbed criticism of columnists and editorial writers or the amused commentary of the conservative Republicans who enjoyed seeing the righteous Jimmy Carter brazenly stooping to crass political threats and retribution.

Representative John M. Ashbrook, a conservative Ohio Republican, called the attention of the House of Representatives to a directive issued by one of Mr. Carter's Cabinet members which he said was an effort to block Congress from obtaining information from the executive branch. The controversial departmental order stated:

"There are to be no meetings, calls or staff contacts with members of Congress or staff . . . regarding proposed or pending legislation, 1980 authorizations or appropriations without prior consultation with me."

Ashbrook declared that if that restrictive order had been issued by a Nixon Cabinet member in 1973, "it would have been headlined from coast to coast for exactly what it is: an action by the executive branch to keep Congress as ignorant as possible of what is going on in the federal bureaucracy."

Then Ashbrook revealed that the author of the directive was President Carter's Secretary of Health, Education and Welfare, Patricia Roberts Harris, and said that it "has the same objective as it would have if issued by a Nixon appointee six years ago. It slams the door in the face of congressional efforts to oversee the activities of the cabinet department."

Ashbrook found "particularly appalling" the fact that the directive was issued when President Carter "was traveling around the country at taxpayers' expense, telling our constituents how he deplores a closed Government and secretiveness in Washington.

"This is not a partisan issue," Representative Ashbrook declared. "It is a matter of the executive branch using its power to prevent Congress from obtaining information to which it has a right. I attacked such efforts under the Nixon administration, and it is my duty as a Member of Congress to attack the same practices by Carter. Moreover, it is the Carter administration's response to the announced policy of both parties in the 96th Congress to increase congressional oversight of Federal agencies."

The *Federal Times,* a perceptive Washington newspaper that specializes in civil service matters, noted that Secretary Harris's action was in violation of Mr. Carter's new Civil Service Reform Act.

That law, enacted in October 1978, stated:

"The right of employees, individually or collectively, to petition Congress or a Member of Congress, or to furnish information to either House of Congress, or to a committee or member thereof, may not be interfered with or denied."

Secretary Harris's memorandum started with the following paragraph of intention: "This is to ask that no communication be sent to Members of Congress or staff on any pending or proposed legislation without express approval by me through the Assistant Secretary for Legislation."

Inderjit Badhwar, the perceptive reporter-columnist for the *Federal Times,* noted that the Harris memorandum was in keeping with a paranoia in the Carter administration that was comparable to that which enveloped the Nixon White House. He characterized it as follows:

"In order to function, indeed even exist, we've got to tighten up on security, trust nobody but the palace guard, speak to nobody, let no one into our inner sanctums, and treat any sinner breaking these codes as an informer deserving whatever punishment is due traitors."

He referred to the attitude as "this Nixonian intelligence agency mindset" that flourished in the Carter administration without the kind of sharp criticism from the press or Congress that it would have faced in a Nixon or Ford administration.

Badhwar noted that Mrs. Harris, as Secretary of HUD, became so frightened by the demonstrators she continually encountered in her travels that she retreated into a specially fortified office at HUD headquarters. "She insisted on expensive fortifications such as special elevators to transport her out of sight of the public, as well as elaborate modification—special bullet-proof walls and glass partitions—in her office," Badhwar wrote in the *Federal Times* of October 1, 1979.

The *Federal Times* editorially chided Secretary Harris in a gentler tone, noting that "it is well and good, and refreshing for a cabinet secretary to have backbone and be a strong leader." But the *Federal Times* declared that Mrs. Harris had "demonstrated enormous misuse of power when she batted out a memo that told all federal workers in her mammoth HEW shop that they are henceforth forbidden to 'call' or 'contact' any member of Congress or any congressional staff worker.

"We assume that any HEW employee would be similarly forbidden to discuss such matters with *Federal Times,* too, but that was not a part of her written order," the editorial said.

It was suggested in the editorial that Mrs. Harris read the section of Mr. Carter's Civil Service Reform Act, which is supposed to protect a federal employee's right to furnish information to Congress.

"That's against the law, Patricia," the editorial said. "Strong, take-charge leadership is fine. But leaders have got to know the rules of the game. And in this case, it's not just a game, it's what the United States—as stated by the Constitution—is all about."

It was not immediately clear whether Secretary Harris's memorandum to bar contact with Congress was her own idea or whether it was in keeping with the new ideas of leadership that were emerging from a panicky Carter White House. It was unlikely that either President Carter or Attorney General Civiletti would take the initiative to tell the outspoken and unusually independent Mrs. Harris that they believed she was breaking the law and violating the United States Constitution, even if they disagreed with the memorandum barring federal employees from contacting their Congressmen and Senators.

Mrs. Harris was no stranger to controversy. Only a few weeks after Pat Harris was sworn in as the new Secretary of HEW with unrestrained plaudits from President Carter on the great job she had done at HUD, the *Washington Post* published a series of stories on a HUD scandal that reflected directly on Mrs. Harris' stewardship over the huge housing agency. The *Post* revealed that a large HUD financed housing project operated by Secretary Harris' friend, Mary Treadwell, had been victimized by outrageous mismanagement and thievery estimated to be from $600,000 to $1,000,000 over a four year period. The *Washington Post* placed the responsibilities for the massive mismanagement and thievery on Mary Treadwell and two associates. Treadwell, former wife of Washington, D.C. mayor Marion Barry, was Chief Executive Officer for P.I. Properties, Inc., the offending corporation. Although Secretary Harris was not in charge of HUD when Mary Treadwell arranged federal funding for P.I. Properties, the mismanagement and thievery continued throughout the time Harris was Secretary of HUD. The *Washington Post* series was published in the third week in October 1979, and on October 31, 1979, Senator William Proxmire made a Senate speech stating, "What is particularly distressing about Clifton Terrace (the apartment project operated by P.I. Properties) is that it happened right here in Washington, right under the eyes of HUD and, in fact, under the eyes of not one, but three, different HUD Secretaries. I find it shocking to read that HUD continued to provide assistance to the project despite early warnings from some HUD staff and despite the fact that required audits could not be conducted because, as one HUD agent said, 'How can we investigate records that weren't there?' " Proxmire said he found it "incredible that so many (HUD auditors) could be intimidated for so long by so few and that, from the beginning, 'deep interest' by top HUD officials in the project shielded it from objective evaluation and sound management practices." The Wisconsin Democrat, Chairman of the Senate Banking, Housing and Urban Affairs Committee, said reports indicate that "three officials of P.I. Properties, Inc. diverted, misappropriated and stole at least $600,000 from the U.S. Government and from low-income tenants during the past four years." Although the Justice Department was already reported to be conducting a criminal investigation of the frauds reported by the *Post,* Chairman Proxmire asked for a full investigation by the General Accounting Office to establish responsibility in the top HUD management for permitting frauds to be continued long after top officials, including Mrs. Harris, had been told of evidence of massive irregularities.

"This new disclosure should give us pause when we realize we are spending over four billion dollars a year to assist low and moderate income persons to secure decent housing," Proxmire said. "How much of that money is being siphoned off by crooks?"

"Why did it take HUD a full 15 months after an unsatisfactory audit by its Inspector General to take back a project in which only four mortgage payments had been made in three years?" Proxmire asked in a question directed at the time period when Mrs. Harris headed HUD. But by the time Proxmire asked that question, Pat Harris was no longer at HUD for the reason that President Carter had promoted her to head the biggest spending department in the United States, the Department of Health, Education and Welfare.

While President Carter's motivations may have been among the highest of our presidents, it had to be concluded that he somehow missed his mark by a wide margin. Whether because of the enormity of the problems he faced, or his poor selection of personnel for many key posts, he lost the confidence of the voters. In his frustration with the ineffectiveness of his appointees to make government perform, he moved further and further along the line of the authoritarian methods of deception, secrecy, and bitter political retaliation.

As Mrs. Rosalyn Carter prepared for a major role in the 1980 political campaign, the Carter White House abandoned completely the 1976 campaign pledge to cut the White House staff. Mrs. Carter's staff that had swollen to more than 20 full-time people—the largest staff ever for a First Lady—was augmented further by appointment of a $56,000-a-year staff director, Kit Dobelle. Mrs. Dobelle, wife of Carter Campaign Director Evan Dobelle, was placed on the same White House salary level as White House Chief of Staff Hamilton Jordan and National Security Advisor Zbigniew Brzezinski.

While this was undoubtedly a convenient arrangement for coordinating the campaign activities of Jimmy and Rosalyn Carter, it was a highly questionable use of federal tax money. But the widespread criticism of a government-financed million-dollar "imperial court" for Rosalyn Carter was shunted aside by the White House press office in a general atmosphere of political arrogance as Carter vowed an all-out campaign to win the Democratic presidential nomination.

A million-dollar-a-year budget for the First Lady's staff was somehow insignificant at a time when multi-billion-dollar programs were being allocated and timed for maximum political benefit in Florida, Illinois, New Hampshire and other key primary states. Raw hardball politics prevailed, and Tim Kraft, one of the top figures in the Carter campaign, bluntly warned that federal government officials who defected to Senator Ted Kennedy would be summarily fired.

The rhetoric of populist idealism that had characterized the Carter campaign in 1976 was gone, and in its place was the ruthless resolve to use the power and the purse of the federal government to win the nomination and re-election. It had been done before, but never with such brutal frankness. Even Lyndon Johnson and Richard Nixon had felt constrained to deny that the power and money of the government agencies were being used for such purely political objectives.

Even Neil Goldschmidt, the new Secretary of Transportation got into the hardball politics of use of government programs to win the Democratic presidential nomination for Jimmy Carter. Chicago received a $196 million transit grant from the Department of Transportation on October 2, 1979—just six days before Chicago Mayor Jayne Byrne indicated to Rosalyn Carter that she would support Jimmy Carter's bid for re-election.

After Mayor Byrne reversed herself 20 days later and endorsed Senator Ted Kennedy, Transportation Secretary Goldschmidt expressed his anger to a group of Washington reporters and volunteered that future calls from Mayor Byrne would receive little consideration. He indicated his inherent threat to use DOT decisions for politics had the approval of the Carter White House.

Washington Post Columnist Richard Cohen noted the contrast between Jimmy Carter's idealistic campaign rhetoric of 1976 and the cynicism of Goldschmidt's comments in November, 1979. In a November 23, 1979 column, Cohen wrote, "The plain fact of the matter is that if someone in the Nixon administration said what Goldschmidt had said, everyone would have yelled bloody murder . . . Jimmy Carter is a long way from Richard Nixon, but what is wrong for one is just as wrong for the other."

Although President Carter boldly pledged to fight Senator Kennedy or any other Democratic opponent all the way to the convention, he seemed a political klutz. He spoke constantly of "my leadership," but acted like a wooden clown or a caricature of a clumsy ward heeler politician.

The story of Mr. Carter winning in an eyeball-to-eyeball confrontation with a fierce and aggressive swimming rabbit brought cruel comments implying that Jimmy Carter was finally fighting in his own class. The President's collapse in the arms of a Secret Service agent on a long distance run seemed to forecast a shattering and humiliating defeat at the hands of Senator Kennedy or one of the Republican contenders for the presidency.

Unfortunately, there were many who perceived the Carter administration failures as evidence that an honest, God-fearing, intelligent man could not be a good president. There were those who accepted in whole or in part Mr. Carter's often-stated characterization of himself, and did not examine the details of the actions of Mr. Carter or his appointees.

The tragedy of the Carter administration was that the President failed to live up to the ideals that he preached on the campaign trail in 1976. He did not select "the best" men and women for office from a standpoint of either competency or higher standards of honesty. He permitted personal cronyism and pressure group politics to dictate essentially all of his appointments.

He did not eliminate partisan politics from the selection process for judges or for key officials in the Justice Department. Merit was not the sole standard, and often it was disregarded.

Standards of Carter loyalty, difficult to distinguish from the Nixon loyalty test of the Watergate period, dominated.

President Carter declared a war on the energy problem and then crippled his own war machine by permitting White House tampering with top personnel, which delayed the effective operations of the new Energy Department for at least two years and perhaps more.

The Carter "reform" of the civil service was typical of all of his reforms—mostly political window dressing and little substance.

His eagerness to accommodate all sides on all issues resulted in his pleasing no one and being regarded as a weak and wishy-washy president. The greatest tragedy of all was that President Carter's performance created an unreasoned national craving for a strong and forceful leader—any strong leader. Carter's weakness set the political stage for a bold, strong leader who might be too bold, too strong, too ruthless and too authoritarian to tolerate opposition and more skillful in the exercise of the authoritarian tools of secrecy and political retribution that Jimmy Carter and Richard Nixon used quite clumsily.

INDEX